DATE DUE

Demco, Inc. 38-293

JAN 1 0 2012

Mozart and Enlightenment Semiotics

The publisher gratefully acknowledges the generous support of the Ahmanson Foundation Humanities Endowment Fund of the University of California Press Foundation.

The publisher also gratefully acknowledges the generous contribution to this book provided by the University of Washington.

Mozart and Enlightenment Semiotics

STEPHEN RUMPH

UNIVERSITY OF CALIFORNIA PRESS
Berkeley Los Angeles London

University of California Press, one of the most distinguished university presses in the United States, enriches lives around the world by advancing scholarship in the humanities, social sciences, and natural sciences. Its activities are supported by the UC Press Foundation and by philanthropic contributions from individuals and institutions. For more information, visit www.ucpress.edu.

University of California Press
Berkeley and Los Angeles, California

University of California Press, Ltd.
London, England

Library of Congress Cataloging-in-Publication Data

Rumph, Stephen C.
    Mozart and enlightenment semiotics : Stephen Rumph.
        p.   cm.
    Includes bibliographical references and index.
    ISBN 978–0-520–26086–3 (cloth : alk. paper)
    1. Mozart, Wolfgang, 1756–1791—Criticism and interpretation.
2. Music—18th century—History and criticism.   3. Music—Semiotics.
4. Enlightenment.   I. Title.
    ML410.M9R86   2012
    780.92—dc23   2011020890

Manufactured in the United States of America

20   19   18   17   16   15   14   13   12
10   9   8   7   6   5   4   3   2   1

In memory of my mother,
Carolyn Oleman Smith (1930–2009)

I cannot write poetically; I am not a poet. I cannot arrange my words so artfully that they reflect shadow and light; I am not a painter; I cannot even express my feelings and thoughts through gestures and pantomimes: I am not a dancer. But I can do it with the sounds of music; I am a Musikus.

Wolfgang Amadeus Mozart, letter of 8 November 1777

Contents

Musical Examples

Acknowledgments

This book has benefited from the insights and critiques of many keen minds. I learned much from conversations with Michael Spitzer, Richard Will, Laurence Dreyfus, Marshall Brown, Matthew Head, Peter Hoyt, Lawrence Zbikowski, and Jacqueline Waeber. Robert Hatten kindly read portions of the manuscript, as did the late Raymond Monelle. Wendy Allanbrook also found time to offer generous, at times appropriately stern, comments on my work. I have appreciated the opportunity to preview chapters at Stanford University, the University of British Columbia, Duke University, the University of Oxford, and the Centre for Research in the Arts, Social Sciences and Humanities (CRASSH) at the University of Cambridge. Special thanks are due to my anonymous reviewers, whose unsparing comments prompted me to clarify many a vague idea and hazy passage.

Among my colleagues at the University of Washington, Robin McCabe, Judy Tsou, Larry Starr, JoAnn Taricani, Aine Heneghan, George Bozarth, Jane Brown, Joel Durand, and Shannon Dudley deserve special thanks. I have cherished the ongoing friendship of Berkeley acquaintances, especially Peter Mercer-Taylor, Steve Swayne, and my advisor, Joseph Kerman.

Richard Taruskin has remained a trusted mentor, unflagging in his encouragement and advice. I have enjoyed stimulating conversations with James Hepokoski, Stephen Hinton, Nick Matthews, Carlo Caballero, Dean Sutcliffe, Richard Wattenbarger, Sherry Lee, Vera Micznik, and Caryl Clark and have valued the openness and generosity of spirit of Elaine Sisman, James Webster, Mary Ann Smart, Karol Berger, Anna Maria Busse-Berger, Bob Judd, and many other musical scholars. Outside the academy, I have treasured the opportunity to work with outstanding coaches, conductors, and directors, from whom I have learned invaluable lessons about Mozart, opera, and musical meaning. A short list must include Jonathan Khuner, Erich Parce, Dean Williamson, Katherine Cathcart, Christophe Chagnard, the late George Shangrow, Jeffrey Simon, Gerard Schwarz, Fred Carama, and the late Richard Miller.

Mary Francis and her team at University of California Press once again made the publication process an effortless joy. Mary has been a dream editor—encouraging, wise, tactful, efficient. Many thanks also to Eric Schmidt, Suzanne Knott, Rolf Wulfsberg, and Mary Ray Worley.

I am grateful to *Music and Letters* and the *Journal of the Royal Music Association* for kind permission to reprint, respectively, chapters 2 and 6.

Many wonderful friends have accompanied me during the writing of this book, including Laura Kakis Serper, Philip Mote, Rebecca Martin, Arne Lim, Ken Knutzen, Paul Spinrad, and Timothy Dunne. To Marilia Roman . . . *você é linda mais que demais*. Deep thanks and love go to my stepfather, Chalmers Smith; my father and stepmother, Charles Rumph and Shirley Johnson; my daughter, Nastasja; and my numerous siblings, in-laws, nieces, and nephews, among whom I must single out my stepsister, Sarah Smith.

This book is dedicated to the memory of my mother, Carolyn Oleman Smith, a woman of legendary warmth and compassion, as well as a superb collaborative pianist. She was my first and best musical companion, and not a day passes that her memory does not inspire me.

I close with a quote that reveals my deepest acknowledgment and which seems fitting for a book on signs: "And the Word became flesh and dwelt among us." To Him be glory both now and forever. Amen.

Introduction

In 1717 Alphonse Costadau, an obscure Dominican friar, published the
first installment of his *Traité des signes*. He set himself an ambitious task:
"My plan has been nothing less than to assemble in a single corpus the
principal signs that serve to express our thoughts and that have been instituted for each purpose, whether to form and entertain a perfect human
society or to serve the pleasures and commodities of life, signs that, so far
as I know, have only been discussed piecemeal."[1] The *Traité* eventually
filled twelve volumes and covered a formidable range of material. Costadau cataloged linguistic, gestural, sculptural, pictorial, religious, military, and sartorial signs; he even analyzed the *signes diaboliques* through
which necromancers communed with demons. His first volume also featured a long chapter on musical signs from antiquity to the present.

Costadau's project may surprise readers accustomed to thinking of semiotics as a twentieth-century discipline, founded by Charles Sanders Peirce and Ferdinand de Saussure. In fact, signs fascinated eighteenth-century writers, and they elaborated a sophisticated theory that embraced epistemology, language theory, psychology, economics, and aesthetics. The concern with signs stemmed largely from the new empiricist philosophy, codified by John Locke and ratified by Sir Isaac Newton's titanic achievements. If, as Locke claimed, all knowledge entered through the senses, then philosophy needed to study how the mind represented, ordered, and circulated sensory ideas. Aesthetic writers also gravitated to semiotics as they sought to define the precise nature of imitation; thus, Alexander Baumgarten, the founder of modern aesthetics, defined the poet's task as *"heuristica, methodologia, semiotika."*[2] The famous treatises of the Abbé Du Bos, Charles Batteux, James Harris, Moses Mendelssohn, Gotthold Ephraim Lessing, Edmund Burke, and Johann Gottfried Herder all rely upon a careful analysis of signs and representation. Finally, the rampant speculation on language gave a mighty boost to the semiotic enterprise.

Enlightenment sign theory has attracted much attention since the 1960s. The simultaneous publication in 1966 of Noam Chomsky's *Cartesian Linguistics* and Michel Foucault's *Les mots et les choses* exposed a wide audience to eighteenth-century linguistic and semiotic thought. The most thorough research has come from historians of linguistics like Hans Aarsleff, Lia Formigari, Ulrich Ricken, Marcelo Dascal, and Sylvain Auroux.[3] When David Wellbery published his important study of Lessing's *Laokoon* in 1984, he planted Enlightenment sign theory firmly within Germanics, art history, rhetoric, and literary studies.[4]

Yet this research has made few inroads into music history or theory. While a handful of scholars have explored eighteenth-century sign theory, the subject still hovers on the interdisciplinary periphery.[5] This seems a curious lacuna, considering how much of the best recent scholarship on Mozart, Haydn, and Beethoven concentrates upon rhetoric and semiotics. Inspired by Leonard Ratner's groundbreaking *Classic Music* (1980), Wye Jamison Allanbrook, Elaine Sisman, Mark Evan Bonds, James Webster, George Barth, Tom Beghin, Elisabeth Le Guin, Matthew Head, Danuta Mirka, and other musicologists and performers have explored the important role of rhetoric and topics in late eighteenth-century music.[6] Meanwhile, Kofi Agawu, Raymond Monelle, Robert Hatten, David Lidov, and Michael Spitzer have offered distinguished semiotic studies of the Viennese masters.[7] These scholars have revolutionized eighteenth-century studies, scotching forever the myth of a formalist "Classical style." Comparatively little attention has been paid, however, to how Mozart, Haydn, and their contemporaries understood language, rhetoric, or signs. The research into musical meaning awaits a fuller engagement with the general issues of Enlightenment representation.

In a nutshell, we lack a "historically informed" semiotics of eighteenth-century music. Scholars can now hear Mozart's music played on period instruments, according to eighteenth-century precepts. They can analyze his scores with the benefit of contemporary theory treatises. They can even learn how audiences might have listened to his music. Semiotic research has yet to reconstruct a comparable "native" perspective. Such an enterprise begins with the recognition that musical signification, like performance and theory, differs between cultures and epochs and, therefore, demands different modes of interpretation. We listen for text-painting in Bach cantatas, but not in Frankish chant; we search for autobiographical expression in Mahler's symphonies, but not in Sammartini's. Such assumptions do not merely influence our interpretation. They also shape our research, determining the sources we consult and the directions we pursue.

This book makes a start at reconstructing this context, exploring the ideas that informed the production and reception of meaning in Mozart's music. It offers analyses of selected works, illuminated by eighteenth-century writings on signs and language. The musical analyses range among Mozart's symphonies, concertos, operas, and church music; the written sources also cover a wide spectrum, representing French, British, German, and Italian traditions. Rather than sprinkle the text with isolated quotations, I have chosen to concentrate upon a small number of thinkers, presenting each author's semiotic writings within the context of his entire oeuvre. Admittedly, this approach runs the risk of reducing intellectual history to a portrait gallery of great thinkers. Yet it has the advantage of showing how sign theory fit within the fabric of eighteenth-century intellectual life.

These authors appear as witnesses, let it be stressed, and not as influences. In the case of a *musicien philosophe* like Jean-Jacques Rousseau, we might well argue that ideas flowed directly from treatise to score. This book makes no such claim for Mozart. Of course, as Nicholas Till, Volkmar Braunbehrens, and Robert Gutman have documented, Mozart enjoyed wide intellectual contacts through Melchior Grimm's Parisian circle, the Countess Thun's Viennese salon, and the learned brethren of his Masonic lodge.[8] His collaborations with erudite librettists and choreographers like Giuseppe Parini, Lorenzo Da Ponte, and Jean-Georges Noverre would have offered the composer further access to aesthetic and philosophical ideas. Indeed, the leading book dealer and publisher in Vienna, Johann Thomas von Trattner, rented rooms to Mozart and even stood godfather to both his sons.

Nevertheless, this study does not argue for direct influence. It explores instead the common foundations of music and ideas, unearthing those basic assumptions about signs, language, and representation shared by composers, librettists, and philosophers. This is not to imply that Mozart or his fellow composers consciously realized the ideas of philosophers (although these figures people their operas).[9] Leopold Mozart need not have read Locke to assert in his 1756 violin method that "all our perceptions originate in the external senses. There must therefore be certain signs which, through the eyesight, affect the will instantly, and cause the production of various tones either with the natural voice, or on different musical instruments, according to these various signs."[10] Mozart's father was simply passing on received wisdom, echoing ideas that circulated among the educated classes during the eighteenth century. As Till put it, Leopold was "doing no more than reiterating the basic premise of John Locke's empiricism, the very foundation of bourgeois freedom to which he aspired."[11]

If this approach seems perilously abstract, let us consider the alternative. Suppose that we discovered a "smoking gun," that we could prove that Mozart read a particular treatise. In fact, such an example exists. In a letter of 4 April 1787, Mozart seems to have paraphrased a passage from Moses Mendelssohn's *Phädon*, a book he owned.[12] If Mozart read the short dialogue in its entirety, as seems not unlikely, he came across this account of human cognition: "With every sensation a multitude of cognitions streams into [the individual], which are inexpressible to the human tongue; and if he juxtaposes the sensations to each other, if he compares, judges, decides, chooses, rejects—he multiplies this multitude into infinity. At the same time, an unceasing activeness unfolds the capabilities of the spirit innate in him."[13] The passage faithfully expounds Christian Wolff's faculty psychology, rehearsing the Leibnizian theory of the mind as a "power of representing" *(vis representativa)*. Based on this evidence, we might plausibly argue that Mozart was acquainted with a fundamental component of German rationalism.

Yet we would still need to explain how the composer bridged the abyss between word and tone, philosophical argumentation and musical structure. As Bonds and Spitzer have emphasized, even the most "transparent" music-theoretical writing involves a metaphoric leap between verbal and musical domains.[14] We must eventually appeal to some mediating construct, whether homology, episteme, systemic metaphor, or *mentalité*. Without such a deep structure, interdisciplinary connections remain a matter of random contiguity, like treetops blown together in the wind. Critics can either take refuge in a mystical zeitgeist or simply confine themselves to "the music itself."

This study (to pursue the Herderian metaphor) reaches back through branch, bough, and trunk into that *terroir* from which the different arts and sciences spring. I shall argue that Mozart's musical expression reflects a core of assumptions that permeated late eighteenth-century thought. Specifically, his music reveals a new understanding of the relationship between the senses, signs, and human understanding. The question is not, did Mozart study Mendelssohn, or Rousseau, or Locke? But rather, what shared premises guided each man's work within his chosen métier?

French thinkers figure prominently in this study, as befits France's leading role in European intellectual life, including the Austrian Enlightenment. Franz Szabo has documented reading habits within late eighteenth-century Vienna: "We get a clear picture of just how au courant Viennese high society was with an amazingly broad spectrum of Western (especially French) books. Voltaire and the *Encyclopédie* were apparently common currency with both men and women and passed from hand to hand and were avidly devoured by each in turn."[15] The diary of Karl von Zinzendorf, a major source on Viennese musical life, provides a taste of this Francophilia.

On 5 October 1762, Zinzendorf read Rousseau's *Discours sur l'origine et les fondements de l'inégalité parmi les hommes,* which includes the author's famous polemic with Étienne Bonnot de Condillac over the origins of language. The following day Zinzendorf completed François Veron de Forbonnais's *Éléments du commerce,* then went to hear Gaetano Guadagni sing arias from Gluck's newly premiered *Orfeo ed Euridice.*[16]

Mozart also enjoyed wide access to French ideas. While in Paris he came in close contact with Melchior Grimm, a family friend to whose *Correspondance littéraire* Leopold Mozart subscribed. Grimm belonged to the inner circle of Encyclopedists, which included Rousseau, Condillac, Denis Diderot, and Jean le Rond d'Alembert. Mozart also hobnobbed with the ballet reformer Jean-Georges Noverre ("with whom I can dine as often as I like"), author of the influential *Lettres sur la danse* (1760).[17] Mozart, as Georg Knepler put it, "spent almost three solid months living in a bastion of the French Enlightenment."[18] French ideas also permeated intellectual life in Milan during Mozart's operatic apprenticeship. Giuseppe Parini, librettist for *Ascanio in Alba,* was spearheading a literary reform based on *il sensismo francese,* drawing upon the theories of Condillac, Diderot, and Batteux. Even Mozart's childhood opera *Bastien und Bastienne* originated in a French source, an adaptation of Rousseau's *Le devin du village.*

Of course, this study ranges beyond France, to encompass German, Italian, and British thinkers. This cosmopolitan approach matches the reality of intellectual life during the Enlightenment. Books circulated rapidly within the Republic of Letters in numerous translations, broadcasting ideas beyond national boundaries (Zinzendorf read Adam Smith's *Wealth of Nations* in 1778, only two years after its publication).[19] The most gaping lacuna, as with most studies of Mozart and Haydn, is the Austrian tradition. Faced with the paucity of philosophical, literary, and music-theoretical texts, critics have understandably reached for intellectual contexts beyond Vienna—Sturm und Drang drama, the Lutheran *musica poetica,* Kant's theory of the sublime, Laurence Sterne's ironic narratives. The present study takes the same approach, although it perhaps casts a somewhat wider net.

Methodologically, this book owes much to Wellbery's study of Lessing's *Laokoon.* Wellbery analyzed Enlightenment sign theory within a holistic context, synthesizing intellectual and sociological analysis. Likewise, I have aimed to situate Mozart's semiotic practice within a larger cultural web, exploring the ways in which his music participated in the intellectual and ideological life of the later eighteenth century. Unlike Wellbery's study, however, this book does not adhere to Foucault's theory of successive and discontinuous "discursive formations." I have inclined instead toward the dialogic critique of Mikhail Bakhtin and Julia Kristeva, which recognizes the multiplicity of genres, styles, dialects, and other social traces within the individual text. This "heteroglossia" traverses historical eras, as well as class and geographical boundaries, as Bakhtin explained: "A dialogue of languages is a dialogue of social forces perceived not only in their static co-existence, but also as a dialogue of different times, epochs and days, a dialogue that is forever dying, living, being born."[20] This book approaches musical meaning in Mozart as a dialogue of heterogeneous practices, each with its own intellectual and sociological entailments.

Enlightenment sign theory itself discourages a more unified approach. For all their fascination with signs, eighteenth-century writers never produced a systematic semiotics. They discussed signs in multiple contexts—linguistics, epistemology, aesthetics, psychology, logic—but did not subsume these diverse studies within a single theory. The term *semiotika* itself appears sporadically, but without consistent meaning. For Locke, it meant the science of verbal communication; for Baumgarten, a general theory of representation. Meanwhile, the *Encyclopédie* article "Sémiotique" discusses the term exclusively in the ancient sense of medical symptomatology. As Sylvain Auroux explained: "The use of the concept 'sign' is not in itself governed by any direct definition. Its sense is purely operational."[21] Accordingly, the six chapters of this book progress through linguistics, psychology, rhetoric, musical aesthetics, theology, and logic, unfolding the diverse functions of the sign within eighteenth-century thought.

While this study approaches Enlightenment sign theory on its own terms, it also brings that historical theory into dialogue with modern semiotics. Some preliminary definitions will help prevent confusion. Following Peirce, I shall refer to that which represents as the *sign* and that which is represented as the *object* (terms which correspond to Saussure's signifier and signified). Sign and object belong, respectively, to what Louis Hjelm-slev termed the *expression* and *content planes*.[22] The relationship between the two planes determines the further opposition between *syntax* and *semantics*. Unless otherwise specified, *syntax* will refer to the structure of a single plane, *semantics* to the correlation between the two planes. For example, the hierarchy of musical meters (expression plane) and the hierarchy of social classes (content plane) each constitutes a syntactic structure; their correlation in dance topics forms a semantic relationship. The sign-object relation thus involves a mapping between structures, rather than a simple one-to-one correspondence. A major task of this book will be to define the intellectual, cultural, and social rationales that govern the correlation of signs and objects in Mozart's music.

This brings us to the most original and elusive element of Peircian semiotics, the *interpretant*. According to Peirce, the sign-object relation is always mediated by a second sign, provoked by the first: "A sign, or *representamen*, is something which stands to somebody for something in some respect or capacity. It addresses somebody, that is, creates in the mind of that person an equivalent sign, or perhaps a more developed sign. That sign which it creates I call the *interpretant* of the first sign. The sign stands for something, its *object*."[23] As Lidov put it, "the interpretant is the factor of the sign that instantiates, or realizes, the relationship of the representamen to the object."[24] The interpretants of a musical sign might include a related work, a genre, a poetic text, a title, or the composer's biography. The interpretant can also be a structural concept, inherent in the syntax; hence, the idea of "hierarchy" allows us to correlate 6/8 gigues with the peasantry and 3/4 minuets with the nobility.

The learned ideas of a culture, however diluted, also function as interpretants. Modern audiences steeped in Freud may find latent fantasies in an artwork, where an earlier age imbued with Romantic mythology would have heard traces of the artist's life. In the same way, I shall argue, a common stock of ideas concerning signs, language, and cognition informed the way Mozart and his contemporaries constructed musical meaning. This entire book amounts to a search for intellectual interpretants, those shared ideas that determined how Mozart's music signified.

Finally, we should note the subtle distinction between *arbitrary* and *conventional* signs. Eighteenth-century writers, like modern theorists, classified those signs as arbitrary whose relation to an object relied solely upon human agreement; such signs (above all, words) correspond to the Peircian *symbol*. Yet nonarbitrary, or "natural," signs, which correspond to Peirce's *icon* and *index*, were also governed by human convention. Pamina's portrait in *Die Zauberflöte* illustrates this point. The portrait represents by resemblance, like an icon; yet, unlike an icon, it does not represent merely a possible object. A specific woman, Pamina, dictates the painted features, a causal relationship that makes the portrait an index. Nevertheless, this "natural" sign confounds Papageno as he seeks to identify Pamina (Act 1, scene 2):

> Die Augen Schwarz—richtig, schwarz. Die Lippen roth—richtig, roth. Blonde Haare—Blonde Haare. Alles trifft ein, bis auf Händ und Füße. Nach dem Gemählde zu schlüßen, sollst du weder Hände noch Füße haben; denn hier sind auch keine angezeigt.

> (Black eyes—right, black. Red lips—right, red. Blond hair—blond hair. Everything matches, except the hands and feet. Judging by this painting, you shouldn't have either hands or feet, because none are shown here.)

Alas, Papageno has not learned the conventions of portraiture, which allow a part to stand for the whole. In Enlightenment anthropology, mastery of signs went hand in hand with human progress, distinguishing civilized man from the primitive *Naturmensch*.

The reader may perhaps be wondering, why is this book about Mozart? Why should a general study of Enlightenment semiotics focus on a single composer? To some extent, the answer comes down to personal preference. Yet I cannot escape the conviction that Mozart's music embodies the ideals of his age with unusual clarity. His theatrical bent, cosmopolitan upbringing, position within the emerging capitalist economy, and even his highly impressionable personality seem perfectly suited to the empirical, extroverted impulse of Enlightenment representation. Critics have hinted as much, as when Ratner claimed that Mozart was "the greatest master at mixing and coordinating topics, often in the shortest space and with startling contrast," or when Daniel Heartz concluded his magisterial *Music in European Capitals* (2003) with the suggestion that "the ultimate heir and greatest genius of the galant style, it could be argued, was Mozart."[25] This book aspires, however, to being more than a study of Mozart. Hopefully, the ideas explored here can be extrapolated to Haydn, Boccherini, Salieri, Kraus, or any other composer of the age.

Before getting on with the study, I feel compelled to enter a final caveat. In some quarters, intellectual history is still regarded as peripheral to musicological research, an indulgence readily sacrificed to Occam's razor. On this view, composers would seem to be swimming in a transparent sea through which ideas pass like bright tropical fish. I hold emphatically to the opposite belief: that a society's intellectual presuppositions shape every aspect of cultural life, including music, and that our understanding of intellectual history, far from being superfluous, informs all our interpretations of musical composition, theory, and reception. As I see it, composers are the little fish and ideas the sea through which they swim. The task of criticism is to describe those fascinating patterns of turbulence where talent beats against the currents of history.

ONE From Rhetoric to Semiotics

"I no longer know what I am, or what I do." *Non so più cosa son, cosa faccio.*
Cherubino's first aria in *Le nozze di Figaro* betrays a surprising uncertainty.
Traditionally, operatic characters knew precisely what they were and what
they did. Above all, they knew what they felt. Aria texts abound in emotive words, as when the Queen of the Night exclaims, "Hell's vengeance
cooks in my heart! Death and despair flame about me!" *(Der Hölle Rache
kocht in meinem Herzen, Tod und Verzweiflung flammet um mich her!)* The
Countess Almaviva also spells out her feelings in her opening aria: "Grant,
Love, some remedy for my sorrow, for my sighs" *(Porgi amor qualche ris-
toro al mio duolo, a'miei sospir!)*. These characters know their minds. They
enjoy transparent access to their thoughts and emotions.

Yet Cherubino cannot name what he feels. He can only list symptoms—
he burns, he freezes, he palpitates, he blushes. He feels a desire, but can-

not explain it. The page resembles Tamino gaping at Pamina's portrait in *Die Zauberflöte:* "I cannot name this something, yet I feel it burning here like fire!" It takes Tamino half of "Dies Bildnis" to discover what he is feeling, and the other half to decide what he should do about it. For Cherubino, too, reflection awaits the end of his aria, when he finally turns inward to consult his heart: "I speak of love with myself." *Parlo d'amor con me.*

And herein lies the difference with the Queen and Countess. Neither woman is singing for herself. Each seeks to persuade a listener—the Queen incites Pamina to murder; the Countess implores Cupid for mercy. In a word, "Der Hölle Rache" and "Porgi amor" exemplify rhetoric, persuasive speech designed to move an audience. As Julian Rushton put it, "Speech and music are devised to convince the listeners, who are divided into those on stage and those in the auditorium."[1] Cherubino's aria does something entirely different. While Susanna may be listening, he is not trying to persuade her. How can he, since he does not even know what he desires? Like Tamino, he enters his aria in search of self-knowledge, seeking to understand his powerful yet obscure emotions.

Cherubino does not lack skill in rhetoric. After all, he has just handed Susanna an original composition, the *canzonetta* he will perform in Act 2. "Voi che sapete" also describes the page's Petrarchan turmoil, how he burns, freezes, trembles, and palpitates. But Cherubino here displays his adolescent confusion strategically, in order to win over the Countess. He has not destined the *canzonetta* for solitary introspection, as he makes clear at the end of the recitative preceding "Non so più":

Leggila alla padrona,	Read it to your mistress,
leggila tu medesma;	Read it yourself;
leggila a Barbarina, a Marcellina;	Read it to Barbarina, to Marcellina;
leggila ad ogni donna del palazzo!	Read it to every woman in the palace!

These final verses prepare us for an aria about language whose key verb is *parlare*, to speak. But "Non so più" will reveal a linguistic model diametrically opposed to formal rhetoric.

Operatic rhetoric relied upon a lexicon of conventional signs through which characters could communicate their emotions and desires. Mozart equipped the Queen of the Night with a familiar arsenal—*coups d'archet,* string tremolos, iconic thunderbolts, fanfare-like melodies. Likewise, he gave the Countess sighing appoggiaturas, chromatic inner voices, and a vocal intonation derived distantly from Gluck's plaintive "Che farò senza Euridice," and immediately from the prayerful Agnus Dei of his own Mass in C, K. 337. The Countess even names her musical figure, singing an accented passing tone on the word *sospir.* These conventional signs belong to a code shared by the onstage and offstage audience and correlate with an equally conventional set of affects.

Cherubino begins his aria bereft of such conventional figures. This is not to say that his aria fails to signify. The churning accompaniment, *subito forte* accents, and breathless vocal writing might well represent the page's amorous state, if we interpret these musical features as indices of bodily experience. Yet, unlike rhetorical figures, these indexical signs do not correlate with a specific affect; they can represent any excited or agitated state. We find the same features in the Count's Act 3 vengeance aria (beginning "Ah no, lasciarti in pace"), Don Alfonso's mock lament in *Così fun tutte* ("Vorrei dir"), and Leporello's terrified description of the stone guest in *Don Giovanni* ("Ah! Signor! Per carità!"). Cherubino's opening music may represent an inchoate physical excitement, yet, like his poetic text, it fails to articulate a distinct affect.

Cherubino's galloping anapests, which might seem a clear expression of adolescent ardor, prove equally polysemous. The identical rhythmic pattern will return at the beginning of the following Terzetto, where it underlines the Count's spluttering fury, and again in Antonio's vinous diatribe during the Act 2 finale.[2] Descending anapestic sequences like Cherubino's opening phrase regularly occur at the end of coloratura passages, as in Belmonte's "Ich baue ganz" *(Die Entführung aus dem Serail)* or the Queen of the Night's first aria (see example 1). These cadential flourishes, however, suggest bravura, triumph, heroic resolve—qualities that hardly fit "Non so più." While the opening music vividly represents a labile excitement, yet it denies Cherubino the conventional figures through which he might articulate a precise emotion.

Yet Cherubino's melody does harbor one conventional figure, embedded within the prosody. Each of his first three phrases ends with an accented passing or neighbor tone on the penultimate syllable, what Will

Example 1.   Examples of descending anapestic sequences: a. *Die Entführung aus dem Serail,* "Ich baue ganz," mm. 153–55; b. *Die Zauberflöte,* "O zittre nicht," mm. 88–90.

Crutchfield collectively dubbed the "prosodic appoggiatura."[3] The harmonic accents match the strong-weak ending of the standard Italian poetic line *(verso piano)* and might thus represent nothing more than scrupulous text-setting; according to Crutchfield, Mozart may have intended every *verso piano* to be sung this way. But the appoggiaturas also suggest the most clichéd of galant figures, the so-called Mannheim sigh. The musical sigh was a thoroughly conventional sign by Mozart's time. As Raymond Monelle has shown, the iconic sign originally represented a sob *(pianto),* and only later became arbitrarily associated with sighing.[4] This interpretation sits uneasily, however, with the opening mood of the aria. Sighs typically evoke lassitude, despondency, or amorous surrender, as in "Porgi amor," while the rhythm, accompaniment, and tempo of "Non so più" suggest vigor and forward drive. It remains unclear whether we should hear the appoggiaturas as part of Mozart's expressive design or simply as a prosodic convention.

Clarity emerges in the second strophe, as Cherubino's music undergoes two notable changes (see example 2). First, his melody broadens and begins to separate out from the underlying eighth-note pulse, suggesting a new sense of composure. Despite the anapestic meter, each verse now begins on the downbeat, the first two with a dotted half note; the phrases stretch to three then four measures, and a contrapuntal bass line undergirds the vocal melody. Second, the appoggiaturas grow more frequent and intense. Chromatically inflected in mm. 18 and 21, they pervade 22–25 in both melody and bass line. The word *desio* (desire) inspires a particularly lush accented neighbor tone (mm. 26–27, 31–32). Delivered at a

Example 2.   *Le nozze di Figaro*, "Non so più," mm. 16–36.

So - lo ai no - mi d'a-mor, di di - let - to, mi si

tur - ba, mi s'al - te-ra il pet - to, e a par - la - re mi

sfor - za d'a - mo - re un de - si - o, un de -

- si - o ch'io non pos - so spie - gar, un de - si - o,

(continued)

Example 2.   (continued)

un   de - si - o   ch'io non   pos - so   spie - gar.

languorous *alla breve* pace, this exquisite dissonance sounds unmistakably like a conventional sigh. Moreover, it falls within the line, rather than at the end: text expression, rather than prosody, dictates this figure.

Significantly, this second strophe concerns language. Cherubino refers to names and speaking, *nomi* and *parlare:*

Solo ai nomi d'amor, di diletto,	Simply at the name of love, of delight,
mi si turba, mi s'altera il petto	I become upset, my heart races,
e a parlare mi sforza d'amore	And I am compelled to speak of love
un desio ch'io non posso spiegar.	By a desire I cannot explain.

The most important name is *desio,* which inspires the first unambiguous rhetorical figure. Cherubino still cannot explain his affect; yet, in enunciating it, he takes command of a conventional sign. After repeating the opening strophe (mm. 37–51), Cherubino returns to the topic of language: "I speak of love while awake, I speak of love while dreaming" *(Parlo d'amor vegliando, parlo d'amor sognando).* The poetic meter now switches from *decasillabi* to *settenari,* erasing the anapests altogether.[5] A deeper sense of calm emanates from this music, with its orchestral interludes, static harmony, pastoral pedal points, and subdominant inflections. As he speaks of his desire, Cherubino progressively liberates himself from the torrent of immediate experience.

Example 3. *Le nozze di Figaro,* "Non so più," mm. 91–100.

Yet language still disperses him. He scatters his words throughout nature, until the winds "carry away the vain accents," with jagged bounding lines that recall his opening melody. Only in the final measures does Cherubino turn inward to the true subject of his speech: "And if there is nobody to hear me, I speak of love with myself" *(E se non ho chi m'oda, parlo d'amor con me).* Delivered in a hushed adagio, free from the coercive rhythm of the orchestra, these words complete the reflective arc (see example 3). As the page pronounces the word *me,* he sings the most poignant and audible sighs in the aria. These figures also sever the last ties with the prosody, falling on a *verso tronco* that lacks an unaccented final syllable. At last, Cherubino transcends blind passion and begins to reflect.

What is the instrument of his mastery? A mere sigh, half buried in the prosody. When plucked free, it becomes a powerful tool, a lever that raises him above the torrent of passions and physical desires. Cherubino ends where the Queen of the Night and Countess began, with a transparent understanding of his own mind. He has discovered . . . a sign.

.   .   .   .   .

Like Cherubino, Mozart enjoyed a precocious talent in the rhetorical arts. As Daines Barrington reported to the Royal Society in 1769, the child prodigy could perfectly mimic the conventional rage and love arias of Italian opera.[6] The last music Mozart ever wrote epitomizes the art of *musica poetica*. The unfinished "Lacrimosa" from the Requiem condenses an awesome battery of rhetorical devices (see example 4). The orchestra evokes the lachrymose mood with its dragging offbeat melody, thin texture, slowly pulsing bass line, and dissonant appoggiaturas. The soprano line begins with two figures associated with pathos, the minor-sixth leap from $\hat{5}$ to $\hat{3}$, and the sighing dissonant suspension on the penultimate note. The vast chromatic resurrection, described by the chorus in awestruck gasps, exemplifies the vivid text-painting, or *hypotyposis,* prized by theorists of musical rhetoric.

No ambiguity can survive this juggernaut of musical signs. The "Lacrimosa" begins with a precise affect, announced by the opening word and hammered home by every possible means. Mode, tempo, texture, figure, and text-painting combine to express a single unmistakable emotion; this is a massively redundant message that requires no clarification. But Mozart's music rarely works this way. He delighted in the play of contrasting signs, and his scores abound in the most jarring shifts of style and character. Mozart embraced every influence in his musical environment, whether from the ballroom, theater, parlor, countryside, or cathedral. As Wye Allanbrook put it, he commanded "a musical style in which echoes abound, in which listening is to a great extent negotiating with echoes."[7] Or, in Boris Asaf'ev's words, "The creation of Mozart is always an art of experiencing, the experiencing of a limitless world of sensations, and through it, of objective reality."[8] This motley, extroverted style seems antithetical to the older rhetorical model.

To appreciate the difference, let us consider a work that draws upon the same signs as the "Lacrimosa." The famous Symphony in G Minor, K. 550,

Example 4. Requiem, "Lacrimosa," mm. 1–8.

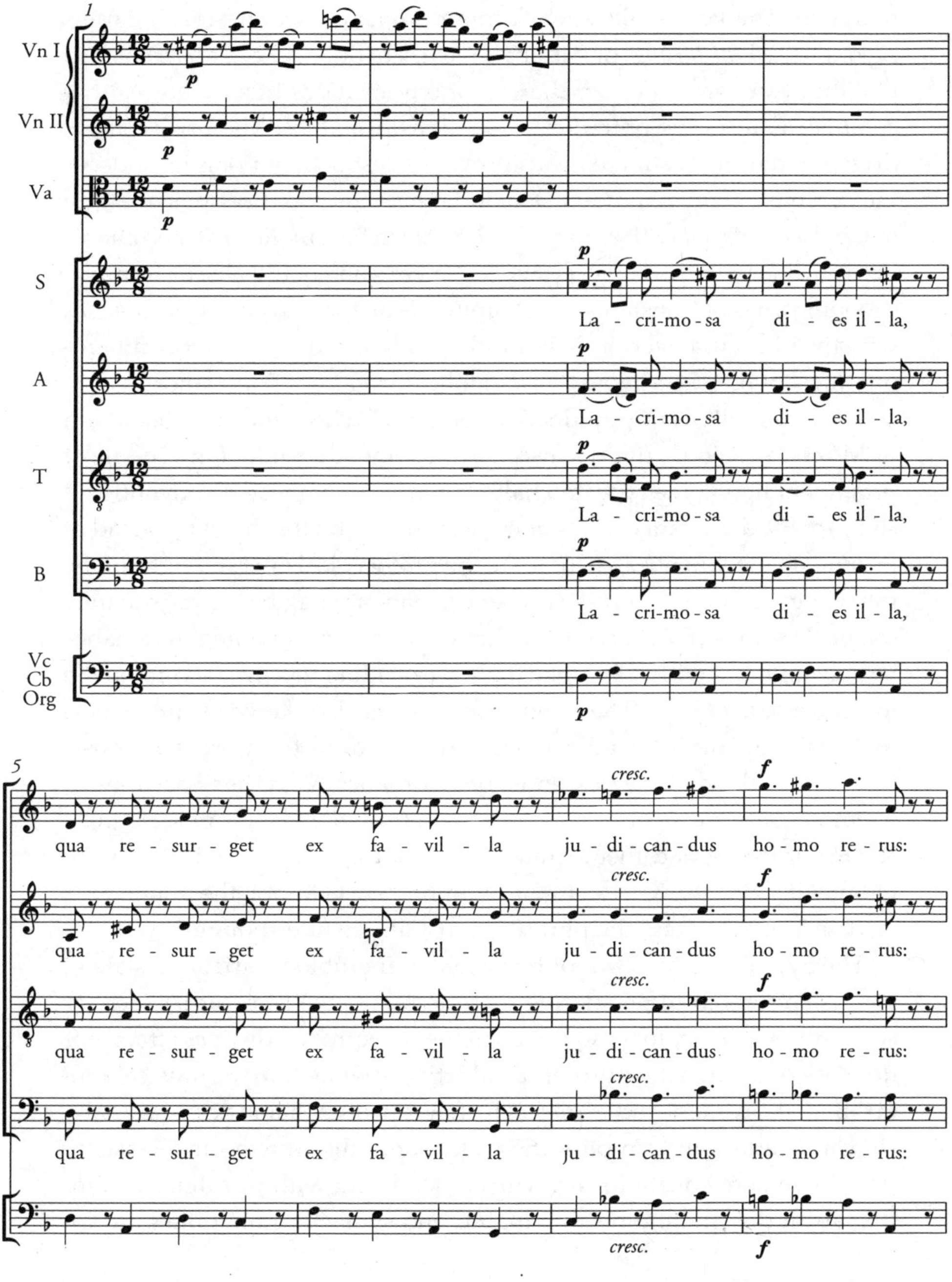

also begins with exposed strings accompanied by a monotonous pulsation in the bass. Sighing half steps pervade the melody, which also leaps a minor sixth. The key recalls such G-minor laments as Constanze's "Traurigkeit" *(Die Entführung)* or Pamina's "Ach, ich fühls" *(Die Zauberflöte).* Unlike the Requiem, however, the symphony includes other features that complicate, or even contradict, these signs of pathos. The brisk tempo, driven by the viola ostinato, scarcely evokes despondency or grief; indeed, the nervous energy reminded Donald Francis Tovey of Rossini's overture to *Il barbiere di Siviglia.*[9] The anapestic rhythm, which replicates Cherubino's decasyllabic pattern, suggests an excitement and energy absent from the drooping arias of Constanze and Pamina, as do the descending sequences with their bravura overtones. We seek in vain for the distinct, unambiguous affect of the "Lacrimosa," "Der Hölle Rache," or "Porgi amor."

The ambiguity is not confined to semantics. The syntactic articulation of Mozart's melodic figures also muddies the interpretation. The most prominent figure, the repeated half-step motive, suggests a conventional sigh. Yet the dissonant e♭" falls unconventionally on the upbeat, instead of leaning on the downbeat. (Compare the prototypical operatic sighs in the following Andante, mm. 5–6, whose chromatic appoggiaturas fall squarely on the downbeat.) Mozart has further weakened the opening dissonance by subsuming it within an upbeat phrase, leading to a firm accent on the lower consonant tone. The minor-sixth leap is also skewed from its normal position. This intervallic figure normally forms the apex of a phrase, from which the melody descends to the cadence, as in the "Lacrimosa." (Compare also the opening of the Adagio from the Piano Concerto in A, K. 488; or the second theme, mm. 29–35, of the Allegro from the String Quintet in G Minor, K. 516.) In the Symphony in G Minor, the minor sixth is tossed off at the end the phrase, almost like an afterthought.

The Symphony in G Minor begins, like Cherubino's aria, in a state of confusion foreign to persuasive rhetoric. While we can readily identify conventional signs, they do not combine to express a distinct affect, nor do they conform to their prototypical articulation within the musical syntax. Both the content and expression of the opening theme demand analysis, clarification, and simplification. Of course, these are normal tasks for first-movement sonata forms, which often begin with puzzling features that await digestion. Indeed, semantic and syntactic ambiguities are entirely normal for Mozart and his contemporaries, especially Haydn, and contribute to the high wit of their music. As Michael Spitzer has explained: "Parametric congruence is more typical of Baroque music than of Classical. In a concerto grosso, the parameters tend to march in single file within a unified *Affekt*. The Classical style, by contrast, is characterized by the play of the eighteenth-century *ars combinatoria*."[10] Formal rhetoric may account for a Corelli concerto or Bach aria, but it offers a dubious guide to Mozart's symphony—by most accounts, a paragon of Classical style.

Mozart's procedure does match a different paradigm, however, which pervades eighteenth-century writing on signs and language. This alternative linguistic model contradicts the underlying premises of persuasive rhetoric—indeed, it challenges the very notion of language as communication. This model makes sense of Mozart's treatment of signs in the Symphony in G Minor and, indeed, suggests a general semiotic framework for late eighteenth-century music. The best introduction leads through the writings of the most influential linguist of the age, Étienne Bonnot de Condillac.

. . . . .

Condillac's *Essai sur l'origine des connoissances humaines* (1746) largely dictated the history of eighteenth-century language and sign theory. Published with the help of Denis Diderot, the *Essai* left its imprint on all of the Encyclopedists, including Rousseau, who had to fight free of its influence. Condillac's sensualist philosophy spread rapidly through Pierre de Maupertuis's *Réflexions critiques sur l'origine des langages et la signification des mots* (1748) to the Berlin Academy, where it stimulated notable responses from both Johann Georg Sulzer and Johann Gottfried Herder. Giuseppe Parini, the leading poet of Hapsburg Milan and the librettist of Mozart's *Ascanio in Alba*, based his reform of Italian letters upon *il sensismo francese*. Melchiore Cesarotti, the eminent Venetian linguist and translator of Ossian, also absorbed Condillac's theory in his *Saggio sulla filosofia delle lingue* (1785). Condillac's influence peaked during the French Revolution, when the Idéologues adopted sensualism as the national educational program. Suppressed by both Napoleon and his reactionary opponents, Condillac's philosophy faded into oblivion during the Restoration.[11]

Condillac wrote his *Essai* in response to John Locke's *Essay Concerning Human Understanding* (1689). Locke had attacked the rationalist doctrine of innate ideas, claiming that all knowledge originated in sensation. He rejected the introverted path of René Descartes, who had demanded that we "set aside all the prejudices of the senses and in this regard rely upon our understanding alone, by reflecting carefully on the ideas implanted in it by nature."[12] Locke responded that "to ask *at what time a man has first any* ideas is to ask when he begins to perceive."[13] He carefully distinguished "real essences" from the "nominal essences" of human language, dismissing those thinkers who treated *genera* and *species* "as if they were things regularly and constantly made by nature and had a real existence in things, when they appear upon a more wary survey to be nothing else but an artifice of our understanding."[14] To remedy this abuse of language, Locke concluded his *Essay* by calling for a science of "*sēmeiōtikē*, or the doctrine of signs."[15]

Condillac answered the call, carrying Locke's empiricism to more radical conclusions. The French philosopher aimed to purge the residual dualism of Locke's *Essay*, which still distinguished between ideas of sensation and reflection. The French philosopher proposed the concept of *sensation transformée*, claiming that not only perception but also abstract thought itself originated in the senses. Where Locke had portrayed the mind as a passive tabula rasa, Condillac emphasized the active mechanisms through which sensation developed into cognition. The process began with attention, as physical instincts (hunger, fear, desire) isolated stimuli from the perceptual field. Imagination sustained these impressions in memory, permitting comparison between past and present ideas. Comparison of ideas led to judgment, reasoning, and, finally, reflection. Physical needs drove the entire process, as the mind recalled past objects to satisfy present desires. Guided by this *liaison des idées*, or connection of ideas, the mind progressively analyzed the confused tableau of sensation, composing and decomposing experience in accordance with the physical laws of nature. The mechanism ran continuously from body to mind, eliminating the last vestiges of Cartesian dualism.[16]

Condillac's signal contribution, which shaped the work of Rousseau, Herder, Sulzer, and countless other thinkers, was to demonstrate the interdependence of signs and thought. As he declared, "The use of signs is the principle that develops the seed of all our ideas."[17] Condillac distinguished three categories. *Signes accidentels* (natural objects associated with ideas by chance) activated memory, but only reflexively. *Signes naturels* (instinctual expressions of emotion) communicated needs, but also remained beyond conscious control. Only *signes institués* (signs established by convention) permitted humans to develop rational thought: "But as soon as someone begins to attach ideas to signs that he himself has chosen, one sees memory form in him. Having acquired memory, he begins to control his imagination and give it new exercise. For with the help of signs he can recall at will, revive, or at least can often revive, the ideas that are attached to them."[18] Signs thus guided the evolution of human thought, from the simplest sensory comparison to the most abstract syllogism. The subject, like Cherubino, is now liberated from immediate sensations and drives: "As soon as memory is formed and the exercise of the imagination is within our power, the signs that it recalls and the ideas that these awaken begin to free the soul from its dependence upon the objects that act upon it. It now has the ability to recall and pay attention to things it has seen, and to disregard those immediately before its eyes."[19]

Condillac's sensualist philosophy both mirrored and influenced a sharp turn within aesthetic theory. During the 1740s, the rationalist rhetoric of Nicolas Boileau-Despréaux, Bernard Lamy, and other spokesmen of French neoclassicism lost ground to a new empiricist poetics that prized transparency and verisimilitude. Johann Christoph Gottsched, who had promoted French ideals in Germany through his *Critische Dichtkunst* (1730), came under attack from the Swiss critics Johann Jakob Breitinger and Johann Jakob Bodmer (with whom Sulzer studied). Breitinger dismissed Gottsched's rule-bound poetics in his own *Critische Dichtkunst* (1740), praising instead the "precise correspondence of the painted likeness with such originals that, being found in the realm of nature, are possible."[20] Likewise, Diderot would argue in his *Entretiens sur Le fils naturel* (1757): "Beauty has in the arts the same basis as truth in philosophy. And what is truth? The conformity of our judgments with phenomena. What is beauty in the imitative arts? The conformity of the image with the thing itself."[21] Parini upheld the same ideal in his *Discorso sopra la poesia* (1761), locating the poet's aptitude in "a certain disposition of the organs and a certain temperament that allows him to feel in a manner both strong and delicate the impressions of exterior objects."[22] Parini's *Lezioni di belle lettere*, delivered in Milan the year before his collaboration with Mozart, spelled out the secret of artistic creation: "This can only be accomplished by gathering together, in one connected and coherent work of art, the greatest possible number of diverse objects that, by nature or circumstances, can arouse delight."[23]

One of the strongest challenges to neoclassical rhetoric came from within the rationalist tradition itself. In his *Meditationes philosophicae de nonnullis ad poema pertinentibus* (1735), Alexander Gottlieb Baumgarten revived the Aristotelian term *aisthēta* to designate the science of sensory experience. He opposed *aisthēta* to *noēta*, the science of logical argumentation. Poets should eschew noetic abstraction, Baumgarten urged, and confine themselves to sensory representations drawn from the lower faculties.[24] Instead of *les idées claires et distinctes* prized by Gottfried Wilhelm Leibniz and his pupil Christian Wolff, the poet should aim for clear but confused (i.e., indistinct) ideas. The goal was "extensive clarity," an abundance of vivid sensory representations: "The more that is gathered together in a confused representation, and the more extensive clarity the representation has, the more poetic it is."[25] In his later *Aesthetica* (1750–58), Baumgarten defined the poet's task as "*heuristica, methodologia, semiotika*"—a Greek translation of the rhetorical triad *inventio, disposition, elocutio* that replaced the art of style with the science of representation.[26]

To ground his sensualist theory of knowledge, Condillac appealed to human origins, both onto- and phylogenetic. He found a model of sound philosophy in the innate reasoning of children, as he explained in his mature *Logique* (1780): "It will be sufficient if we continue as nature made us begin; that is, observing and putting our judgments to the test of observation and experience. This is what we all did in our earliest childhood; and if we could recall that age, our first studies would put us on the road to other fruitful studies."[27] Human language evolved historically from the same pure origin. According to Condillac, speech developed from an innate *langage d'action*, or gestural language, which gradually fell away as words multiplied and grammar grew simpler. This natural language left its traces in primitive speech, which abounded in sensual tropes and figures. Human language thus began as a primitive poetry and evolved into prose only as humans learned to analyze and reason. As Condillac explained: "At its origin, style was poetic because it began by painting ideas in the most sensible images, and was also strongly rhythmic [mesuré]. But as languages became more elaborate, the langage d'action gradually disappeared, the voice became less varied, and the taste for figures and metaphors imperceptibly declined (for reasons that I will explain) as the style began to resemble our prose."[28]

The poetic origins of language became a commonplace of eighteenth-century aesthetics, thanks to Rousseau and Herder, which has obscured the radical implications of Condillac's argument. In fact, he turned classical rhetoric on its head, reversing the Five Canons. Language now originated in innate gestures (actio), gave rise to poetic language (elocutio), gradually took on connection and order (dispositio), and culminated in rational thought (inventio). As the Idéologues recognized, Condillac's theory amounted to a revolution in language. The Essai inverted the hierarchy of reason and sensation, dethroning metaphysics and placing language at the service of scientific progress.

Judged against Condillac's semiotic theory, the confused opening of K. 550 makes good sense. On this reading, the Symphony in G Minor would not be expected to obey the dictates of neoclassical rhetoric, expressing a distinct affect through conventional signs. On the contrary, it begins with a confused tableau that the movement must analyze and reduce to order, precisely by developing signs. Such a reading treats Mozart's symphony less as an act of communication and more as a process of cognition; less as an expression of emotion, more as an exploration of the feeling subject. David Wellbery summarized this paradigm in his study of Lessing's Laokoon: "For Enlightenment semiotics, then, the progress of knowledge toward ever greater distinctness of thought, toward an ever more refined analysis of our representations, is likewise a progress into language, a transition from perception and imagination to the manipulation of arbitrary signs in symbolic cognition."[29] Let us return to Mozart's symphony and explore the way such a process might play out across the Molto Allegro.

.   .   .   .   .

The Symphony in G Minor would seem to begin if not with an arbitrary sign, certainly with a highly conventional one. The opening e♭"–d" semitone suggests the musical sigh, a figure associated with pathos and languor. Alfred Heuss took this view, tracking the "passus duriusculus" through all four movements of K. 550.[30] Repeated insistently at the beginning of a somber G-minor movement, the half-step motive might seem to function as a symbol, a musical "word" that expresses a codified meaning. Yet, as argued above, the brisk tempo, surging anapests, and hints of bravura style complicate this interpretation. Moreover, the dissonant notes occur on the upbeat, a deviation from prototype that clouds the figure's identity. While the motive may suggest a conventional sign, conflicting factors, both semantic and syntactic, force us to suspend judgment.

In Peircian terms, the beginning of K. 550 fails to provide a reliable interpretant, that element of the semiotic triad that mediates between sign (half step) and object (sigh).[31] Certainly, the half-step motive can provoke any number of interpretants, whether a genre (aria patetica), a related piece ("Traurigkeit"), or in Heuss's case, a code (musica poetica). Yet conflicting information undermines each of these interpretive contexts, leaving the meaning indeterminate.

The missing interpretant emerges within the musical syntax itself. The process begins in mm. 14–16 as the theme reaches the half cadence (see example 5). The thematic sentence ends with an expansive semitone (d"–c♯"–d"), stretching over three bars. In mm. 17–20, the woodwind return to the c♯"–d" neighbor motion, repeating the half step five times. The augmented rhythm separates the motive from the nervous anapests, granting it the languorous pace appropriate to a sigh. Moreover, as the winds isolate the melodic figure, the strings reiterate the anapestic rhythm on a single note. In Gestalt terms, the division into two choirs effects a "figure-ground segregation," disentangling the melodic figure from the relentless anapestic rhythm.

This analytical process continues in the transition, which now realigns the melodic figure metrically. In mm. 30–33, the lower melodic notes trace

Example 5.   Symphony in G Minor, K. 550, Molto Allegro, first theme, mm. 14–18.

a foreground descent through two accented passing tones (e♭"–d", c"–b♭"), moving in sixths with the bass. The upper notes now fall on the downbeat, creating the prototypical "tension-release" pattern of the sigh figure. The passage culminates in a chromatic neighbor-motion (e♮"–f"), whose dissonant first note leans on the downbeat (mm. 34–37). Repeated three times with sforzando accents and wind reinforcement and balanced by a

Example 6.   K. 550, Molto Allegro, second theme, mm. 56–60.

dissonant d♭ neighbor-tone in the bass, the half-step motive begins to sound distinctly like a conventional sigh.

The half-step motive also haunts the second theme, whose descending chromatic line recalls the traditional figure of *pathopoeia* (see example 6). Yet the metrical disposition of the theme again undercuts the figure, with the chromatic tones falling on weak beats. A simple metrical shift, however, unleashes the expressive force of the chromatic melody. The final phrase of the theme extends the descent by one crucial note, so that m. 59 begins on a dissonant d♭". The new half step, $\hat{4}-\hat{3}$ of a parenthetical A♭ harmony, repeats three times with stabbing echoes in the woodwind. In Heuss's phrase, the interval can finally "wield its poisonous needle."[32]

The second theme also hones the half-step figure harmonically. Previously, the neighbor note inflected the fifth degree, from either above or below ($\hat{6}-\hat{5}$ or ♯$\hat{4}-\hat{5}$). In mm. 58–62, the half step shifts to a $\hat{4}-\hat{3}$ neighbor motion, balanced by $\hat{7}-\hat{1}$ in the flute. As Robert Gjerdingen and others have noted, this $\hat{1}-\hat{7}$ . . . $\hat{4}-\hat{3}$ schema pervades late eighteenth-century music.[33] The potent configuration, which combines two semitones around a tritone, heightens the poignancy of Mozart's accented passing tone. At the same time, the A♭ parenthesis introduces an element of dialogue, transforming the aria-like melody into a rudimentary duet.

This passage bears a striking resemblance to the chromatic setting of *desio* in Cherubino's aria. Both "purple patches" arrive at the end of a secondary key area in B♭, and both emphasize the identical d♭"–c" half step. In each passage, moreover, the chromatic sigh is repeated verbatim, once in the aria and thrice in the symphony. For Cherubino, the chromatic sigh initiates a new stage of consciousness as he first articulates his emotions through a conventional sign. The symphonic passage evokes the same sense of epiphany, as if an obscure feeling had finally risen to conscious attention. The music seems to stop in its tracks, fixating upon the crystallized sign.

Full clarity awaits the closing theme (see example 7). The half-step motive retains the $\hat{1}-\hat{7}$ . . . $\hat{4}-\hat{3}$ schema of the second theme, along with its duet texture. But now, transformed into a fourth-species suspension, the appoggiatura leans achingly across the bar line. The anapestic rhythm has faded into the background, murmuring subliminally as a dominant pedal. And the echoing antiphony of the second theme blossoms in a dialogue between first violin and lower strings; the opening figure has truly become a subject of discourse. As in Cherubino's aria, this moment of reflection only emerges in the final measures, in the inward dialogue between melody and bass. "I speak to myself of sorrow," the closing theme seems to say. *Parlo di dolor con me.*

Example 7.   K. 550, Molto Allegro, closing theme, mm. 68–72.

The Molto Allegro, on this reading, seeks neither to persuade nor to communicate. Rather, it charts a journey into consciousness, enacting the process by which reflection emerges from the confused immediacy of experience. This process unfolds dynamically, as the musical syntax—texture, harmony, meter—gradually constructs an interpretive context for the opening half-step motive. Only in the closing theme does the recollected motive crystallize as a *signe arbitraire*, capable of uniting past memory and present experience. Arriving after the exposition has reached the decisive cadence in the secondary key, the little canon provides a moment of reflection and introspection.[34] It suggests, as Leo Treitler put it, "the quality of a meditation on a remembered past, after the turmoil and before the silence."[35] Here, perhaps, is a musical equivalent to Condillac's *sensation transformée*. By a steady, almost imperceptible series of steps, we have climbed from the lowlands of sensation to the peak of reflection. Our guide? A sign, of course.

.   .   .   .   .

Language and logic treatises from the eighteenth century typically follow the order of study established in the Port-Royal *Logique* (1662). They begin with individual signs, proceed to propositions and syllogisms, and conclude with a consideration of method. In keeping with tradition, therefore, we turn now to the musical analogue of a proposition, the phrase. Specifically, we shall explore the linguistic context of galant periodicity, the phrase structure that largely defines Mozart's inherited style.

Eighteenth-century writers devoted considerable attention to the verbal period, which they usually defined as a complex hypotactic sentence. Music theorists widely adopted the literary term, as Leonard Ratner and Mark Evan Bonds have documented.[36] Joseph Riepel, Heinrich Christoph Koch, Johann Nikolaus Forkel, and Anton Reicha all discussed phrase structure in terms of rhetorical composition. As Elaine Sisman, Tom Beghin, and George Barth have admirably demonstrated, this rhetorical model can yield sensitive analyses and performances when applied to the music of Haydn, Mozart, and Beethoven.[37]

This approach, however, has not met with universal enthusiasm. In an important study of Beethoven's phrase structure, Dénes Bartha rejected appeals to traditional rhetoric, which he felt obscured the deeper influence of folk music. Bartha sought "to relieve our great classic heritage of music from the anachronistic burden of sterile late-Baroque rhetoric, and to establish its intimate basic relationship to one of its main sources, popular song and popular dance."[38] Spitzer also has drawn a sharp distinction between galant periodicity and rhetorical argumentation. According to Spitzer, periodicity redefined the metaphor of music as language, locating the shared domain in syntax rather than semantics: "In a formulaic phrase, the material has literally no signification. The content of such melodies can be scooped out and replaced with no loss to their intelligibility, so that the material is completely assimilated by the syntax."[39] Moreover, as Matthew Riley has shown, the rhetorical theory of the north German theorists reflected the specific concerns of late German rationalism—a dubious context for a cosmopolitan style that originated in southern Italy.[40]

Given these divergent opinions, it will be helpful to examine eighteenth-century theories of verbal syntax (understood here as sentence structure). The topic attracted keen interest, sparking surprisingly fierce debates. Moreover, the debate peaked at midcentury, as the balanced periods of the new Neapolitan style were supplanting the asymmetrical phrases of Scarlatti, Vivaldi, and Handel. Once again, Condillac's writings were at the center of the imbroglio.

As we have seen, Condillac proposed a semiotic theory of human understanding in which signs fixed, recalled, and combined sensory ideas in response to bodily needs. To avoid relapsing into Cartesian dualism, Condillac had to explain this process through a purely physical mechanism. His solution was the *langage d'action*. Early humans, he conjectured, originally communicated their needs through passionate cries and gestures—in effect, primitive life was a continuous opera. Gestures accompanied instinctual cries, reinforcing those natural signs: "They usually accompanied [their cries] with some movement, gesture, or action of an even more sensible expression. For example, he who suffered because he lacked an object that his needs demanded would not merely cry out; he made efforts as if to obtain it, moved his head, his arms, and all the parts of his body."[41] Such pantomimes bridged the gap between natural and instituted signs, establishing arbitrary meanings through ostension: "They articulated new sounds, and by repeating them many times to the accompaniment of some gesture that indicated the objects to which they wished to draw attention, they became accustomed to giving names to things." The *langage d'action* persisted in the pictorial metaphors and figures that enshrined the images of the gesturing body. Condillac could thus claim that gestures were "the seed of language and all the arts that can serve to express our thoughts."[42]

Both poetry and music originated in the *langage d'action*, as humans sublimated bodily impulses into intonation and meter: "To take the place of the violent bodily movements, the voice was raised and lowered by strongly marked intervals . . . Just as inflections by perceptible intervals had introduced a singing declamation, so the marked inequality of the syllables also added a difference of time and measure."[43] Music and verse evolved simultaneously, as this primitive prosody developed: "Having noted the uniform and regular cadences that appeared by chance in discourse, the different movements caused by the inequality of the syllables, and the pleasing impression of certain vocal intonations, men formed patterns of rhythm and harmony from which they gradually derived all the rules of versification. Music and poetry were therefore naturally born together."[44]

Indeed, as Downing Thomas has explained, music plays a privileged role in Condillac's theory of language origins. As the preceding quotations show, the *Essai* attributes musical properties to instinctual vocal cries, the *signes naturels* from which *signes institués* evolved. The speech inflection of preverbal humanity already possessed a clear intervallic and metrical structure (which Condillac traced to Rameau's generative *corps sonore*), a structure that expressed itself in the gestures of the *langage d'action*.[45] The inherent musicality of the *signe naturel* thus ensured an unbroken continuity between the innate expression of emotion and the use of conventional signs. As Thomas explained: "In the context of Condillac's system, this musical language could be said to constitute an anthropological 'missing link,' bridging the gap between the pre-history of language and the development of conventional sign systems."[46]

Like Rousseau, Condillac drew inspiration for his theory of language origins from the newer Italian music. Thus, he explained that the Italians wrote simpler recitatives than the French because the passionate southern nations preserved more vigorous gesticulation in their speech. Conversely, Condillac's theory of gesture exercised an influence on musical developments, helping to inspire the *ballet d'action* that played so important a role in Gluck's reform operas. As Sophia Rosenfeld wrote of Mozart's acquaintance and collaborator, "[Jean-Georges] Noverre's writings marked the first major attempt to resuscitate Condillac's model of a *langage d'action* for modern, didactic ends."[47]

Condillac's *langage d'action* suggests an intriguing analogy with galant periodicity. Let us approach this carefully. According to the *Essai sur l'origine des connoissances humaines*, language began as a simple nomenclature, without verbs or syntax. Humans connected nouns solely through gestures: "Before people had the use of verbs, the name of the object they wished to talk about was pronounced at the very moment when by some action they indicated the state of their minds." Even as grammar supplanted gesture, word order continued to mirror patterns of physical ostension: "Thus the most natural order of ideas caused the object to be placed before the verb, as in 'fruit to desire.' "[48] As grammatical structure evolved toward an ever-greater uniformity and simplicity, the *ordo naturalis* vanished and languages assumed the familiar order of subject-verb-object. Modern syntax was thus an artificial construct that distanced humans from the sensual origins of human understanding. As Ulrich Ricken explained, "Condillac's theory of word order is an expression of the concern that stood at the center of philosophical interests during the Enlightenment, namely, to place human beings in an immediate relationship to reality by excluding all metaphysical intervention."[49]

Departures from normal word order, or inversions, became a cause célèbre for Enlightenment writers, a weapon against the Académie française and the entire system of authority it embodied.[50] Early reformers had grouped inversion with the rhetorical figures, specifically, *hyperbaton*. The Port-Royal *Logique* thus contrasted *le style scholastique* and *le style figuré;* the latter, by inverting normal syntax, could capture the emotional connotations, or *idées accessoires*, of language. Bernard Lamy, leading rhetorician of *le grand siècle*, defended inversions similarly in *L'art de parler* (1676): "One can say that an arrangement is 'natural' when it presents all the parts of a proposition united the way they are in the spirit."[51] Likewise, the Abbé Du Bos found Latin a more poetic language than French, claiming in his *Réflexions critiques sur la poésie et sur la peinture* (1719) that "Latin construction allows one to reverse the natural order of words, and to transpose them until one finds an arrangement that affords both effortless pronunciation and an agreeable melody."[52] These critics did not deny the universal validity of S-V-O order; they merely defended syntactic liberties as a means of enriching the sensible properties of language. In his study of "Cartesian linguistics," Noam Chomsky justly hailed such surface transformations as precursors of generative grammar.[53]

The deep structure itself came under attack during the 1740s, as empiricists like Condillac tore down the Cartesian wall between soul and body. Charles Batteux's *Lettres sur la phrase française comparée avec la phrase latine* (1748) upended the rationalist model, claiming that *l'ordre métaphysique* had corrupted *l'ordre naturel*. Johann Gottfried Herder would argue similarly in his influential *Fragmente. Über die neuere deutsche Literatur* (1768): "The languages of savages and the ancients, original tongues which bear the stamp of an early sensual way of life, abound in inversions. Gestures and accent help to make this chaos of words comprehensible."[54] Melchiore Cesarotti summarized the sensualist position in his *Saggio sulla filosofia delle lingue* (1785): "Inverted syntax is the spontaneous daughter of nature."[55]

The debate impacted Mozart's milieu through the writings of operatic reformers. Francesco Algarotti lampooned traditional word order in his *Saggio sopra la lingua francese* (1750): "The noun must always lead the column, adjective in hand, followed by the verb with its faithful adverb. And the direct object always brings up the rear and would not desert its post for anything in the world."[56] Rousseau's *Lettre sur la musique françoise* (1753) argued that "the inversions of the Italian language are more favorable to good melody than the didactic order of our own."[57] Heinrich Christoph Koch tapped the French tradition when he formulated his "mechanical rules of melody." His *Versuch einer Anleitung zur Composition* (1782–93) refers several times to Batteux's *Cours de belles-lettres* (in Karl Wilhelm Ramler's translation). Koch's term for a phrase articulation, "Ruhepunkt des Geistes," is a direct translation of Batteux's "repos de l'esprit," culled from *Les beaux-arts réduits à un seul principe* (1746).

This grammatical debate, I would suggest, lends a crucial insight into musical periodicity and what it meant to Mozart's age. According to Condillac and his followers, verbal syntax originated in gesture. The phrase structure of galant music also derives from gesture, enshrining the symmetrical patterns of courtly dance. François Chastellux early on recognized this connection: "[The Italians] saw very well that they could not invent a melody unless they held to a simple and unique idea and gave this idea proper expression in form and proportion. This observation led them to discover the musical period. A minuet, a gigue have their definite measures; melodies form phrases, and these phrases have their regular and proportional elements."[58] The balanced phrases that enabled composers to combine signs so flexibly originated in the movements of the dancer's body. Mozart's own education and teaching demonstrate the primacy of dance: he learned to compose by copying out scores of minuets and began his student Thomas Attwood on the same regimen.[59] Late eighteenth-century music takes shape around the choreographic symmetries of the body. And, as in Condillac's theory, this binary structure operates at every level, from the smallest phrase to the grandest sonata form. As Sisman has noted, this hypotactic organization is especially evident in Mozart's music.[60]

In effect, the new dance-based syntax emancipated music from voice source. In the early eighteenth century, composers organized virtually all music according to the disposition of voices. Trio sonata, aria, concerto, fugue, ritornello—each form and genre is defined by a relationship among voices. To ask how this music is organized amounts largely to the question, who is speaking? This vocal model reflects, above all, the pervasive understanding of music as rhetoric. It corresponded to the method of *Fortspinnung* by which the composer elaborated affective figures across an entire movement, like an orator amplifying a simple argument.[61]

Galant periodicity, rooted in dance, replaced the oratorical model with a purely kinesthetic principle. Ideas cohere simply because they balance metrically, obeying a logic that originated in bodily movement. Composers no longer needed to present contrasting ideas through a dialogue of voices, as in the trio sonata, concerto, or fugue; dialogue is built into the phrase structure itself. As Mozart's music demonstrates, the balanced period accommodates a variety of signs, allowing the composer to juxtapose the most diverse styles and gestures. Signs circulate freely within this kinesthetic syntax, like words within a Latin sentence, and can be inverted with no loss of coherence (consider the trio of the "Jupiter" Symphony, whose opening period begins with a V-I cadence). Periodicity thus provided an optimal vehicle for the representational aesthetic of Mozart's age. It allowed composers to "stage" musical signs objectively, free from the illusion of an orating subject.

The erosion of voice nowhere appears more clearly than in Ratner's discussion of *ars combinatoria*. Writing in the late 1960s during the heyday of chance music, Ratner showed how eighteenth-century composers invented dice games to generate marches, minuets, and other simple binary pieces. Mozart himself may have written a "musikalisches Würfelspiel."[62] Composers would choose randomly from a collection of interchangeable phrases, which they could then insert into appropriate slots in the musical period. Galant phrase structure, Ratner noted, encouraged such mechanistic operations: "The short, well-defined melodic stereotypes available to all composers; the few established paths taken by the harmonic-rhythmic periodicity—these invited the manipulations, the juggling and substitutions that make up combinatorial play."[63] Two centuries before John Cage discovered the *I Ching*, Mozart's generation had found a way to exclude the metaphysical subject from musical composition. They did not abandon themselves to blind chance, however, but embraced the logic of the moving, gesturing body.

Critics may continue, of course, to interpret Mozart's works within the categories of the Lutheran *musica poetica*. Certainly, the writings of Koch, Kirnberger, Forkel, and Sulzer lend encouragement. But we should remember that the north German critics were describing a cosmopolitan style that originated in Italy during the 1720s, a style that both inspired and drew nourishment from a literary culture dominated by French thought. If, indeed, musical style participates within the intellectual context of its time, then the new phrase structure of galant music would seem to point directly away from neoclassic rhetoric, with its basis in seventeenth-century rationalism, and toward the naturalistic poetics of the Enlightenment. It will not suffice merely to update an old tradition to explain the new style. New wine demands new wineskins.

According to Condillac and his followers, sentence structure originated in expressive gestures, the "natural" signs from which human language evolved. They did not view syntax as an a priori mental structure, but as the transformation of a more primitive (and reliable) mode of expression. To interpret Mozart's symphony in this light, we need to treat his phrase structure as a sign in its own right, charged with gestural meanings. The rhythmic-metric structure of K. 550 is not a neutral grid. Like Condillac's *langage d'action*, it provides an expressive substrate from which conventional signs emerge, and against which they take on meaning. This process involves every level of the Molto Allegro, from the individual measure to the overall form.

At the lowest level, the anapestic rhythm of the opening theme indexes the expressive world of Italian opera. The first four phrases create a perfect quatrain of *decasillabi*, the ten-syllable lines with which "Non so più" begins. Indeed, the theme exactly replicates the anapestic rhythm of Cherubino's aria, composed two years before K. 550. This connection might well encourage a rhetorical interpretation. After all, the instrumental theme seems directly inspired by vocal music, mimicking the accents of operatic discourse. Moreover, it begins with what appears to be a conventional figure, spun out in the manner of a single-affect aria. K. 550 would seem to exemplify the wordless oration prescribed by Koch, Sulzer, and other theorists of *musica poetica*.

Yet, as we saw, the Molto Allegro progressively separates the anapestic rhythm from the half-step figure. This analytic process begins in mm. 16–20, as the wind and string choirs segregate the rhythmic and melodic motives. When the opening theme returns at the end of the exposition, the anapests have receded fully into the rhythmic background, while the half-step appoggiatura emerges most clearly as a conventional sigh. And as melody and rhythm separate, the inchoate agitation of the opening theme finally gives way to a single distinct affect. Ironically, Mozart's theme draws closest to operatic rhetoric as it severs its ties with operatic prosody.

The irony vanishes when we adopt the perspective of sensualist linguistics. According to Condillac's theory of origins, prosody and conventional signs lay at opposite ends of a historical continuum. The accents of passionate speech sprang from the innate *langage d'action* and faded in proportion as instituted signs developed. Likewise, Mozart's motive leaves behind its vigorous rhythmic origins as it crystallizes into a conventional figure. Indeed, the half-step motive ends as a fourth-species suspension in the *alla breve* rhythm of the learned style—the most rational, incorporeal style available to Mozart.

The process of crystallization occurs within the metrical structure, beginning at the level of the individual measure. As argued above, the opening half-step figure begins on an upbeat, and gradually shifts to the downbeat over the course of the Molto Allegro, realizing the prototypical form of the sigh figure. An analogous process occurs at the level of the period. Mozart's symphony opens with a famously ambiguous phrase structure. As Leonard Bernstein pointed out in his Harvard Norton lectures, the theme supports contradictory hypermetrical interpretations.[64] Most obviously, the two-bar phrases suggest a strong-weak pattern, with accents on the even measures. Yet, as Bernstein argued, the hypermetrical accents actually fall on the odd measures, creating a weak-strong pattern. Several factors support this interpretation: the harmonic changes coincide with the odd measures, as do the lower notes of the octave-leaping bass line; and the nested anapestic rhythm creates a sense of forward motion, driving toward the second measure of each phrase.

The resulting metrical ambiguity is not simply a structural curiosity. Upbeat and downbeat phrases index different physical and emotional states, and thus function semantically. The meaning of the opening theme largely depends on whether we hear the phrases as "yearning" or "straining" toward a goal, or "receding" or "drooping" from an initial impulse. Such kinesthetic signs are not codified like rhetorical figures, yet they play no less a role in musical signification.[65] They index those gestural patterns that eighteenth-century thinkers located at the root of language and music, and which music semiotics has only begun to chart.[66]

The twin metrical "problems" in Mozart's theme—the displaced sigh figure and the ambiguous hypermeter—are worked out together across the Molto Allegro. As the opening thematic sentence continues (mm. 10–13), the melody traces a foreground passing motion, $\hat{3}$–$\hat{2}$–$\hat{1}$, moving parallel to the bass. The dissonant harmony supporting $\hat{2}$ twice resolves to I^6, creating the "tension-release" pattern typical of the operatic sigh. This first "correction" of the opening half-step figure simultaneously disrupts the hypermeter. The accent now falls on the even measures, a shift confirmed by the arrival of the structural downbeat in m. 16. The passage clarifies the melodic figure, while also establishing an unambiguous hypermeter for the repetition of the opening theme.

The tandem process continues in Mozart's second theme, whose hypermeter is also ambiguous. The transition has prepared a strong-weak grouping (mm. 28–43), yet the harmonic structure of the theme supports a competing weak-strong interpretation. Each two-bar phrase moves from a stable root-position triad to either a dominant-seventh chord or $I^{6/4}$ suspension, imparting an accent to the second bar. The metric interpretation again affects the meaning of the phrase, determining whether we hear it as gaining or losing energy, moving toward or receding from the downbeat. And, again, the extension of the theme settles the matter. To this point, as noted, the chromatic passing tones fall on weak beats, dampening their expressive impact. The "purple patch" in mm. 58–66 decisively shifts the dissonance to the downbeat, with two important results. First, the half-step motive now sounds like a prototypical sigh; second, the harmonic accent now falls on an even bar, confirming the strong-weak grouping from the transition. The metrical "correction" elucidates both figure and phrase structure.

It is the overall form, with its clear binary divisions, that conclusively resolves the metrical ambiguity of the first theme. As Monelle has noted, the original confusion stems from the abrupt introduction to the theme, a mere three beats that fail to establish a hypermetrical context. By adding either one or two measures, he explained, Mozart could have removed the ambiguity.[67] This "missing" introduction materializes after the first statement of the theme, following the half cadence (mm. 16–20). The emphatic postcadential gestures hammer home an unmistakable hypermeter. Prepared by this passage, the theme drops securely into a weak-strong grouping, guided by the descending line in the bassoons. The binary schema of sonata form, with its symmetrical repetition of the opening theme, supplies the context missing from the opening bars.

The retransition, with its more decisive cadence, creates an even clearer context for the theme (see example 8). Six measures of dominant pedal

Example 8. K. 550, Molto Allegro, retransition, mm. 160–66.

prepare the reprise of the first theme, carving out a two-bar hypermeter. Another descending line leads into the cadence; but this time Mozart has stretched it out, filling in the *Quintzug* chromatically and projecting it into the flute's upper register. The theme emerges unmistakably as an upbeat, completing the structural cadence and removing any lingering ambiguity about the phrase structure.

The first movement of K. 550 brilliantly exploits the semantic potential of sonata form, with its predictable binary patterns. The phrase structure of the first theme, ambiguous at the beginning of the Molto Allegro,
gradually assumes a clear meaning as it becomes embedded within the
larger patterns of tension and release that span the movement. The form
no longer functions, as in the oratorical model, to elaborate signs presented clearly at the outset. On the contrary, it progressively clarifies the
meaning of those signs, constructing an interpretive context for the ambiguous ideas. In this way, the rhythmic-metric structure of K. 550, from
the individual measure to the overall form, functions as a Peircian interpretant, determining the correlation between signs (half step, phrase) and
their objects (sigh, "upbeatness"). It plays an integral role in creating musical meaning.

Therefore, it does not suffice to argue, as Ratner did, that Mozart's
generation simply transformed an earlier rhetorical tradition: "Classic
music inherited its expressive attitudes from the baroque era, but mod-
ified the formalized sustained unity of baroque expression by means of
frequent contrasts to create a kaleidoscopic, sharply etched, subtly nuanced, and sensitive expressive palette, with a considerable admixture
of humor."[68] The Symphony in G Minor sustains a thoroughly unified
expression, with little contrast and even less humor. Unity comes, however, from a new source. It arises from the symmetrical, repetitive movements of the human body, from that gestural substrate that precedes verbal discourse. Mozart's generation had moved beyond baroque rhetoric,
and not simply because they allowed a more varied expression of affects.
The rhetorical model itself, based on the assumption that music should
communicate the contents of a self-reflective mind, had given way to a
new paradigm.

·   ·   ·   ·   ·

The older rhetorical paradigm, of course, did not simply wither away. It
continued to thrive in the serious operas, fantasias, variation sets, caden-
zas, and learned finales of Mozart and his contemporaries. Sisman's
rhetorical readings of Haydn, Mozart, and Beethoven have proved so per-

suasive precisely because she has studied these older genres and styles. Even within the new sonata style, as Bonds has amply demonstrated, the traditional model of rhetorical *elaboratio* lived on, whether in Haydn's monothematic sonata forms or in the vaunted *thematische Arbeit* of the high Viennese style.

This chapter, then, leaves an important question dangling: How do old and new paradigms interact within Mozart's music? This question falls within the purview of *méthode*, the crowning section of the Port-Royal *Logique*. It must await the following chapters, which explore the diverse ways Mozart navigated the complex, often contradictory currents of late eighteenth-century musical thought. For the moment, however, perhaps we can suspend judgment about Mozart's method and simply confess (with apologies to Cherubino) that we no longer know what it is, or what it does.

TWO The Sense of Touch in *Don Giovanni*

Of all Mozart's operas, *Don Giovanni* has inspired the richest intellectual speculation, attracting such diverse commentators as E. T. A. Hoffmann, Søren Kierkegaard, George Bernard Shaw, Albert Camus, Jacques Lacan, and Bernard Williams.[1] Yet while Giovanni himself has fascinated posterity, the Commendatore may have resonated more deeply with Mozart's age. Living statues pervaded late eighteenth-century culture, as the Pygmalion myth fired the imaginations of poets, musicians, and philosophers. Winckelmann, Rousseau, Klopstock, Schiller, and numerous lesser authors embraced Ovid's myth of the living artwork. During Mozart's lifetime no fewer than fifty Pygmalion operas, ballets, melodramas, and pantomimes graced the European stage; the same years saw twenty-seven other statue operas.[2] Beethoven crowned this tradition in the "Eroica" Symphony, whose finale enshrines the ballet of Prometheus and his clay statues.

Giovanni Bertati's *L'antiquario burlato, ossia La statua matematica* gives a taste of this theatrical fashion. Bertati, whose *Don Giovanni* served as a model for Da Ponte's libretto, wrote his statue opera for San Moisè, Venice (1780), where it helped launch the career of Giovanni Valentini. Luigi Caruso composed a new setting for Pesaro in 1786, the year before *Don Giovanni* premiered. Bertati's libretto concerns a Milanese burgher who attempts to marry off his daughters to a wealthy dotard and his dimwitted son. He possesses, besides two nubile daughters, a famous museum housing a "mathematical statue" that can move and respond to questions. The plot reaches a climax when the dashing Cavaliere Balena, offended by the mechanical speech, draws his sword upon the statue. Whereupon, the "statue"—actually the cavalier's elderly rival in disguise—flees with his son, freeing the daughters to marry their aristocratic suitors.

Bertati's farce illustrates the several allures of the living statue. As scientific metaphor, the automaton, or *homme machine,* embodied the mechanistic theory of human nature. As aesthetic symbol, the animated statue allowed artists to explore the membrane between reality and representation, nature and artifice. François Hemsterhuis, author of the well-known *Lettre sur la sculpture* (1769), described the uncanny effect of plastic art: "When I contemplate some beautiful thing, a beautiful statue, I am in truth only seeking to unite my being, my essence, with this heterogeneous being; but after much contemplation I become disgusted with the statue, and this disgust arises uniquely from the tacit reflection I engage in about the impossibility of a perfect union."[3] Johann Gottfried Herder ascribed the Hebrew ban on graven images to the peculiar realism of sculpture in *Plastik* (1778): "The God of Israel knew to warn his sensual people against images and statues, for where there was an image they also perceived an indwelling demon and could not avoid idolatry."[4] Joseph II evidently shared this concern, for in 1784 he forbade the Viennese to place garments and wigs upon their church statues.[5]

The living statue, through its palpable immediacy, expressed another intellectual value—the primacy of touch. In Jean-Jacques Rousseau's melodrama *Pygmalion* (1762–70), which inspired many imitations, Galatea awakens to life through touch:

GALATHÉE: *[se touche et dit] Moi!*

PYGMALION: *[transporté] Moi!*

GALATHÉE: *[se touchant encore] C'est moi.*

PYGMALION: *Ravissante illusion qui passes jusqu'à mes oreilles, ah !*
              n'abandonne jamais mes sens.

GALATHÉE: *[fait quelques pas et touche un marbre] Ce n'est plus moi.*

[. . . Elle pose une main sur lui; il tressaille, prend cette main, la porte à son
coeur, et la couvre d'ardents baisers.]

GALATHÉE: *[avec un soupir] Ah! encore moi.*

GALATEA: [touches herself and says] Me!

PYGMALION: [transported] Me!

GALATEA: [touching herself again] It is I.

PYGMALION: Ravishing illusion that penetrates even to my ears, oh,
              never leave my senses! [Galatea takes a few steps and
              touches a marble]

GALATEA: That is not I.

[. . . She rests a hand on him; he shivers, takes that hand, presses it
to his heart, and covers it with passionate kisses.]

GALATEA: [with a sigh] Ah! Me again.[6]

Rousseau's *scène lyrique* models the psychological theory of his popular
novel *Émile* (1762), which traced human consciousness to the infant's tactile explorations: "He wants to touch everything, handle everything. Do
not oppose yourself to this restlessness. . . . It is only by movement that we
learn that there are things which are not us, and it is only by our own movement that we acquire the idea of extension."[7] Both *Émile* and *Pygmalion*,
in turn, betray the influence of Rousseau's friend Condillac, whose rose-
sniffing statue remains the most famous image of the French Enlightenment. Condillac's living statue, featured in the *Traité des sensations* (1754),
first attains self-awareness through touch: "Our statue, unreflective with the
other senses, begins to reflect with touch."[8] Herder later absorbed the Encyclopedists' sensualist psychology in his *Kritische Wälder* (1769) and *Plastik,* which explicitly link sculpture to the sense of touch. Herder traced art,
language, and knowledge to touch, and even rewrote Descartes's *cogito ergo*

sum as "Ich fühle mich! Ich bin!"—"I touch myself! I am!"[9] Immanuel Kant summed up the new value of touch in his *Kritik der praktischen Vernunft* (1788): "Empiricism is based on touch, but rationalism on a necessity that can be seen."[10] For the empiricist Enlightenment, touch served as a court of final appeal, adjudicating the claims of both truth and beauty.

The sense of touch plays the same veridical role in *Don Giovanni*. Ottavio and Anna take hands to swear vengeance, Giovanni and Zerlina to vow nuptials. Zerlina wins back Masetto's trust by begging him to touch (or even beat) her.[11] And in the banquet scene, the living statue demands Giovanni's hand in pledge. This climactic scene recalls the other fatal contact in *Don Giovanni*, which Mozart has evoked through a rare recollection of earlier music (see example 9). As the Commendatore enters, the orchestra thunders the identical diminished-seventh chord on which Giovanni struck his mortal blow in the Act 1 duel (No. 1, m. 175). The duel returns more overtly as Giovanni actually clasps the stone hand. A rising scalar motive had accompanied the clashing of swords, condensing into an accelerating sequence as the final thrust neared. In the banquet scene, the identical motive materializes as the Commendatore commands Giovanni to repent. As the argument reaches a climax, the motive is again condensed sequentially (since the basses now play the motive, Mozart has inverted it to preserve the wedge-shaped counterpoint). In effect, Mozart has united the two most decisive moments of touch in *Don Giovanni*.

Of course, cultural values should emerge not only in masterpieces like *Don Giovanni* but also, perhaps especially, in the works of Mozart's "anonymous" contemporaries. In fact, Giuseppe Gazzaniga, who set Bertati's *Don Giovanni* in 1787, forged the same link between duel and handshake (see example 10). As the statue offers his hand, the rushing violin scales return from the sword fight. At the moment of contact, tremolos in E♭ minor recall the fatal sword thrust; and Giovanni delivers his mortal *oimé* on the identical ♭c' and diminished-seventh harmony as the Commendatore's *ahi*. These subtle recollections, so foreign to the light spirit of the Venetian one-act, suggest that tactile experience was indeed an eerie attraction of theatrical statues.

The importance of the sense of touch in *Don Giovanni* points toward a

Example 9. Mozart, *Don Giovanni,* parallels between duel and banquet scenes: a. Duel (no. 1), mm. 166–75; b. Banquet scene (Act 2 finale), mm. 536–44.

Example 9.   (continued)

new philosophical interpretation of the opera. Yet unlike the host of existing interpretations, this chapter does not propose a symbolic or allegorical reading. It probes a more basic level—indeed, the very conditions of
representation. Having examined the cognitive function of the Enlightenment sign, we now explore its formation, seeking the psychological
foundations upon which the new empiricism constructed its semiotic theory. Like Leporello groping in the dark for a passageway, we shall trace
the contours of Mozart's intellectual environment, running our fingertips over rough, unfamiliar textures. For guides we shall lean upon three
thinkers representing British, French, and German traditions. An analysis
of three scenes will then suggest how the new psychology informed Da
Ponte's and Mozart's expressive design. Uniting poetry, music, and ideas
is the rich, ubiquitous figure of the living statue.

·   ·   ·   ·   ·

George Berkeley first championed touch in his *Essay towards a New Theory of Vision* (1709). Berkeley sought to explain how secondary visual qualities (color and light) represent the primary qualities of objects (shape, size,
distance). How, he asked, does the image painted on the retina teach us

Example 10.   Giuseppe Gazzaniga, *Don Giovanni,* parallels between duel and banquet scenes: a. Duel *(introduzione)*, mm. 115–22; b. Banquet scene *(finale)*, mm. 339–42.

about a three-dimensional world? The *Essay* addresses the famous problem posed by William Molyneux: could a man born blind who recovered his sight recognize the shapes he had learned by touch? Berkeley's startling answer revolutionized the science of vision and provides important insights into Enlightenment sign theory.

Example 10. *(continued)*

In the *Essay* Berkeley attacked the "geometrical" theory of Cartesian optics. As Margaret Atherton has shown, Berkeley targeted the account proposed by Descartes's disciple Nicolas Malebranche in *De la recherche de la vérité* (1674).[12] Malebranche had attributed spatial perception to a combination of binocular vision and rational calculation. In perceiving an object, he claimed, the eyes formed a triangle with the object at its apex. The mind then calculated the distance of the visual rays, according to the angles the eyes formed in focusing. Finally, reason accommodated this perceptual judgment to the innate idea of extension, correcting the inaccuracies of sensation. Since extension is a rational (supersensory) idea, it organizes both sight and touch. Therefore, the blind man would indeed recognize the same shapes with either hand or eye.

Berkeley attacked this cumbersome theory by arguing for the heterogeneity of sight and touch: "That which I see is only variety of light and colors. That which I feel is hard or soft, hot or cold, rough or smooth. What similitude, what connection have those ideas with these? . . . The two distinct provinces of sight and touch should be considered apart, and as if their objects had no intercourse, no manner of relation one to another."[13] He thus ruled out appeal to either innate ideas or a synesthetic "common sense." Molyneux's subject would experience light and colors but would have no way of identifying such sensations with the cube or sphere pressed into his palm.

How then do we orient ourselves in the world visually? Berkeley claimed that we must learn to associate sight and touch. Like Rousseau's grasping infant, we connect what we see and feel by sheer force of habit. In this way, visual sensations come to function as signs of tactile objects: "Visible figures represent tangible figures much after the same manner that written words do sounds. . . . And the manner wherein they signify and mark unto us the objects which are at a distance is the same with that of languages and signs of human appointment, which do not suggest the things signified by any likeness or identity of nature, but only by an habitual connection that experience has made us to observe between them."[14] Berkeley thus banished innate ideas and calculation in favor of signs and experience.

Berkeley elaborated the language metaphor in his *Treatise Concerning the Principles of Human Knowledge* (1710), in which he famously denied the existence of matter. Berkeley abolished causality, together with all abstract ideas, ascribing the regularities of nature to a purely semiotic relationship: "The connexion of ideas does not imply the relation of *cause* and *effect*, but only of a mark or *sign* with the thing *signified*. The fire which I see is not the cause of the pain I suffer upon my approaching it, but the mark that forewarns me of it."[15] Since tactile sensations (like pain) directly concern human survival, God has made them the objects of visual signs: "Visible ideas are the language whereby the governing spirit, on whom we depend, informs us what tangible ideas he is about to imprint upon us."[16] Therefore, Berkeley concluded, "It is the searching after, and endeavoring to understand those signs instituted by the Author of Nature that ought to be the employment of the natural philosopher, and not the pretending to explain things by corporeal causes."[17] As Colin Turbayne explained, Berkeley has replaced the scientific metaphor of Clockwork with that of Divine Language; nature is now God's book and the scientist an expert linguist.[18]

The Divine Language differed from the Babel of human tongues. Eighteenth-century thinkers categorized signs as either "natural" or "arbitrary," a distinction that underwrites Berkeley's argument of touch in the *Essay*: "A visible square, for instance, suggests to the mind the same tangible figure in Europe that it doth in America. Hence it is that the voice of Nature which speaks to our eyes is not liable to that misinterpretation and ambiguity that languages of human contrivance are unavoidably subject to."[19] In eighteenth-century thought, the natural sign is both a semiotic and cosmological entity, instituted by God himself to instruct humanity. Natural signs included not only physical sensations, but also gestures, facial expressions, instinctual cries, and even physiognomies.[20] Arbitrary signs, on the other hand, were invented by humans and, thus, subject to human error and prejudice—hence, the repeated protests against the "abuse of words."[21]

Therefore, those arts that used natural signs—painting, sculpture, dance, and music—were thought to speak a more universal language than words. The Abbé Du Bos thus argued in his *Réflexions critiques sur la peinture et sur la poésie* (1719): "Just as painting imitates the shapes and colors of nature, so the musician imitates the tones, accents, sighs, vocal inflections, indeed, all the sounds through which nature herself expresses the sentiments and passions. . . . Words draw their meaning and value solely from human institution, and enjoy currency only within a particular country."[22] The Scottish philosopher Thomas Reid would claim in his *Inquiry into the Human Mind on the Principles of Common Sense* (1764) that the fine arts were "nothing but the language of nature, which we brought into the world with us, but have unlearned by disuse. . . . Abolish the use of articulate sounds and writing among mankind for a century, and every man would be a painter, an actor, and an orator."[23] As Mozart's ballet collaborator Jean-Georges Noverre put it in *Lettres sur la danse et sur les ballets* (1760), music and dance speak "the language of sentiment; it is universally expressive and seducing, as it is universally understood."[24]

In this sense, we can understand the reported exchange between Mozart and Haydn, as the older composer was embarking for London: " 'Oh, Papa, you have had no education for the wide world, and you speak so few languages.' 'But my language is understood all over the world.' "[25] Haydn's answer hinges on the distinction between the arbitrary signs instituted by humans and the innate signs given by nature. This distinction can help explain the puzzling new prestige of wordless music in the late eighteenth-century (Haydn went to London to write symphonies, not operas), an age still dominated by imitative aesthetics.[26] Bemused by this apparent conflict between theory and practice, critics have appealed to earlier traditions of musical oratory or later theories of "absolute music." Yet Enlightenment semiotics provides a perfectly adequate rationale for instrumental music. The doctrine of the natural sign resolves that paradox that neither Baroque rhetoric nor Romantic metaphysics can explain— that is, how composers could uphold an imitative aesthetic, indeed, embrace it most faithfully, while rejecting language itself.

·   ·   ·   ·   ·

The sense of touch seized the attention of European philosophy with Condillac's *Traité des sensations* (1754). His waking statue, whose senses gradually open onto the world of experience, became the very emblem of Enlightenment sensualism. The *Traité* belongs within Condillac's larger critique of rationalism, which he had introduced in the *Essai sur l'origine des connoissances humaines* (1746). Like Berkeley, Condillac attacked the mind-body dichotomy, specifically, John Locke's separation of sensation and reflection. And, even more rigorously than Berkeley, he elaborated a semiotic theory of knowledge.

In the *Essai*, as we have seen, Condillac pioneered a purely physical theory of human understanding in which signs played an unprecedented role.[27] Signs allowed the mind to recall, compare, and order sensory ideas, according to the *liaison des idées;* they thus guided the evolution of human thought, from the simplest sensory impression to the most abstract syllogism. The centrality of signs led Condillac, like Berkeley, to a linguistic interpretation of nature; as he claimed in the *Logique* (1780), "The study of a well-conducted science amounts to the study of a well-made language."[28]

In the *Traité des sensations* Condillac tempered his emphasis on the constitutive function of language, which had veered toward cultural relativism.[29] The waking statue is meant to illustrate the universal principles of the mind before it masters signs. Condillac now conceded that sensation alone could activate human understanding, indeed, that a single portal sufficed: *"With only one sense the mind has the seed of all its faculties."*[30] Yet the statue first awakens in solipsistic isolation. It mistakes the sensations of smell, hearing, taste, and even sight for modifications of its own being. "If we present it with a rose," explained Condillac, "to us it will seem a statue that smells a rose; but to itself, it will be nothing but the smell itself of this flower."[31]

Only touch alerts the statue to external reality. As the statue handles solid objects, it perceives an immovable Other: "Since the essence of this sensation is to represent at one and the same time two things that exclude each other, the mind will not perceive solidity as one of those modifications in which it finds merely itself. It will perceive it necessarily as a modification in which it finds two things that exclude one another."[32] This rupture gives birth to reflection as the statue, like Rousseau's Galathée, touches its own body and then compares it with other tactile objects. Finally, the statue explores the outer world by combining touch with the other senses. It now learns that it is not a rose: "Placing its hand by chance on the objects that it encounters, [the statue] grasps a flower, which remains in its fingers. As the arm moves it aimlessly, now towards its face, now away, it experiences itself in a certain manner with more or less vividness. . . . Finally, it begins to suspect that the change in state is due to the flower."[33] Touch thus contains the seed of scientific discovery, allowing the mind to predicate qualities of the sensory world. The primal rupture between self and Other also makes possible representation, that fissure between sign and object.[34]

What then bridges the gap between sensation and language, *Traité* and *Essai*? Condillac found the answer within the body itself, in the *langage d'action*. As he claimed in the *Essai*, gestures were "the seed of language and all the arts that can serve to express our thoughts."[35] Likewise, Condillac's statue learns to orient itself in the world by manipulating objects. Touch may awaken the subject to external reality, but bodily movement must complete the education.

Condillac advanced his strongest claims for the *langage d'action* in the *Logique*, arguing that all analytical thought originated in gesture. As he explained, "Men begin to speak the language of action as soon as they have sensations," so that "there is an innate language, even though there are no innate ideas."[36] The *langage d'action* began instinctually, but as individuals observed other humans, they learned to interpret and manipulate gestures consciously. They now began to order their perceptions sequentially, reducing the confused tableau to a logical succession.[37] Whence the origins of analytic thought: "So little by little, he will form the habit of repeating, one after another, the movements which nature caused him to make all at once; and the language of action will naturally become an analytic method for him. I say a *method* because the succession of his movements will not occur arbitrarily and without rules."[38] This pointed reference to *méthode* signals Condillac's complete inversion of Descartes's rationalist epistemology. The *Logique* banishes innate ideas and replaces the transcendent *cogito* with a purely physical mechanism.

In his later work Condillac renounced the arbitrary sign altogether, speaking instead of *signes artificiels*. In the *Grammaire* (1775) he dismissed arbitrary signs as "chosen without reason and by caprice." Artificial signs, on the other hand, arose through analogy with the analytic mechanism of the *langage d'action*: "We did not choose the first signs. It is Nature who gave them to us. But in giving them, she set us on the path towards imagining others for ourselves. . . . Artificial signs are signs whose choice is founded on reason; they must be imagined through the skill with which known signs have prepared our intellect."[39] All reliable signs were physically motivated, springing from the gesturing body. To interpret *Don Giovanni* in this spirit, we must burrow through the poetic and musical signs to the underlying logic of the body—a journey that only terminates in the sense of touch.

.   .   .   .   .

Condillac's statue lived on in Herder's aesthetics and language theory. Herder drew inspiration from both Berkeley and Condillac in his systematic aesthetic theory, the *Kritische Wälder* (1769) and the essay *Plastik* (1778). Like them, he fiercely opposed dualism, whether rationalist or (later) Kantian. Like many progressive Germans, Herder embraced a form of pantheistic naturalism; as he professed in his essay on the sense of touch, "I am truly in a chain with God, just as I am in a chain with the worm that I tread underfoot."[40] His theory of art, language, and knowledge radiates from an unshaken conviction in the order, goodness, and sufficiency of nature. And like his forebears, Herder enlisted touch in the campaign against metaphysics.

In the *Kritische Wälder* (1769), Herder responded to the semiotic theory of Lessing's *Laokoon* (1766). Lessing had famously distinguished between the natural signs of painting and sculpture, and the arbitrary signs of poetry; the first operate in space, the second through time. In the first *Wäldchen* Herder refined Lessing's categories in two ways. First, he expanded the natural sign to include music and granted poetry a new mode. Painting and sculpture now operate in space, music through time, and poetry through force *(Kraft)*, the capacity for summoning absent objects. Second, he followed James Harris in reviving Aristotle's distinction between work and energy, *ergon* and *energeia*. Painting and sculpture produce static works; music and poetry, active discourse.[41]

. In the fourth *Wäldchen*, Herder refined his categories further. Inspired by Condillac and Diderot, he assigned each art a separate sense.[42] Sculpture, music, and painting form a progressive hierarchy, corresponding to touch, hearing, and sight *(Gefühl, Gehör, Gesicht)*. Touch enjoys pride of place. Herder adduced Berkeley's theory of vision, claiming that "only through touch and lengthy, repeated handlings can we gain any concept of bodily space, spherical angles, and solid forms."[43] Indeed, all sensation originated with touch: "Touch is the primary, certain and true sense that develops; it already develops within the embryo, and from it the remaining senses gradually unfold." Vision, on the other hand, is "the coldest, most philosophical of the senses." The ear mediates these extremes: "Hearing alone is the most inward and deep of the senses. It is less distinct than the eye, but also less cold; less basic than touch, but also less crude."[44]

Herder ordered the arts according to this sensory hierarchy. Sculpture appeals most directly to the aesthetic subject, engaging touch through its mass and solidity. The statue addresses the beholder as pure individuality, isolated and unconstrained by laws of perspective; as Herder would claim in *Plastik* (1778), the statue represents "the *embodied* soul."[45] Painting, on the other hand, subjects the individual figure to the collective composition: "Each painted figure is nothing in itself; it belongs entirely to the overall surface of the eye. Each sculpted figure owes little to the whole; it exists in itself, and is *all* to the feeling hand—what a difference!"[46] Music reconciled touch and sight, immediacy and abstraction, through its properties of energy and movement. Finally, poetry triumphantly synthesized the other arts: "Poetry is more than mute painting and sculpture. . . . It is discourse, music of the soul. The sequence of thoughts, images, words, and tones is its expressive essence . . . . Its energy works more deeply upon the soul with each word and tone, and all works together towards the whole."[47]

The same sensory hierarchy informed Herder's prize-winning *Abhandlung über den Ursprung der Sprache* (*Treatise on the Origin of Language*, 1772). In the best-known passage, Herder attacked Condillac's mechanistic theory of language, specifically, the French philosopher's emphasis upon instinctual needs. The human animal, he argued, was defined precisely by its freedom from instinct. Humans do not innately build dams, spin webs, or perform other complex tasks. In recompense, however, they enjoy a far wider sphere of activity. Condillac's prime movers, need and attention, do not motivate Herder's rational animal: "The forces of his soul are spread out over the world; [there is] no direction of his representations on a single thing; hence *no drive to art, no skill for art*—and, most pertinent here, *no animal language.*"[48] Humans possess instead *Reflexion*, or *Besonnenheit*, the power to integrate sensations within a perceptual schema: "The human being demonstrates reflection when the force of his soul works so freely that, in the whole ocean of sensations which floods through all the senses, it can, as it were, separate off, hold fast, and focus attention upon a single wave, while being conscious of its own attentiveness."[49] Language thus begins in freedom from physical impulse: in forming the simplest sign, humans exercise self-awareness. Attention is both in and for itself, directed outward to the object and reflected back upon the subject.

Herder ascribed *Reflexion* to the same sensory hierarchy that governed the arts. Hearing again mediated between touch and sight: "Touch senses only within itself and its organ; vision throws us great distances outside of ourselves: hearing stands in between in its degree of mediation."[50] Thus, for example, a human being presented with a sheep neither preys upon it (touch), nor loses its woolly contour in a profusion of light and color (sight). Rather, he singles out its sound: "He recognized the sheep by its bleating; this was a *grasped sign by means of which the soul distinctly recalled to awareness* [besann] *an idea.* What else is that but a word? And what is the *entire human language* but a *collection of such words?* "[51] All signs emerged from this interior balance of the senses; as Herder put it, "I cannot think the first human thought, nor frame the first human judgment, without dialoguing, or at least striving to dialogue, within my soul."[52]

Herder revolutionized language theory by demonstrating how a holistic mental schema underlay the formation of even the simplest word, an insight that eluded Condillac. After Herder, as Charles Taylor wrote, "an atomism of meaning becomes as untenable as the parallel atomism of perceptions does after Kant."[53] Nevertheless, the theory of *Reflexion* is grounded within the mechanisms of sensualist psychology. When he later attacked Kantian idealism in his *Metakritik zur Kritik der reinen Vernunft* (1799), Herder revived the hierarchy of *Gefühl-Gehör-Gesicht* in his revision of the Transcendental Aesthetic.[54] *Kalligone* (1800), his rebuttal to Kant's Third Critique, marshals Berkeley's theory of touch and embraces Condillac's account of language origins.[55] From first to last, Herder remained within the sensualist tradition of the Enlightenment.

· · · · ·

A shadowy world arises from the pages of Berkeley, Condillac, and Herder. Truth no longer presents itself before the tribunal of reason. It must be patched together from the testimony of the different senses, witnesses of varying reliability. Ideas no longer sparkle, clearly and distinctly, within the theater of the mind. They hide behind signs whose interpretation demands experience and critical judgment. Poetry and music no longer serve as earthly ambassadors of a sovereign, immaterial soul. Signs spring instead from the moving, gesturing body, and they can easily deceive. In summary, this sounds very much like the world of *Don Giovanni.*

A new subject inhabits this world, an elusive self who resembles neither the transcendent *cogito* of rationalist rhetoric nor the productive *Ich* of idealist aesthetics. The Enlightenment subject, Mozart's subject, is a creature of experience and signs. He comes alive only when he senses, grasps, gestures, speaks, and interacts with other subjects. Characters like Don Giovanni or Faust embodied this new appetite for experience. Yet empiricism also dispersed the subject—or, as David Hume insisted, dissolved personal identity altogether.[56] The sense of touch seemed capable of grounding this restless subject and providing a post-Cartesian foundation for experience. Let us enter this world and experience life through the eyes and fingertips of the Mozartian subject.

·   ·   ·   ·   ·

1	Vedrai, carino,	You will see, my dear,	[Bars 1–52]
2	se sei buonino,	If you're good,	
3	Che bel rimedio	What a lovely remedy	
4	ti voglio dar!	I have for you!	
5	È naturale,	It's natural,	
6	non dà disgusto,	It doesn't taste bad,	
7	E lo speziale	And the apothecary	
8	non lo sa far.	Cannot make it.	
9	È un certo balsamo	It's a special balm	
10	ch'io porto addosso,	That I carry within;	
11	Dare tel posso,	I can give you some,	
12	se il vuoi provar.	If you want to try it.	

13	Saper vorresti	Do you want to know	
14	dove mi sta?	Where it is?	
15	Sentilo battere,	Hear it beating,	[Bars 53–104]
16	toccami qua!	Touch me here!	

Zerlina's second aria progresses explicitly from vision ("vedrai") to hearing ("sentilo") to touch ("toccami"). The text falls into four quatrains of *versi quinari,* or five-syllable lines. Musically, the aria divides cleanly in half (52 + 52 bars). Yet Mozart has devoted the entire second half to the last two verses, where Zerlina commands Masetto to hear and touch her beating heart. Musical heartbeats were an opera buffa cliché, from the final duet of Pergolesi's *La serva padrona* to the Guglielmo-Dorabella duet in *Così fan tutte.* These numbers merely represent the sound of the heart, however, as in Serpina's "Senti il tipiti." Zerlina's aria drives beyond hearing to physical contact; as the stage direction in mm. 59–60 specifies, she is "making him touch her heart." This trajectory, coupled with the lopsided proportions of the setting, suggests that the relationship between the senses plays a more than incidental role in Da Ponte's and Mozart's expressive design.

Poetically, the vision-touch progression corresponds to a movement from imagination to perception, discourse to intuition. Da Ponte's first three strophes spin out an elaborate metaphor whose target remains hidden until the end. His use of future conditional ("Vedrai . . . se sei buonino") further abstracts Zerlina's discourse, both temporally and modally. The delicate eroticism and diminutives suggest Mary Hunter's category of the "serva/contadina" aria, in which a rustic minx enjoys "both an acute awareness and an astute summing-up of her audience (often with the intention of teasing, deceiving, or manipulating them)."[57] Zerlina controls Masetto rhetorically, enticing him with erotic *double entendre* ("un certo balsamo"), and then reining in his fantasy with the chaste literal meaning.[58]

Poetic artifice evaporates in the final verses, where Da Ponte has abandoned metaphor and mannerism in favor of two simple commands. The switch to imperative plucks the discourse out of the hypothetical future, precisely as Zerlina reveals the target of her metaphor. Yet she does not name the hidden object (her heart) with a verbal symbol, but invites Masetto instead to hear and feel it beating. The omission also invites text-painting, encouraging the composer to substitute a musical icon, as Mozart did. As vision gives way to hearing and touch, communication reverts to nonverbal "natural" signs.

The final deictic, *qua*, completes the regression from the symbolic realm. Deictics are words whose meaning depends upon the speaker's context (here, now, I). As Mauro Calcagno has shown, these "pointing" words helped librettists create a distinctively theatrical poetry, allowing them to locate the singers within the spatiotemporal coordinates of the stage action.[59] Zerlina's *qua* focuses attention on the act of enunciation, emphasizing her actuality in theatrical space. It also serves as a gestural cue: even without the stage direction, Da Ponte's omission of the "naming" word *core* requires the singer to indicate her breast.[60] To establish her sincerity, Zerlina dispenses with arbitrary signs and offers Masetto the audible, tangible evidence of her body.

Mozart responded to Da Ponte's opening strophes with a rarefied musical sign, the siciliano topic. Dance topics, Monelle has explained, signify through a double process of indexicality, the second of Peirce's sign-object relations.[61] The musical sign indexes the object by replicating distinctive features—in this case, the musette pedal, 3/8 meter, and characteristic dotted rhythm. The object, in turn, indexes associated cultural meanings. Unlike the minuet or contredanse, however, the siciliano was no longer danced in eighteenth-century ballrooms; it did not belong to the occasional music of Mozart's age.[62] Its connotations of simple innocent nature were purely arbitrary, derived from the conventions of the pastoral genre. The siciliano topic functions, in Matthew Head's phrase, as "a copy of a copy."[63] It thus provides a fitting complement to the discursive abstraction of Zerlina's first three strophes.

The siciliano vanishes in the second half of "Vedrai carino," together with Zerlina's metaphor (see example 11). Like Da Ponte, however, Mozart withholds the "name" of the hidden object; the musical heart, with its conventional tick-tock oscillation, does not materialize until mm. 76–77. The second half begins instead with a cluster of physical indices, as Zerlina's performance draws closer to the body. The bass begins to pulse with eighth notes, suggesting a quickening of vital signs; a sinuous melody coils downward through three octaves, evoking intimacy and envelopment; the vocal melody shifts to a low monotone, like a gentle murmur; and the rising sequence and upbeat rhythms indicate urgency, anticipation, and excitement.

These indices do not submit easily to naming or verbal paraphrase, like dance topics or iconic text-painting. Yet such signs, which appeal directly to kinesthetic and emotional experience, lie at the heart of musical expression. Certainly, they are what eighteenth-century writers had in mind when they distinguished the "natural" signs of music from the arbitrary signs of language. Lawrence Zbikowski has offered a recent explanation of the same distinction: "The primary function of language within human culture is to direct the attention of another person to objects or concepts within a shared referential frame. The primary function of music, by contrast, is to represent through patterned sound various dynamic processes that are common in human experience."[64] Such evocative patterns are the most characteristic musical signs, but also the most elusive.

It is remarkable, therefore, how systematically Mozart has derived the indices in mm. 53–75. Every sign we have identified comes directly from the siciliano. The pulsing bass transforms the musette pedal, energizing the static bass line. Zerlina's opening phrases preserve the characteristic dance rhythm, while eliminating its lilting melodic contour: even her monotone declamation derives from m. 1, with its repeated c". The rising tetrachordal motive is a written-out extension of the grace-note ascent in m. 2, which draws out the yearning, upbeat impulse of the ornament. The sequence in mm. 61–63 restores the rising motive to its $\hat{1}$–$\hat{2}$–$\hat{3}$ origin, while preserving the written-out rhythm. Moreover, the sequenced motive is an exact 2:1 diminution of the opening two-bar rhythm. The winds proceed to isolate the first four notes (mm. 63–66), hammering out the diminished upbeat rhythm on a single chord as Zerlina commands, "Hear it beating." This insistent motive, derived impeccably from the opening bars, reveals the pulse that has been beating throughout the aria. In summary, Mozart has dissolved the complex dance topic into its distinctive features and realized the expressive potential of these simple units. His semiotic transformation of the siciliano displays the same technical finesse and sophistication we expect of his motivic, tonal, and formal procedures.

Example 11.   Mozart, *Don Giovanni*, "Vedrai carino," mm. 53–85.

Mozart's transformation of the opening rhythmic motive reveals another generative process, which engages both poetry and music. The rhythm in mm. 1–2 (♪♪♪ | ♪.♪♪) is not only a distinctive feature of the siciliano, but also a common prosodic formula. As Friedrich Lippmann has shown, this basic rhythm was a staple for *quinari sdruccioli* from Gluck's "Chorus of the Furies" in *Orfeo ed Euridice* ("Chi mai dell'Erebo") to Verdi's "La donna è mobile" in *Rigoletto*.[65] To understand the interaction of topic and prosody in "Vedrai carino," let us consider two neighboring examples from Mozart's

Example 11.   (continued)

Da Ponte operas (see example 12). Despina's "In uomini" alternates *quinari sdruccioli* and *piani*, beginning at "Di pasta simile / son tutti quanti." As in Zerlina's aria, the rhythmic motto, coupled with compound meter and bass pedal, index a pastoral dance. Yet Mozart has carefully respected the prosody, modifying the dotted rhythm for each *verso piano*. Figaro's "Se vuol ballare" begins with the same rhythm, this time indexing a minuet. The text, however, contains only one *sdrucciolo*, which falls within the following 2/4

Example 12. Related prosodic rhythms: a. *Così fan tutte,* "In uomini," mm. 25–27; b. *Le nozze di Figaro,* "Se vuol ballare," mm. 1–8.

Di pa - sta si - mi-le son tut - ti quan - ti,

Se vuol bal - la - re si-gnor Con - ti - no,   se vuol bal - la - re si-gnor Con - ti - no,

section. In this case, Mozart chose the rhythm solely to represent a dance. As these arias demonstrate, two independent systems generate Zerlina's vocal rhythm, the topical (musical) and the prosodic (poetic).

"Vedrai carino" plays between the two systems. As in Figaro's aria, the dance topic clearly dictated Mozart's choice of rhythm. Zerlina's entire aria contains only two *sdruccioli,* verses 9 and 15; Mozart simply imposed the dance rhythm on the *quinari piani.* Moreover, only the second *sdrucciolo,* "Sentilo battere," matches the rhythmic motive. The accents fall on the first and fourth syllables, and the double consonant of *battere* even implies a dotted rhythm. Topic and prosody first coincide on this pivotal line, as metaphor gives way to literal meaning, symbolic discourse to sensory intuition. Rhythmic priority shifts from topic to prosody, from the represented object to the act of enunciation itself. Prosody, in turn, becomes transformed into a bodily index, as the speech rhythm is isolated, diminished, and, finally, truncated in the winds' "beating" motive.

The question remains, how did Mozart realize musically the experience of touch? Harmony proves the most telling parameter. The aria's second half begins, like the first, with a static tonic pedal point. The rising sequence in mm. 61–63 leads to a V_7 chord, which is prolonged for three measures while the winds repeat their four-note motive. This prolongation adds weight to the final verse, "Toccami qua," which finally completes the cadence. The repetition of the passage (mm. 67–75) stokes the tension further. Zerlina repeats her diminished-fifth leap twice, extends the V_7 chord by repeating *qua* three times, and finally pauses on a deceptive cadence. Instead of resolving to the tonic, however, Mozart has finally deployed his musical "heart," with its quaint *staccato* tick-tock, suspended on a ii$_6$ chord. Only now does the conventional pictorialism arrive, after Zerlina has wound harmonic tension to a peak and riveted attention with her insistent deictics. The icon emerges as a palpable object, as if Zerlina were handing Masetto a heart locket. And finally, after having bared the pulsing body beneath the siciliano, the orchestra triumphantly restores the dance topic in the coda.

Zerlina's aria leads patiently to the foundations of the Enlightenment sign. Representation recedes continuously into the body, from dance to prosody to pulse, ending with unmediated contact. After Zerlina's first aria, Masetto exclaims, "Just see how that enchantress could seduce me!" Her second aria leaves him dumbstruck. Zerlina has guided her lover to a space beneath language, truly, to the bedrock of communication.

.   .   .   .   .

"Là ci darem la mano" might appear to trace the same path. This seduction also begins with a visual invitation, as Giovanni shows Zerlina his "casinetto," and it ends with explicit physical contact—according to the stage direction, Giovanni and Zerlina exit "abbracciati." A closer look reveals that this duplicitous giving of hands follows the opposite trajectory from "Vedrai carino," from sensory intuition into the airy reaches of symbolic discourse. Unlike Zerlina, Giovanni does not return to the solid foundations of the natural sign; he is, quite literally, building castles in Spain.

Giovanni's opening quatrain begins and ends with locational deictics, *là* and *qui*. His preceding recitative has prepared a visual reference field, specifying "quel casinetto" and even flagging it with a *là*, sung on his highest note. Each verse locates the actor physically, defining his position in theatrical space:

> *Là* ci darem la mano;
> *là* mi dirai di si.
> Vedi, non è *lontano*,
> Partiam, ben mio da *qui*.

(*There* we shall take hands;
There you will say yes to me.
See, it is not *far*,
My love, let us depart *from here*.)

As in Zerlina's arias, these "pointing words" invite physical gesture. They anchor language in the *hinc et nunc,* emphasizing the enunciation of the message. Verb tense and mood again help to situate the discourse. Giovanni begins in the future indicative, then switches to the imperative to actualize the projected events—a temporal shift that parallels the spatial progression from *là* to *qui*. Even the expression for marrying, *darsi la mano,* draws on a tactile image and invites stage business.

As Zerlina weighs Giovanni's offer, she distances herself from the enunciatory context. Spatiotemporal perception gives way to emotional introspection, while the shift to the conditional mood whisks the discourse into the realm of the hypothetical imagination:

Vorrei e non vorrei,
mi trema un poco il cor;
felice è ver sarei,
ma può burlarmi ancor!

(I would, yet I wouldn't,
My heart is trembling a bit.
True, I would be happy,
Yet he could still deceive me!)

Zerlina's response also shows a new rhetorical finesse. The quatrain is structured around the figure of *antithesis,* both within verse 1 and between verses 3 and 4. Zerlina has already strayed from the certainty of the senses into the deceptive web of language.

Giovanni's verse also undergoes a prosodic transformation in Zerlina's response. All but one of his verses began with a trochee; all but one of hers begins with an iamb. The alternation of trochees and iambs continues in the third strophe as they begin to trade lines, with Zerlina finally echoing Giovanni's pattern:

GIOVANNI: Vieni mio bel diletto!

ZERLINA: Mi fa pieta Masetto!

GIOVANNI: Io cangeró tua sorte!

ZERLINA: Presto, non son più forte!

Giovanni's trochees accent his deictics and imperatives, emphasizing his command of the physical space *(là, vedi, vieni, io)*. Zerlina smoothes away these gestural accents as she explores her inner world *(vorrei, mi trema, felice, mi fa pietà)*. Her graceful iambs triumph in the final strophe, as Giovanni's seduction succeeds:

Andiam, andiam, mio bene,
a ristorar le pene
d'un innocente amor.

These suave verses complete the transition from gesture to prosody. In Condillac's terms, they sublimate the innate impulses of the *langage d'action*, "the seed of language and all the arts that can serve to express our thoughts."[66]

The final strophe wafts the characters into the artificial realm of the pastoral. Giovanni and Zerlina leave behind all particulars of space, time, and bodily orientation, and frolic in the Arcadian fantasy of "innocent love." As in "Vedrai carino," Da Ponte has exploited the dual perspective of trope, in this case, irony. Zerlina accepts the invocation of "innocent love" at face value, while the audience (represented onstage by the eavesdropping Donna Elvira) grasps Giovanni's true intentions. The duet ends where the aria began, in deceptive artifice.

Mozart responded to Da Ponte's opening strophe with music of utmost simplicity. He set Giovanni's blunt verses syllabically (aside from a brief flourish in the final phrase), scrupulously following the accentual pattern. The melody orbits tightly around the tonic, just as the deictics rivet the discourse to the enunciatory context. Nor does the famous melody seem to index any dance, genre, or style. Allanbrook detected a serenade, but this seems dubious.[67] The opera contains two explicit serenades, "Deh vieni alla finestra" and Giovanni's related solo in "Ah, taci inguisto cor."

These outdoor songs are set in a pastoral 6/8, like Susanna's "Deh vieni, non tardar" *(Figaro)* or Pedrillo's "Im Mohrenland" *(Die Entführung)*, and even feature the characteristic siciliano rhythm. The duet opens with a striking absence of topical reference, complementing Giovanni's artless speech.

As the discourse shifts to emotive introspection, Giovanni's melody sprouts new flourishes—an upbeat, a falling fifth on "cor," a cadential extension. Throughout the Andante, Zerlina adorns Giovanni's melody with sighs, swoops, and descending chromatic lines. These melodic figures do belong to a conventional code, the vocabulary of operatic rhetoric. Indeed, her decoration of Giovanni's melody exemplifies the principle of *elaboratio* or *amplificatio* that Mark Evan Bonds and Bettina Varwig have identified as central to eighteenth-century musical rhetoric.[68] Here, too, Mozart's procedure runs opposite to "Vedrai carino." The aria breaks down the siciliano, releasing the bodily indices within the topic; the duet constructs a conventional figuration, obscuring the "natural" simplicity of the melody.

Mozart responded to Da Ponte's ironic final strophe with another rarefied pastoral topic. The lilting 6/8 enhances the iambic verse, while the pedal point and siciliano rhythm evoke the nostalgic realm of innocent lovers. The melodies of the Andante and Allegro share a similar contour, pushing upward against $\hat{3}$ and leaping a fourth at the cadence. Yet, the Allegro softens the bare outlines of the opening melody, filling in the leaps and rocking between $\hat{3}$ and $\hat{2}$. These gentle undulations already begin with Zerlina's chromatic palpitations in mm. 25–27 and 43–46, and complete her ornamental elaboration of Giovanni's melody. Not even the exclamations of "Andiam!" at the end of the duet (mm. 64–72) can disturb the new *soavità*. They echo Giovanni's urgent entreaties at the end of the Andante, but Mozart has coaxed the libidinous cries into a balanced period, floating above the graceful dance rhythm. Art refines nature, as music and poetry sublimate the crude signs of emotion.

"Là ci darem la mano" vindicates that mistrust of signs that haunts Enlightenment thought. While signs played an indispensable role in freeing the mind from brute instinct, they could also lead humanity astray into false metaphysics and superstition. This ambivalence toward human progress, so familiar from Rousseau, did not escape Condillac: "We find that the epoch of [languages'] decadence occurs at the very time that they seemed to attain the greatest beauties. We see figures and metaphors accumulating and overloading the style with ornamentations, to the point where the foundation seems merely an accessory. When this moment arrives, we can slow down, but cannot prevent, the decline of a language."[69] Or, as Herder complained: "We know words and believe that we know things themselves; we embrace the shadow, rather than the body that casts the shadow."[70] Mozart's operas demonstrate the mixed blessing of representation. By playing with signs, Mozart could dislodge his characters from their fixed social positions and reconstruct a utopian world. Yet in the hands of Giovanni, Vitellia, or the Queen of the Night, the same signs become instruments of seduction and deceit. The Enlightenment had a sure remedy—tear down the rotten edifice and build anew on the foundations of nature and the senses. The antidote to "Là ci darem la mano" is "Vedrai carino."

. . . . .

For Romantic critics, the Act 2 banquet scene epitomized Don Giovanni's tragic grandeur, his Miltonian struggle against divine authority. Recent commentators have cast a more jaundiced eye on the Don, noting the unreflective, parasitic nature of his music. In her valuable study of Aristotelian recognition (*anagnorisis*), Jessica Waldoff questioned Giovanni's tragic stature: "But the true tragic hero always has his moment of recognition—compare Hamlet, Macbeth, Othello, Faust. Don Giovanni is no tragic hero. Heroic though his defiance may seem, he stands in the place where a hero should be."[71] For Allanbrook, Giovanni was simply "No-Man."

This final analysis proposes a different view of the Don from the vantage point of sensualist psychology. As with "Vedrai carino" and "Là ci darem," we shall probe beneath the surface of musical representation and character analysis, plumbing that more obscure region in which both signs and the reflective self were thought to originate. I shall argue that, from this perspective, Don Giovanni does indeed achieve self-knowledge in the banquet scene, attaining if not heroic at least human stature.

The Act 2 finale begins with the most artificial, "metalinguistic" signs in the entire opera. The scene not only contains diegetic music, remarked on by the characters, but even includes a selection by Mozart himself. As Daniel Heartz has suggested, the texts of the three quoted arias may even provide a commentary on the dramatic action.[72] As he mocks Elvira, Giovanni spouts yet another buffa aria; accompanied by obbligato winds and capped by a singsong refrain, his little *brindisi*, "Lascia ch'io mangi," could pass for a fourth quotation. (In the Bertati-Gazzaniga version, Giovanni improvises a 3/4 toast to the city of Venice at this point, "Far devi un brindisi.") The banquet scene introduces Giovanni as a glib actor whose signs have slipped their moorings in sensual reality. Hovering in this rarefied ether, Giovanni awaits his downfall.

The Man of Stone immediately drags him to earth (see example 13). Mozart marked the statue's arrival with two musical recollections, both of which emphasize his physical presence. The catastrophic opening chord recalls the opera's most decisive moment of touch, replicating the precise harmony on which Giovanni impaled the Commendatore. The aural onslaught can almost mask the second musical reminiscence. Beneath the blaring chords, the basses and cellos rumble a series of ponderous half notes. This *alla breve* rhythm comes from the previous scene (mm. 396–98 and 400–402), where Leporello reports the statue's heavy steps—"Ta, ta, ta, ta!" (These steps should not be confused with the statue's knocking, which Mozart has represented with *coups d'archet* in mm. 406–17). This is no ghost or insubstantial phantasm. The Man of Stone bursts upon the scene as a physical mass, solid, palpable, and moving purposefully through space.

As the Commendatore begins to sing, his footsteps are transformed into the feet of poetic meter. The lower strings shift from half notes to the marchlike ostinato that accompanies the statue throughout most of the scene. Mozart seems to have derived this ostinato directly from the poetic meter. The statue's first words fall into a pair of trochaic *ottonari*: "Don Giovanni a cenar teco, / M'invitasti e son venuto." As Lippmann has shown, dotted rhythms like the statue's ostinato were a standard choice for *ottonari*; the same pattern underlies the final chorus of *Le nozze di Figaro* ("Questo giorno di tormenti"), as well as the third terzetto ("Una bella ser-

Example 13.   *Don Giovanni*, Act 2 finale, mm. 433–43.

enata") and Act 1 stretto ("Dammi un bacio, o mio tesoro") of *Così fan tutte*.[73] In *Don Giovanni*, the statue's ostinato falls into two-bar groupings, the normal length for an Italian verse, articulated by the descending tones of the bass tetrachord.[74] Meanwhile, the Commendatore plods through his *ottonari* in four-bar phrases, in keeping with his *alla breve* gait. As in "Vedrai carino," Mozart seems to have forged a direct link between bodily rhythm and prosody, translating footsteps into poetic feet.

Two epiphanies await Giovanni as he pits himself against the Man of Stone. The first comes with the A-minor cadence in mm. 477–85, the first structural downbeat of the scene (see example 14). Until this point, Giovanni has stammered his responses over syncopated or triplet rhythms. As he composes himself, the Don attempts an authentic cadence in A minor, answering the Commendatore's challenge. The Commendatore rides over Giovanni, however, eliding his phrase with an interrupted cadence. As if deaf to Giovanni's response, the statue repeats his demand: "Parlo,

Example 14. *Don Giovanni,* Act 2 finale, mm. 477–85.

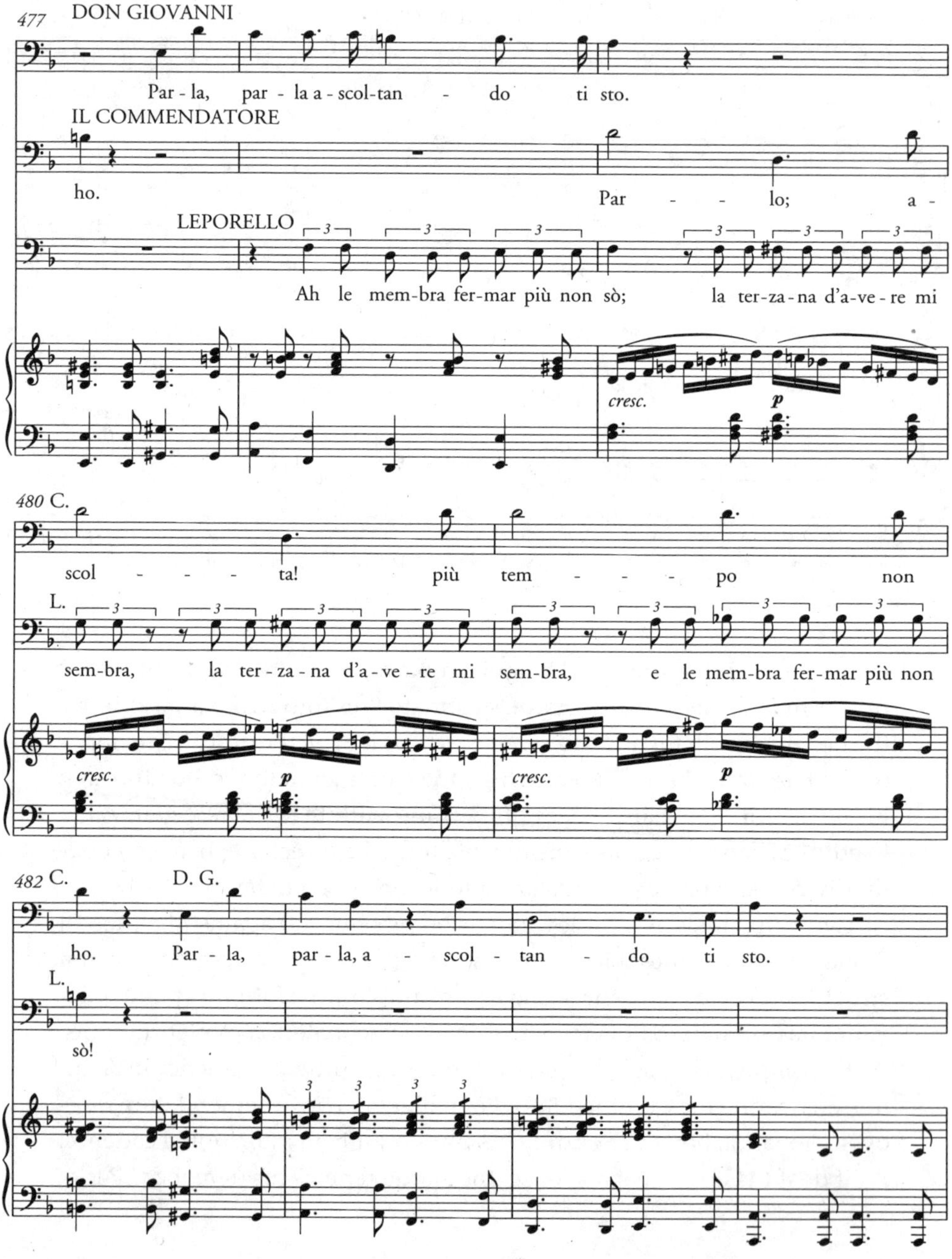

ascolta, più tempo non ho." Giovanni repeats his phrase and succeeds in reaching an authentic cadence, but this time he augments his rhythm to match the Commendatore's *alla breve*. Now, for the first time, the Commendatore's trochaic ostinato accompanies Giovanni's line.

Significantly, this moment hinges on the sense of hearing. Giovanni adopts the Commendatore's ostinato only as he agrees to listen. Mozart has repeated the command for emphasis, his only textual repetition in the scene. Two bars of naked ostinato allow the cadence to sink in, forcing Giovanni (and the audience) to actually listen. The Don, we might say, has begun to exercise reflection in Herder's sense of an inner dialogue mediated by the ear. Yet he learns to listen only as he pushes against the immovable stone. Because the Commendatore does not join in the glib dialogue, he forces the Don back upon the emptiness of his own discourse.

The second epiphany involves the handshake itself. As Giovanni takes the statue's hand, the trochaic ostinato vanishes. The texture now switches to obbligato recitative, as tremolos and rushing scales represent the violent struggle. As noted, these signs derive directly from the Act 1 duel. Yet they no longer depict clashing swords, but a battle of words. Physical aggression, already formalized in the *code duello*, is further sublimated into speech intonation; as Condillac put it, "To take the place of the violent bodily movements, the voice was raised and lowered by strongly marked intervals."[75] Having learned how to listen, the Don now learns how to speak, anchoring his speech in the bedrock of physical gesture.[76]

The tragic aspect now begins to unfold. In his analysis of Rousseau's *Pygmalion*, Paul de Man argued that, ironically, the moment of touch dissolved the self: "The energy that succeeds at last in forcing the exchange is the deconstructive discourse of truth and falsehood that undoes selfhood as tragic metaphor and replaces it by the knowledge of its figural and epistemologically unreliable structure."[77] In other words, the stony surface does not confirm the integrity of the self. Rather, it shatters the fragile shell of signs through which that self has elaborated an identity. De Man's interpretation may repel readers unsympathetic to poststructuralism; yet it underlines a crucial dialectic of Enlightenment linguistics. Earlier theories of language, grounded in the duality of body and soul,

had guaranteed the rational self a life outside of language. Enlightenment sensualism erases that option. To stop signifying is to regress to the
dumb, unconscious body. The subject is suspended between a primal
oblivion and the artificial web of symbols. In the end, Pygmalion chooses
artifice:

> Oui, cher et charmant object: oui, digne chef-d'oeuvre de mes mains, de
> mon coeur et des Dieux . . . c'est toi, c'est toi seule: je t'ai donné tout mon
> être; je ne vivrai plus que par toi.[78]

> (Yes, dear and charming object; yes, worthy masterpiece of my hand, of
> my heart, and of the gods . . . it is you, you alone: I have given you my
> entire being, and I shall no longer live except through you.)

Giovanni faces the same crossroads. The statue has burst through Giovanni's web of signs, wrenching him back to the same preverbal, premu-
sical strata to which Zerlina led Masetto. Repentance seems almost
unimaginable at this point, on purely semiotic grounds. Count Almaviva's
contrition at the end of *Le nozze di Figaro* rings false, not simply because
we doubt his change of heart, but because we no longer trust the musical
language. We have observed how glibly Mozart's characters adopt musical signs to deceive, seduce, and pursue goals. The Count's hymn is just
another sign, paper money without backing. For Giovanni, having reached
the touchstone of meaning, confession can only mean a return to the mi-
rage of signs. As he tears free of the Commendatore's grip, the Don re-
nounces the entire representational system he has exploited so masterfully
throughout the opera.

Giovanni's refusal thus represents, if not heroism, at least an act of integrity. Mozart permits him a valiant death, setting his final "No!" on a
half cadence that demands closure. With this performative, the Don finally
takes control of the tonality, if only to damn himself to oblivion. The No-
Man removes himself from the play of signs and enters into the frozen
constellations of mythology. "He is with Pluto and Persephone," sing the
other characters before they memorialize Giovanni in the *antichissima can-
zone*. The Don ends his career as . . . a mute statue.

·   ·   ·   ·   ·

The Man of Stone has furnished critics with many symbols. For the Romantics, he represented the spirit realm; for Freudians, the Oedipal father; for social historians, the *ancien régime*.[79] Yet, for Mozart's age, the living statue played the opposite role of a symbol. Its solid, unyielding surface drove the subject back into the body and senses, away from the symbolic order. The Pygmalion myth captivated the Enlightenment imagination precisely because it explored the fine line that separated reality and representation, nature and artifice.

And, perhaps, the living statue dramatizes a problem that still haunts modern thought. The Man of Stone exposes the inner contradiction of a subject who must project an ethical and metaphysical persona while knowing he is but flesh and blood. By exploring the limits of representation, *Don Giovanni* probes the tensions within a materialist worldview, tensions that have only deepened since 1787. In this sense, Giovanni remains a compelling protagonist for us moderns, who, despite all our attacks on the Enlightenment, do not easily escape its intellectual orbit.

THREE Topics in Context

John Locke complained in his *Essay Concerning Human Understanding* that "one may observe, in all languages, certain words that, if they be examined, will be found in their first original, and their appropriated use, not to stand for any clear and distinct ideas."[1] Locke's protest against the "abuse of words" reverberated throughout the eighteenth century and even became a political cause during the French Revolution. Following the Terror, the moderate Idéologues took charge of national education, adopting Locke and Condillac as patron saints. They zealously prosecuted Condillac's critique of language, rooting out metaphysical abstractions and restoring words to empirically verifiable referents. The Idéologues reconstituted the Académie française as the Institut national, founded the Écoles normales, published the *Journal de la langue française* (edited by "*grammairien-patriote*" Joseph-François Domergue), and celebrated the

Sabbath by debating neologisms.[2] For a brief glorious moment, lexicographers spearheaded the march of human freedom.

Domergue and his colleagues would have flung up their hands over the word "topic," as popularized by Leonard Ratner. The musical term has gathered a host of meanings that vary widely and often correspond only tangentially to any eighteenth-century usage or compositional practice. Nevertheless, Ratner's concept has proved one of the most fruitful approaches to musical semantics, and it belongs at the heart of any discussion of Mozart and semiotics. If, as Enlightenment writers constantly stressed, language shapes thought, then it behooves us to explore what is meant by a musical topic.

Ratner introduced his lexicon of topics in the 1957 textbook *Music: The Listener's Art.* He did not call them topics, however, but simply referred to "types and styles."[3] Ratner showed how Haydn, Mozart, and Beethoven derived their thematic material from a fund of characteristic gestures, forms, and styles. For example, a Mozart keyboard sonata might combine motives drawn from Italian opera, sacred polyphony, courtly dance, and military marches—all within the space of a few phrases. Ratner's brilliant insight unveiled a wealth of semantic content in both vocal and instrumental music long ignored by formalist critics. Like the paint that once adorned the Parthenon, his types and styles restored the vivid colors to the bleached monuments of Viennese classicism.

Wye Allanbrook has hewed most closely to Ratner's original conception. Classic music, she explained, is "a musical language created out of the ordinary materials of its own musical life."[4] Allanbrook quoted the 1785 statement of Michel Paul Gui de Chabanon: "Imitation in music is not truly sensed unless its object is music. In songs one can successfully imitate warlike fanfares, hunting airs, rustic melodies, etc. It is only a question of giving one song the character of another. Art, in that case, does not suffer violence."[5] As music imitating other music, Allanbrook explained, topics transcended the naive pictorialism that later eighteenth-century writers so disdained. Moreover, as she demonstrated in her elegant study of Mozart's operas, topics encode social meanings. She leaned on the testimony of Heinrich Christoph Koch: "If instrumental music . . . is meant to awaken and maintain specific feelings, then it must be involved in such political, religious, or domestic circumstances and actions as are of pronounced interest for us, and in which our heart is predisposed to the expression of the feelings [the music] is supposed to awaken and maintain."[6] By indexing the occasional music of his time, Mozart represented "the world of men, their habits and actions."[7]

In the second edition of *Music: The Listener's Art* (1966), Ratner's theory took a new direction. He now suggested that, "borrowing an expression that belongs to rhetoric, we might very well say that these materials were musical *topics*."[8] Ratner borrowed another rhetorical expression in the textbook *Classic Music* (1980), where he referred to his types and styles as "a thesaurus of *characteristic figures*."[9] In 1991 he redefined the Classic topic once again as "a subject to be incorporated in a discourse."[10] No longer simply stylistic indices, his types and styles now assumed an oratorical function; they presupposed voice, argument, persuasion, and the other entailments of rhetoric. This interpretation has enjoyed wide currency, as when Elaine Sisman defined topics as "the subjects of intelligible speech and the objects of intelligent understanding," or when Jonathan Bellman referred to topics as "a large number of possible subjects for musical discourse."[11]

Meanwhile, musical semioticians have given Ratner's term different meanings. Kofi Agawu largely ignored the semantic content of topics, using Ratner's lexicon primarily as a way to segment the musical surface.[12] Raymond Monelle has generalized topics to embrace all conventional musical signs, including pictorial icons, rhetorical figures, and even Wagnerian leitmotifs: "The topic is essentially a symbol, its iconic or indexical features governed by convention and thus by rule."[13] Monelle's final study, a magisterial survey of musical semantics from the Middle Ages to Henze and Ligeti, seeks in topics "a map of culture, a map that is more direct, less tendentious, than any essay or exemplary fiction of a writer in words."[14] David Lidov has offered a still more capacious definition of topic, which includes any structural idiosyncrasy: "When a salient characteristic is reversed in a musical composition, we may speak of that characteristic as an idea or topic of the piece. A topic, in general, is the matter at hand."[15] Meanwhile, Robert Hatten has located topics at the center of a semantic hierarchy that begins with simple gestures and harmonies and ascends to complex tropes and expressive genres.[16]

These burgeoning meanings suggest that *topic* has come to function as something of a floating signifier. This will not disturb postmodern readers, who accept (or even revel in) such polysemy. Yet, as the Idéologues insisted, names have the power to shape thought; and, without a doubt, Ratner's term has helped to determine research into the musical semantics of Mozart and his contemporaries. In the nominalist spirit of Locke, therefore, the present chapter will test this elusive term to see how far it corresponds to "clear and distinct ideas." History and analysis will serve as the twin benchmarks. We shall revisit a familiar ensemble from *Le nozze di Figaro* guided by the writings of Giambattista Vico, the most brilliant and original advocate of topics in the eighteenth century. The semiotic analysis relies upon Hatten's theory of musical markedness, but seeks to extend that theory in new directions.

· · · · ·

The term *topic* derives from Aristotle's *topos,* or place. Other translations include *locus topicus, lieu commun, lugar,* and commonplace. In ancient rhetoric, topics referred neither to subject matter, arguments, nor figures of speech. Rather, they were methods or strategies for finding arguments. Examples include Aristotle's *ex horismou* ("from definition and knowledge of what the thing is in itself"), Cicero's *ex notatione* ("from the meaning of a word"), and Quintilian's *a fictione* ("from fictitious circumstances").[17] Topics thus belonged to the first canon of rhetoric, *inventio,* and served orators as algorithms for generating arguments. Topics governed the production of every kind of oration, whether political speeches, eulogies, or legal arguments. In fact, the most familiar modern topic belongs to jurisprudence. In preparing a case, attorneys do not simply weigh physical evidence or the testimony of witnesses; they also consult their law libraries, searching for similar cases. They are using the topic of legal precedent, cited by Adam Smith in 1748.[18] Legal precedent is not itself an argument, but a place in which to find arguments.

Eighteenth-century music theorists defined topics in this classical sense. Johann David Heinichen's *Der General-Bass in der Composition* (1728) recommended the *locus circumstantiarum* as a way to find images for text-setting. Heinichen was referring to a strategy; the actual subject matter he called "inventions" *(inventiones)*.[19] Likewise, Johann Mattheson prescribed fifteen topics to spur invention in *Der vollkommene Capellmeister* (1739). These include *locus descriptionis* (the depiction of affects), *locus oppositorum* (oppositions of meters, tempos, registers, or moods), and *locus exemplorum* (the emulation of other composers). He also recommended the *ars combinatoria* (permutation of melodic material), the one genuine *topos* cited by Ratner.[20] These algorithmic strategies differ in kind from Ratner's types and styles. They most closely resemble the "patterns of invention" that Laurence Dreyfus has identified in Bach's music, such as ROTATE, INVERT, DELETE, or MODE-SWITCH.[21]

Mattheson introduced his topics with an ominous caveat: "The mentioned loci seem to be greatly despised by those who permit nothing which has the slightest relationship with schools."[22] In fact, topics suffered widespread abuse during the seventeenth and eighteenth centuries. The Port-Royal *Logique* (1662) condemned topical invention: "Consult as many lawyers and preachers as there are in the world, as many people who speak and write, and who always have material remaining, and I do not know if you could find among them anyone who has ever thought of making an argument *à causa, ab effectu,* or *ab adjunctis.*"[23] Bernard Lamy's *L'art de parler* (1675), the leading rhetorical treatise of *le grand siècle,* also dismissed topics: "In order to be persuasive, one needs only a single proof that is strong and solid; eloquence consists in extending this proof, and bringing it to light so that it may appear clearly." Lamy proceeded to quote Descartes's verdict on the *ars topica* as "an art that teaches us to discourse without judgment on subjects about which we know nothing, an art not worthy of a reasonable man."[24] (Lamy could have adduced Jean Racine's unabashed claim in the preface to *Bérénice* that "all invention consists in making something out of nothing."[25]) François de Fénelon's *Dialogues sur l'éloquence* (1718) mocked the orator who "never thinks of any subject till he be obliged to treat of it; and then he shuts himself up in his closet, turns over his concordance, his collection of sermons . . . and common-place book of separate sentences and quotations that he has gathered together."[26] When Immanuel Kant proposed his "transcendental topics" in the second edition of *Kritik der reinen Vernunft* (1788), he contrasted them with the Aristotelian *topoi* that had allowed teachers and orators "to reason with the appearance of rigor, or chatter garrulously."[27]

The animus toward topics, as Mattheson intimated, owed to their scholastic taint. Within the medieval trivium, topics had bridged logic and rhetoric. Whereas logic dealt in syllogisms, topics generated enthymemes, arguments that lacked a major or minor premise. For example, Descartes's famous enthymeme "I think, therefore I am" lacks the major premise "All thinking beings exist." In the sixteenth century, the anti-Aristotelian reformer Peter Ramus decisively severed logic and rhetoric. During the following centuries, science and logic increasingly assumed responsibility for invention and proof, confining rhetoric to persuasion and adornment. For writers like Arnauld, Lamy, and Fénelon, the proper source of arguments were *les idées claires et distinctes*. Their "philosophical rhetoric" eliminated the *loci topici*, whose artificial rules could only obscure nature and truth. As Peter Hoyt has noted, even Johann Georg Sulzer and Johannn Nikolaus Forkel dismissed topics.[28]

Thus, Ratner's types and styles violate both the letter and the spirit of the classical *ars topica*. They differ in kind from the topics of Aristotle and Cicero, whose dusty routines had at any rate fallen into disrepute by Mozart's time. Yet his types and styles perfectly match the representational poetics that had supplanted traditional rhetoric by the late eighteenth century. The Classic topic, Monelle has explained, is a Peircian index, a sign that represents its object through causality or contiguity: "The dance measures listed by Ratner and Allanbrook, the 'fanfare' motive, the topics of 'French overture' and 'Turkish music' do not signify by virtue of resemblance, but because they reproduce styles and repertoires from elsewhere. Insofar as the slow movement of the 'Jupiter' Symphony is in sarabande meter it presents the dance measure itself rather than an imitation of it, and thus signifies indexically."[29] Whereas an icon represents a merely possible object, an index is dictated by a real object. Thus, Haydn's *Creation* depicts an imaginary Chaos (icon), while his symphonies and quartets replicate features of actual dances, marches, and vocal styles (indices). Moreover, such indices do not require a metaphoric mapping between music and painting or language; both sign and object belong to the musical domain. Topics approach that transparent representation idealized by Enlightenment poetics, which measured beauty by the correspondence between sign and object.

Monelle's indexical interpretation would also explain the embarrassing absence of topic theory in eighteenth-century musical writings. Ratner's later reference to topics, figures, and subjects of discourse suggests a codified lexicon, akin to the Baroque *Figurenlehre*. As he claimed, "All these idioms were familiar to the eighteenth-century listener. He took delight in observing how a composer managed them during a composition; he, as well as the composer, appreciated the richness of content which the interplay of these various styles provided."[30] James Webster argued similarly that in the eighteenth century "every instrumental work was composed and understood within a context of genre, *Affekt*, and 'topoi' (topics)."[31] According to Harold S. Powers, "topics and styles were taken for granted by writers at the time, who advert to them just often enough to leave modern analysts and critics frustrated at the lack of any really systematic exposition."[32] As several critics have observed, however, such claims are conjectural and tend to elide prescriptive theory with listener competence.[33] In fact, the lack of a systematic exposition says much about the status of Ratner's topics. Certainly, the characteristic styles or dance measures in Mozart's music cannot have been lost on contemporary audiences or theorists. Yet they do not seem to have regarded these indices as codified symbols. Thomas Turino has explained the distinction: "Whereas the meanings of indices are dependent on the experiences of the perceiver, and thus can be quite fluid and varied, the meanings of symbols are relatively fixed through social agreement. Dictionaries, math books, and Morse Code manuals document the conventional meanings of symbols."[34] Much as modern theorists might like to codify a musical *Toposlehre*, eighteenth-century writings lend little encouragement.

For better or worse, Ratner's rhetorical interpretation has shaped the growth of topic theory. Critics have tended to treat topics as codified symbols rather than the fluid indices described by Turino. As a result, they have often taken a facile approach to semantic interpretation, while neglecting the syntactic structures that articulate and transform topics and which govern their dynamic interaction with meter, tonality, rhythm, and texture. Such analysis seems particularly crucial for Mozart, a composer who delighted in combining diverse topics, often in rapid succession. The need for a more rigorous syntactic analysis comes to light when we examine contrasting readings of the opening Duettino from *Le nozze di Figaro* by Allanbrook and Daniel Heartz, two critics equally versed in eighteenth-century opera and dance.

The Duettino would seem to present an uncomplicated example of topical semantics. The number portrays a simple action, as Susanna persuades Figaro to stop measuring the bedroom and admire her new bonnet. The music neatly complements this onstage action (see example 15). Figaro's counting is accompanied by a vigorous four-square theme, which Susanna answers with a more delicate idea. As Figaro turns his attention to Susanna, he abandons his opening music and adopts her theme. Music and drama seem perfectly coordinated.

A closer look reveals significant ambiguities, beginning with the identity of the two topics. Both Allanbrook and Heartz classified Susanna's melody as a gavotte, yet they disagreed on the music that accompanies Figaro's counting. Allanbrook heard a bourrée, noting the characteristic upbeat and caesura after the third beat. Heartz, more impressed by the dotted orchestral rhythms and Figaro's downbeat accents, grouped the theme with the many marches in *Figaro*. The critics based their readings upon different cultural interpretants. For Heartz, the contest of march and gavotte symbolized the triumph of feminine values in *Figaro:* "With this little drama in music, which almost needs no text, Mozart has succeeded in foreshadowing the entire opera in the first number."[35] Allanbrook, on the other hand, grouped bourrée and gavotte together as dances of *mezzo carattere,* as opposed to the noble topics of the Count and Countess.[36] The two interpretants, gender and class, determine the different objects assigned to Figaro's theme. In short, topical analysis does not simply proceed from musical to social interpretation. Even identifying a topic may involve judgments about its extramusical meaning.

The binary oppositions also prove more complicated than at first appears. During Figaro's counting music, whether march or bourrée, the cellos, violas, and bassoons introduce a countersubject, sustaining a series of fourth-species suspensions against the melody. These suspensions index a third topic, the learned or strict style—a curious choice for this lighthearted

Example 15. *Le nozze di Figaro*, Duettino, mm. 1–38.

Example 15. *(continued)*

(continued)

Example 15.   (continued)

movement. On Heartz's reading, *stile antico* counterpoint might symbolize the rational, masculine activity of counting. Yet the sacred style belongs equally to the feminine realm in *Figaro,* as in the Countess's arias with their allusions to Mozart's Salzburg masses, or the *alla breve* hymn that crowns the Act 4 finale.[37] The high church style complicates Allanbrook's reading as well, elevating Figaro's bourrée beyond the domain of the *mezzo carattere.*

Nor do the topics segment cleanly. The distinctive trait that most clearly identifies Susanna's theme as a gavotte is the double upbeat. Her phrases all begin on the second half of the bar, in contrast with Figaro's square downbeats. Yet before Susanna has sung a note, Figaro's phrases have already shifted to the third beat. In fact, his last two phrases anticipate the exact rhythm of her melody (mm. 27–30). And when Figaro repeats his melody, his opening phrases begin on the third beat (mm. 36–46). While this metrical shift cannot be said to introduce a new topic, it does blur the most important distinction between Figaro's and Susanna's themes. Similarly, the fourth-species suspensions shift from the third to the fourth beat in mm. 5–7 and merge imperceptibly into the bourrée upbeat. These ambiguities belong to that twilight region between syntax and semantics, a territory that topic theory has yet to chart.

As the Duettino demonstrates, significant problems arise when we treat topics as merely surface features, like motives or instrumentation. It would seem instead that topics are governed by a deep structure, a possibility that theorists have tended to ignore, if not deny. Kofi Agawu conceded that topics "do not seem able to sustain an independent and self-regulating account of a piece," reasoning that "if expression has no syntax, then topics are ultimately dependent signs."[38] William Caplin also concluded that topics do not possess an independent syntax, adding that, while "many modes of musical organization, such as timbre and dynamics, are clearly nonsyntactic, yet they are no less significant forces for musical expression."[39] Yet, unlike timbre and dynamics, topics do not simply belong to the design of the individual work. As tokens of general types, they share distinctive features that remain constant across different works. A theory of topical syntax must begin, therefore, with a more rigorous account of those features. We need to analyze how topics are articulated within the musical structure, considered as a system of differences.

In approaching this task, let us begin by exploring how the Enlightenment viewed rhetoric, invention, and topics. The topical signs identified by Ratner belong to the larger phenomenon of eighteenth-century representation, and any analysis that would claim pertinence for Mozart's age needs to take that context into account. The writings of Giambattista Vico offer a particularly valuable perspective. Vico was not only the most distinguished Italian linguist and philosopher of the eighteenth century. He also spent his career teaching rhetoric at the University of Naples, just blocks from the theaters where Leonardo Vinci, Nicola Porpora, and Giovanni Battista Pergolesi were forging the new style that would conquer Europe. Vico's writings offer a unique glimpse into the linguistic and philosophical controversies attending the birth of the galant style.

.   .   .   .   .

Vico's oeuvre largely amounts to a refutation of Descartes. The Neapolitan professor's defense of classical rhetoric, including the *loci topici*, must be understood as part of his humanist backlash against Cartesian rationalism, what Isaiah Berlin dubbed his "Counter-Reformation in the history of early modern philosophy."[40] Vico rejected the theory of language that Descartes's disciple Lamy had espoused in *L'art de parler:* "Because words are signs that represent the things that occur in our spirits, one might say that they are like a painting of our thoughts, that language is the brush that traces that painting, and that the words in which the discourse is composed are its colors."[41] This dualistic model assumes a clean division between soul and body, mental ideas and physical signs. The same model underlay the theory of musical figures, which Dietrich Bartel has described as "a calculated and objective presentation of generally accepted affections."[42] Rationalist rhetoric, both verbal and musical, treated language as a channel of communication, expressing independently existing ideas and emotions.

Like Condillac, Vico believed in the interdependence of language and thought. Language did not merely express the contents of the mind; it facilitated the operations by which the mind brought order to sensory experience and obtained knowledge. For Vico, as Alessandro Giuliani explained, "the study of expressive means cannot be disassociated from that of the mental procedures. Linguistic communication is also mental communication."[43] Vico's cognitive orientation suggests a fresh approach to Mozartian invention, antithetical to the rhetorical model that has guided much of the writing on musical topics.

Vico launched his campaign against Descartes in his 1707 inaugural address to the University of Naples, *De nostri temporis studiorum ratione (On the Study Methods of Our Time)*. He deplored the critical spirit of modern philosophy, which deadened the imaginative faculties of young minds. He urged a return to the Aristotelian *topoi*, which stimulated invention: "The art of topics, far from being given first place in the curriculum, is utterly disregarded. Again I say, this is harmful, since the invention of arguments is by nature prior to the judgment of their validity, so that, in teaching, invention should be given priority over philosophical criticism."[44] Vico condemned the sterility of the vaunted *esprit géométrique*: "The person who uses the syllogism brings no new element, since the conclusion is already implied in the initial proposition or assumption."[45] Rhetorical enthymemes, since they harbored an unknown premise, trained the student to reason inductively; they fostered *ingenium*, the ability to grasp hidden or far-flung connections. Vico returned to this point in *De antiquissima Italorum sapientia (On the Most Ancient Wisdom of the Italians, 1710)*: "If [someone] will scrutinize all the 'places' distinguished in [Aristotle's] *Topics* with a critical eye, then he will be certain that he knows the thing clearly and distinctly because he has turned the matter over in his mind and answered all the questions that can be asked with respect to the subject under discussion."[46]

Topics thus conduced to Vico's Ciceronian ideal of the *vita activa*. Education should not produce solitary thinkers, he protested, but citizens capable of navigating public life. Topics trained the mind to grasp the confused manifold of everyday life. Whereas science demanded rigorous proof, rhetoric traded in probabilities, the coin of the real world. Michael Mooney has summarized Vico's project: "Faced with the confident claims of Cartesian science to universal competence, he sought to exempt civil affairs from the constraints of the new method and to regain for rhetoric a share in the task of reasoning."[47]

Vico granted rhetoric a central role in his magnum opus, the *Principj di scienza nuova*, whose theory of language origins anticipated the conjectural narratives of Condillac and Rousseau. According to Vico, every human civilization passed through three periods: the ages of gods, heroes, and men. Theocratic patriarchs dominated the first age, warrior-aristocrats the second age, and legal monarchs the third. The three ages corresponded to different modes of expression, beginning with mute gestures and hieroglyphs, proceeding to poetic figures and emblems, and ending with modern prose. As in the French narratives, language developed analytically, growing increasingly precise as humanity left behind brute nature.

Vico planted his flag firmly within the empiricist camp. The first edition of the *Scienza nuova* (1725) traced philosophy and ethics to the lower faculties of body and emotion: "For, in order that men should reach the sublime truths of metaphysics, and those of morality derived from them, Providence permitted the progress of the nations to be regulated in such a way that, just as individual men naturally sense first, and then reflect, first with souls perturbed by passions, then finally with pure mind, so mankind had first to sense the modifications of the body, then to reflect upon those of the soul and finally upon those of abstract mind."[48] Philosophy germinated in the sensual tropes and figures of primitive language, as Vico explained in the 1744 edition of the *Scienza nuova*: "Everything that the poets sensed in their popular wisdom was later understood by the philosophers in their esoteric wisdom. We may say, then, that the poets were the *sense* of mankind, and the philosophers its *intellect*."[49]

In his celebrated discussion of *logica poetica*, Vico correlated rhetorical categories with stages of human culture. Every language, he claimed, passed successively through the tropes of metaphor, metonymy, synecdoche, and irony. Vico situated the *ars topica* at the earliest stage of human language and culture. Returning to the argument of *De nostri tempori*, he emphasized the inductive nature of topical reasoning, which stimulated discovery and brought new ideas to light. For a primitive people, this was the chief function of language: "Topics make the mind more inventive, just as criticism makes it more exact. In that early age, the institutions necessary to human life had to be invented, and invention is the proper task of ingenuity."[50]

Yet these primitive topics served as tools of empirical rather than rational invention: "The first founders of civilization strove to devise an art of *sensory topics*. This allowed them to combine what might be termed the concrete properties, qualities, and relations of individual objects and their species."[51] Early humans could not yet distinguish genera from species, type from token, sign from object. Sensory topics thus gave rise to "imaginative universals" *(universali fantastici)*, archetypes that embodied, rather than represented, cultural values.[52] Sensory topics preceded invention as understood in classical rhetoric, with its a priori categories of place, time, cause, and definition. As Donald Philip Verene explained, "The sensory topos of Vico differs from Aristotle's conception in that it is a theory of how the background of the mind itself is created."[53]

Significantly, Vico located the fountainhead of language, culture, and reason in an aural experience. The thundering sky first roused humans from bestial stupidity, awakening the idea of Divine Providence: "Suddenly frightened and thunderstruck by this inexplicably great phenomenon, they raised their eyes and observed the heavens. In this state, such people by nature possessed only robust physical strength and expressed their violent passions by shouting and grunting. So they imagined the heavens as a great living body."[54] As Gianfranco Cantelli put it, Vico's primitive speakers represented nature as "an animate being whose members were enlivened by that very force which they felt to be flowing in and animating their own bodies."[55] The first task of topics, therefore, was to stimulate a metaphoric mapping between sound and kinesthetic experience.

Naomi Cumming recently articulated a similar theory as she sought to define the object of musical semiosis. Cumming adduced the popular description of violin timbre as a singing voice, in which listeners can intuit "innocence," "warmth," or "maturity." These qualities, she argued, do not resemble verbal objects, which are represented *in absentia*. Rather, the musical object is present within the sign, as part of the sound itself. The human voice is "in" the violin sound, just as Jove was in the thunderstorm. Such meanings, Cumming explained, remain dormant until awakened by reflection: "Suppose that a particular quality of 'voice' attracts your attention. . . . A recognition of its individual quality implies that some comparison has informed your listening. That comparison can, however, remain entirely tacit until a moment of critical reflection, when it becomes more articulate."[56] We perceive human qualities in the violin sound thanks to the metaphor (or interpretant) of music as voice.

The same metaphoric listening makes possible musical topics. We hear an operatic theme as a bourrée or gavotte in accordance with the metaphor/interpretant of music as cultural index. The bourrée and gavotte are objects, yet their distinctive rhythmic features are present within the musical sign; as Cumming put it, "the 'semiotic' object is that which is being picked out by the metaphoric description."[57] Ratner's topics presuppose the same imaginative capacity that permitted Vico's savages to discover Jove in the storm and begin constructing a civilization. Presumably, topics played a similar role in Mozart's age. They helped audiences orient themselves within their social world, with its divisions, hierarchies, and possibilities for mobility.

Interpreting topics in Vico's spirit means, above all, attending to the physical properties of the musical sign. For Vico, as for so many other eighteenth-century thinkers, music and language intersected at the bodily level, in the innate impulses of gesture and speech accent. He located the origins of language in song: "The authors of the pagan nations must have formed their first languages by singing, and in such dim-witted creatures only the stimulus of violent passions could have awakened consciousness. . . . Even today we see that people break into song when they are moved by strong emotions, especially grief or joy."[58] Ratner's topics spring from the same bodily origins, enshrining the patterns of feet and hands, the voices of divas and choirboys. To understand Ratner's topics in their historical context, we need to abandon the anachronistic model of neoclassical rhetoric, with its Cartesian schism of mind and body, idea and expression. This means attending more closely to the physical articulation of the sign and exploring the way in which topics emerge, develop, and interact within the musical syntax. In short, we need to immerse ourselves in the vivid imaginative world of Vico's primitive humans.

●   ●   ●   ●   ●

Such an approach immediately bumps up against a limitation of topic theory. Critics have explored the classification, cultural meanings, and formal function of topics. Yet they have paid little attention to that "second articulation," analogous to the phonemic level in language, that governs the formation of the topical sign. Agawu, Allanbrook, and Caplin have explored topical syntax, but all three began at the lexical level, bypassing the distinctive features that articulate topics.[59] Robert Hatten has concentrated upon the articulation of semantic units below the level of topics (harmonies, gestures) or above them (tropes, expressive genres). Only in his tantalizing analysis of Schubert's Sonata in G, D. 894, has he explained how an individual topic (pastoral) is articulated through oppositions within the musical structure (complexity/simplicity, tension/release).[60] Michael Spitzer has sketched a brilliant outline of a topical syntax, yet he also presupposes the existence of topics as lexical items.[61]

In Louis Hjelmslev's terms, topic theory has concentrated on the content plane (object) and neglected the expression plane (sign).[62] This focus on semantics has left important questions unanswered: How do topics interact with the basic structures of tonality, meter, rhythm, form, and texture? How do the social meanings of a topic relate to its more immediate gestural meanings? When does a musical entity function as a topic, and when is it topic-neutral? To answer these questions, we need to examine more closely the way topics are articulated within the musical syntax.

Susanna's gavotte topic provides an ideal case study. As noted, each of her phrases begins on the third beat, creating the distinctive double upbeat. In effect, Susanna's theme proposes a competing metrical structure: the phrase grouping and agogic accent imply 3 4 | 1 2, as opposed to the notated meter | 1 2 3 4 |. Indeed, the gavotte belongs to an entire class of topics distinguished by displaced meter. Sarabande, polonaise, and mazurka all stress the second beat in triple meter, imposing a 2 3 | 1 pattern on the | 1 2 3 | meter. Similarly, the syncopated rhythms of *alla zoppa, empfindsamer Stil,* and fourth-species counterpoint all pull against the notated duple meter.

As a distinctive feature of multiple topics, displaced meter suggests the equivalent of a topical phoneme. To use Hjelmslev's less charged term, we might call displaced meter a topical *figura.* Hjelmslev was referring to those nonsignifying features within the expression plane from which lexical items take shape: "A language is so ordered that with the help of a handful of figurae and through ever new arrangements of them a legion of signs can be constructed."[63] Other figurae in Susanna's theme include the horn pedal and concertante winds. Neither feature need be heard topically; as Bojan Bujić has insisted, not every pedal point signifies a musette drone.[64] Yet, by combining them with other distinctive features, composers could form numerous topics, including gavotte, pastorale, gigue, siciliano, and passepied.

Texture provides another important source of figurae. For example, the juxtaposition of a rapid melodic line with a slower bass distinguishes both third-species counterpoint and brilliant style. Conversely, a slower melodic line moving against a quicker accompaniment can indicate singing allegro or *stylus mixtus*. These shared figurae help explain, for instance, the way that topics function across Mozart's "Jupiter" Symphony. The second theme of the first movement exemplifies the singing-allegro texture, with an expansive melody floating above a ticking eighth-note accompaniment. The finale opens with a theme in the related *stylus-mixtus* texture, with a white-note chant floating above an identical eighth-note accompaniment. The common texture allows us to probe beneath the lexical surface and uncover deeper oppositions and processes across the symphony.

Of course, topical figurae differ fundamentally from linguistic phonemes. Because of their affinity with physical and psychic processes, music elements always retain semantic value that vowels and consonants lack, and rarely approach the arbitrary relationship of phoneme and morpheme. While the *g* in *gavotte* does not signify, Susanna's double upbeat is already an index of kinesthetic experience (delicacy, anticipation, weightlessness). As Zerlina's "Vedrai carino" demonstrated, the figurae of a topic can themselves function independently as signs. (The "phonemic" material of topical figurae consists of the systematically ordered elements of pitch, rhythm, meter, texture, and timbre bounded by a given style—in short, everything which falls within the purview of formalist analysis.) Figurae thus have a dual aspect. In relation to topics, they function as nonsignifying elements; yet in relation to kinesthetic-emotional experience, they can function as signs in their own right. For this reason, topical figurae may not be reducible to a finite set, like the roughly forty-four phonemes of English. Nevertheless, they provide a valuable bridge between highly conventionalized signs, like gavottes and sicilianos, and the more immediate indexicality of music.

This approach also accords with eighteenth-century sign theory, which traced music to instinctual gestures and cries. David Lidov has formulated the same idea in modern terms: "An affinity of sound with significant neural-motor impulses is given a priori; it is natural. . . . Composition wrests intellectual freedom from that determinate function by the free play of articulations imposed on the continuities of expression."[65] Consider, for example, the suspensions in Figaro's theme. A listener unfamiliar with Ratner's lexicon will nevertheless feel a sense of yearning in the tied notes, as they "strain" across the bar line. The dissonant suspensions index groans, sighs, leaning, and other bodily signs of emotion. A more informed listener will enjoy the added recognition of fourth-species counterpoint and, hence, the poignant dignity of the *stile antico*. Topical figurae can account for the semiotic experience of both *Kenner* and *Liebhaber*.

Figurae also point the way toward a deep structure that would explain how topics are generated and transformed. For example, such a model would unearth the common source of the *alla breve* suspensions in Figaro's bourrée and Susanna's gavotte rhythm. Semantically, learned style and gavotte belong to opposing realms—ancient/modern, strict/free, sacred/secular, song/dance. Yet the two topics share a common figura, the metrical displacement of duple meter. Thus, the learned style can provide a transition between bourrée and gavotte. From the opening bars, the fourth-species suspensions emphasize the third beat, establishing an alternate grouping long before the gavotte arrives. This persistent stress prepares the metrical displacement of Susanna's theme and already invades the rhythm of Figaro's final phrases. In this way, the Duettino shifts imperceptibly from bourrée to gavotte in accordance with a process set in motion in the opening measures. As cultural items, learned style, bourrée, and gavotte do not suggest an obvious interpretation; yet the underlying syntax reveals an impeccable logic.

The question then arises, how do the two levels interact? How do syntactic features, like displaced meter, correlate with the social meanings of

topics? Robert Hatten's research into musical markedness provides an explanation. Markedness theory originated in the phonological research of
Nikolai Trubetskoy and Roman Jakobson and has been generalized to
every category of language. According to structuralist theory, language
operates through binary oppositions, such as open/close (vowel height),
present/past (tense), or male/female (gender). Each pairing contains a
marked term that occurs less frequently and expresses a narrower range
of meaning. For example, the unmarked term *man* signifies either a male
human or humanity in general, while the marked term *woman* signifies
only a female human. As a musical example, Hatten has adduced the minor mode in late eighteenth-century style: "Minor has a narrower range
of meaning than major, in that minor rather consistently conveys the tragic,
whereas major is not simply the opposite (comic), but must be characterized more generally as nontragic—encompassing more widely ranging
modes of expression such as the heroic, the pastoral, and the genuinely
comic, or *buffa*."[66]

Susanna's gavotte is syntactically marked, with its alternative metrical
grouping, as opposed to Figaro's unmarked bourrée. As the marked term
in the opposition, Susanna's melody has the more defined character; this
explains why Allanbrook and Heartz easily recognized Susanna's theme
as a gavotte, yet disagreed on the identity of Figaro's music. There is a direct analogy, moreover, between syntactic and semantic markedness.
Metrically unmarked topics, like marches and minuets, can function as
signs or simply serve as the default style for a movement in moderate
tempo. The offbeat rhythms of gavottes and mazurkas, on the other hand,
mark these topics as characteristic dances with pastoral, feminine, or na-
tionalist meanings. In this way, as Michael Shapiro has explained, markedness structure functions as an interpretant, connecting sign and object.[67]

The correlation of marked dance rhythms with marked cultural categories exemplifies "markedness assimilation," a valuable concept marshaled by Hatten.[68] According to this principle, as Edwin Battistella explained, "marked values from different oppositions tend to cluster in a
given entity or location, creating or reinforcing larger marked entities."[69]
Battistella adduced the language of official utterances, like "in witness
thereof" or "by the power invested in me," in which the marked speech
act and diction (illocutionary, formal) assimilate to the marked context

(ceremony).[70] This relationship rests upon resemblance rather than mere convention or habit. Sign and object are united by an analogous structure in the expression and content planes (S:S'::O:O'). Markedness assimilation exemplifies Peirce's category of second-order icons, or "diagrams," in which the sign replicates the relationship among the parts of its object. It provides an invaluable key to analyzing topical syntax and semantics, placing musical meaning on a truly structuralist footing.

For instance, assimilation explains why the metrically marked dance "gavotte" correlates with the marked gender "woman" in the Duettino. In fact, Susanna's theme unites a cluster of marked traits, both textural (concertante scoring), timbral (solo winds), and formal (secondary theme). Her theme is also marked harmonically. It changes chords every two beats, like the "bustling" sonata-form second themes identified by James Hepokoski and Warren Darcy.[71] Figaro's bourrée, on the other hand, changes harmony every two bars, a rate more typical of galant style. Susanna's rapid harmonic rhythm complements her gavotte rhythm, enhancing the competing groupings within the measure. Most important, Susanna's theme emphasizes the dominant, the marked tonal center within Mozart's sonata-based style. The horns sustain a dominant pedal beneath her melody, while the melody circles the fifth degree reached by Figaro's ascending line, prolonging the descent to the cadence.

Markedness assimilation goes only so far, however, in analyzing topical meaning. While this principle helps account for the formation of semantic structures, it fails to explain how they change and develop across a movement. In fact, markedness values shift dramatically in the Duettino. The reprise erases the oppositions so carefully constructed at the beginning of the number: the concertante texture disappears as Figaro's strings rejoin Susanna's woodwind, and the opening bourrée vanishes, leaving only the gavotte. Markedness assimilation may prove adequate for early eighteenth-century music, in which the expression of a unified affect dictated a static congruence among parameters. Yet it misses the dynamism that distinguishes Mozart's musical dramaturgy, indeed, late eighteenth-century style.

It will be helpful to introduce a concept from markedness theory not discussed by Hatten, the principle of "neutralization." Neutralization occurs when a particular context removes a markedness opposition by suppressing one term (usually the marked). For example, the distinction between voiced (marked) and unvoiced consonants disappears at the end of German words. In this context, all consonants become unvoiced, turning *Rad* (wheel) and *Rat* (council, advice) into homophones. The opposite occurs in American English when *t* and *d* occur between sounded vowels. Both vowels now become voiced; thus, the distinction between *write* and *ride* disappears in *writer* and *rider.*

Neutralization tends to push meaning to a more general level. By stripping away the specific difference, it leaves only the general category, or "archiphoneme." Interpretation therefore requires other sources of information (are we discussing horses or books?). Jacques Derrida exploited this feature of neutralization in his famous neologism *différance*. Since French nasals neutralize the opposition of [ε] and [a], *différance* and *différence* become homophones. Derrida thus directed attention to the general opposition between speech and writing, *parole* and *écriture.*

Neutralization proves especially valuable in interpreting the music of Mozart's generation, in which so many processes involve overcoming binary oppositions. An obvious example is the sonata-form recapitulation, which neutralizes the tonal opposition between I and V. The recapitulation suppresses the marked secondary key, leaving only the unmarked tonic. As in language, neutralization moves meaning to a more general level: by suppressing the local tonal polarity within the exposition, the recapitulation emphasizes the larger opposition between the two halves of the form.

The *tièrce de Picardie* provides another example of neutralization. The major cadence suppresses the marked minor mode, just as the word-final position in German suppresses the marked voicing. The major cadence also erases the emotional opposition between tragic and nontragic. The opening choruses of Bach's *Mass in B Minor* and *St. Matthew Passion* both end with Picardy thirds, yet the major cadence does not alleviate, let alone reverse, the profound pathos of these movements. Instead, the greater stability of the major triad signifies closure, stability, and finality, values that transcend the tragic/nontragic opposition.[72]

To understand how neutralization operates in the Duettino, we must begin with the libretto. Da Ponte's choice of meters seems largely to have dictated Mozart's choice and treatment of topics. The poet set the first two quatrains as eight-syllable lines, or *ottonari*. Figaro's opening verses establish a rigid trochaic stress pattern that continues through the second quatrain. The third quatrain, however, consists of ten-syllable lines, or *decasillabi*. The stress pattern now shifts to anapests, with three accents per line:

FIGARO: Cinque . . . dieci . . . venti . . . trenta . . .   (Quatrain 1: trochaic
            trentasei . . . quarantatre   *ottonari*)

SUSANNA: Ora sì ch'io son contenta;
            sembra fatto inver per me.

            Guarda un po', mio caro Figaro,   (Quatrain 2: trochaic *ottonari*)
            guarda adesso il mio cappello.

FIGARO: Sì mio core, or è più bello,
            sembra fatto inver per te.

BOTH: Ah, il mattino alle nozze vicino   (Quatrain 3: anapestic
            quanto è dolce al mio/tuo tenero sposo   *decasillabi*)
            questo bel cappellino vezzoso
            che Susanna ella stessa si fe'.

The shift from trochees to anapests coincides with the musical reprise, where Susanna's double upbeat supplants Figaro's heavy downbeats. This raises the distinct possibility that Mozart's choice of topics originated in Da Ponte's contrasting meters.

Decasyllabic meter is marked in Mozart's vocal music, both in frequency and range of meaning. True *decasillabi* (as opposed to *quinari doppi*) occur only eighteen times in all of his Italian operas, oratorios, and arias. Ten examples fall within the Da Ponte operas, and half of those within *Figaro* (see table 1). *Ottonari*, by contrast, are commonplace verses, the workhorses of the Italian librettist. While *ottonari* accommodate many stress patterns, *decasillabi* invariably fall into anapests with stresses on syllables 3, 6, and 9.[73] And while *ottonari* serve for many types of characters, Da Ponte assigned *decasillabi* only to servants (Susanna, Figaro, Leporello), rustics (Antonio, the peasant chorus in *Don Giovanni*), and noble characters in pastoral settings (Ferrando).[74] This makes good sense musically, since the double upbeat and anapestic rhythm of *decasillabi* lend themselves to gigues, pastorales, gavottes, and other dances associated with simple nature.

Table 1.   *Decasillabi* in Mozart's Italian Vocal Works

La finta semplice	No. 15: "Amoretti, che ascosi qui siete"
Betulia liberata	No. 1: "D'ogni colpa la colpa maggiore"
Ascanio in Alba	No. 33: "Alma Dea tutto il Mondo governa"
Il sogno di Scipione	No. 7: "Quercia annosa su l'erte pendici"
	No. 12: "Cento volte con lieto sembiante"
Lucio Silla	No. 5: "Il desio di vendetta e di morte" (first quatrain)
	No. 22: "Fra i pensier più funesti di morte"
Il re pastore	No. 9: "Se vincendo vi rendo felici"
Le nozze di Figaro	No. 1: "Cinque . . . dieci . . . venti . . . trenta" (final quatrain)
	No. 6: "Non so più cosa son, cosa faccio" (first two quatrains)
	No. 10: "Non più andrai farfallone amoroso" (first two quatrains)
	Act 2 finale (mm. 467–695): "Che insolenza! Chi'l fece! chi fu! . . . Vostre dunque saran queste carte"
	Act 4 finale (mm. 275–334): "Pace pace, mio dolce tesoro"
Don Giovanni	No. 4: "Madamina, il catalogo è questo" (first two quatrains)
	No. 5: "Giovinette che fate all'amore"
	Act 1 finale (mm. 273–358): "Riposate, vezzose ragazze"
Così fan tutte	No. 24: "Ah lo veggio, quell'anima bella"
	Act 2 finale (mm. 372–409): "Sani e salvi agli amplessi amorosi"

But Mozart played against expectations in the Duettino, which begins with a disjunction between poetic and musical meter. Despite the *ottonari*, Susanna's theme seems tailored to decasyllabic verse, beginning with a double upbeat and containing three clear stresses. To fill out this frame-work, Mozart had to pad the melody with extraneous slurs. Moreover, the accents fall awkwardly on subsidiary words (*sí, son, sembra, inver*). When *decasillabi* replace *ottonari,* however, poetic and melodic accents line up properly, with only three graceful slurs. The reprise not only settles the contest between surface topics, gavotte and bourrée. At a deeper level, it resolves the tension between musical and poetic structure, uniting Su-sanna's theme with its proper meter.

Figaro's bourrée, on the other hand, has exactly eight notes. It fits the trochaic *ottonari* easily, as we hear when Susanna sings along with the melody in mm. 36–40.[75] While her gavotte seems destined for the third quatrain, his bourrée clearly fits the first two. In short, Mozart has engineered the two themes so that only one can survive the shift to *decasillabi*. This ingenious design engages poetry and music below the lexical level. It is coordinated with the dramatic action and musical topics, yet obeys its own structural logic.

The process of neutralization in the Duettino thus proves more complex than a *tièrce de Picardy*. Normally, neutralization removes the marked term, like the minor mode. In the Duettino, however, both gavotte rhythm and *decasillabi* are marked. The reprise suggests the species of neutralization known as "markedness reversal," in which a marked term becomes dominant within a marked context. Henning Andersen has provided a grammatical example: "In English, for instance, in sentences in a marked status, the assertive vs. non-assertive opposition (*they do know* vs. *they know*) is neutralized, and the normally marked assertive is used to the exclusion of the nonassertive (*Do they know? They do not know.*)"[76] The new context suppresses the unmarked term, replacing it with the previously marked opposite.

The reprise of minor-mode binary forms provides an example of markedness reversal. Minuets, scherzos, and sonata forms in minor typically modulate to the relative major (III); the second half, which must remain in the tonic, recapitulates this material in the minor (i). The context reverses markedness values, suppressing the unmarked major mode. In this case, one form of neutralization trumps another: in order to suppress the marked tonality, the reprise must suppress the unmarked mode. If, on the other hand, the secondary material returns in the tonic major (I), as in the first movement of Beethoven's Fifth Symphony, markedness values are not reversed. Such reprises, like the Picardy third, suppress the marked mode, as well as the marked tonality.

In the Duettino, markedness reversal involves another position within sonata form, the retransition. As noted, Susanna's theme strongly emphasizes the dominant: the horns sustain a dominant pedal throughout, while the melody circles about $\hat{5}$, prolonging the descent to the tonic. Within the harmonic context of a thematic exposition, these features are syntactically marked. They pull against the tonic, just as the gavotte rhythm pulls against the notated meter. Within the retransition, which functions to prepare a V-I cadence, the same features become obligatory.

Example 16. *Le nozze di Figaro,* Duettino, mm. 59–77.

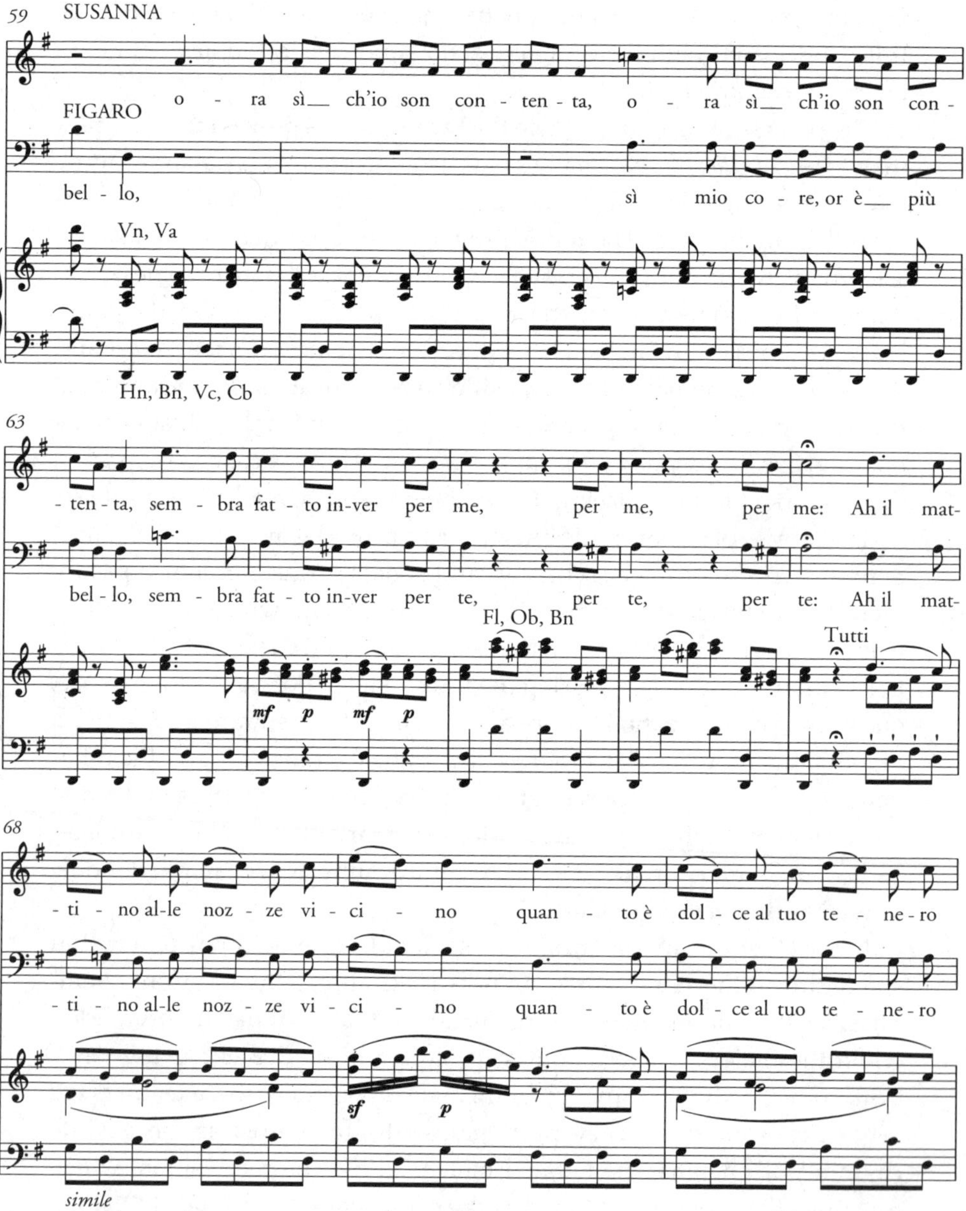

Example 16.   *(continued)*

The retransition reverses markedness values, suppressing the unmarked tonic. The new context thus rules out Figaro's theme, which opens up tonal space with a I-V modulation to the half cadence. Susanna's theme, on the other hand, fits perfectly (see example 16). The eight-bar passage, derived from her theme, winds up tension for eight bars, arpeggiating a V^7 chord over the dominant pedal.

The peculiar construction of Susanna's theme, however, ensures that the cadence does not arrive with the reprise. The pedal point and melodic arabesques continue for another ten bars, delaying closure until the end of her theme. In effect, the retransition and reprise function together as a sixteen-bar period (with two-bar extension), punctuated by a half and full cadence. Mozart has fashioned the retransition-reprise as a single grand upbeat, a design no doubt inspired by Da Ponte's shifting meters. Susanna's theme, which once circled aimlessly, now accomplishes the crucial structural event of the Duettino.

Mozart thus constructed the opening number so that, harmonically and metrically, the retransition and reprise can only accommodate Susanna's theme. Yet her gavotte does not "win" a contest between topics. Rather, the Duettino neutralizes the initial opposition by reversing markedness values. When Susanna's gavotte returns unopposed, the new formal context transforms her sign, endowing its harmonic structure with purpose and direction. The reprise changes the game, rewriting the rules that govern the initial confrontation.

The reprise thus consummates a topical argument that transcends Figaro and Susanna. As we saw, the shift toward the gavotte begins in the first bar with the cello's fourth-species suspensions, long before Susanna's theme emerges. Those suspensions index the learned style, a topic that belongs to neither character (but whose sacred connotations match its reconciliatory role). A structuralist reading of the Duettino, which digs beneath the lexical surface, does not unearth gender or class politics. On the contrary, it reveals a profoundly optimistic teleology that not only tolerates but even celebrates alterity. Figaro does not succumb to Susanna's gavotte. Together they discover a new way of organizing musical time and gesture that transcends gender, class, and topics themselves.

.   .   .   .   .

Critics, conductors, and stage directors can find much grist for interpretation in Mozart's fascinating play with meter and topics. Yet one thing is certain. Any interpretation guided by traditional rhetoric, which treats topics as a codified lexicon, will miss the deepest part of Mozart's art. Such an approach will fall short musically because Mozart was working below the lexical level, playing with more basic patterns of rhythm, meter, texture, and harmony; and poetically, because he was engaging Da Ponte's verses as prosodic patterns, not simply as a repository of images and affects. A more fruitful approach will begin from the sensual particulars and proceed inductively, following the model of Enlightenment language theory from Vico to the Idéologues. Then Mozart's art of invention will shine forth in its true colors, as a dynamic exploratory voyage into the nature of music, poetry, and human culture.

FOUR Mozart and Marxism

When Susan McClary published her critique of Mozart's Piano Concerto in G in 1984, she opened a Pandora's box that her most determined critics have failed to nail shut. Her remarkable analysis of Mozart's "musical dialectic" managed to draw the composer's ineffable art into the orbit of Marxist critique. More precisely, McClary showed how the slow movement of Mozart's concerto might embody tensions brought to light by Theodor Adorno's critical theory. As Adorno's fortunes have waxed within musicology, McClary's dialectical approach has gained traction, even as critics have clawed over her individual analyses. Richard Taruskin ensured the future of McClary's sociological interpretation when he included a respectful, if not uncritical, discussion of her K. 453 analysis in the *Oxford History of Western Music* (2005).[1]

McClary interpreted the Andante as an allegory in which the soloist represents the bourgeois individual, the orchestra the social collective, and Classical tonality the invisible hand that knits them together. The contest between soloist and orchestra thus mirrored "the dramatic tensions between individual and society, surely one of the major problematics of the emerging middle class."[2] Inspired by Adorno's "negative dialectics," McClary probed the Andante for aporias, moments when the synthesis of individual and collective unravels. She found one at the end of the development, where the soloist reaches a half cadence in the distant key of C♯ minor. The willful individual seems to have abandoned the logic of sonata form, blocking the conventional V-I resolution to the recapitulation. Yet the orchestra slices through this "Gordian knot," short-circuiting the conventional root progression with a common-tone modulation back to the tonic. This "irrational" modulation, based on chromatic voice-leading rather than circle-of-fifths harmony, exposes the coercion at the heart of the Enlightenment's social contract. It belies the promise that the individual can freely harmonize its interests with those of bourgeois society.

The five-measure phrase that opens the Andante betrays another chink in Mozart's utopian construct (see example 17). McClary detected a prayerful *Innigkeit* in this gently pulsing music, reminiscent of Bach's cantata arias. Although introduced by the orchestra, the motto transcends individual and collective interests. When the errant soloist returns to the tonic in the recapitulation, it embraces the opening idea with religious zeal: "The soloist 'sees the light,' as it were, and takes the leap of faith necessary to return from its C♯ minor depression to C-major serenity."[3] Yet Mozart's motto glows with the flame of an earthly creed. Beneath the guise of Christian devotion, the concerto sanctifies the ideology of the bourgeoisie: "The individual and social norms are required to submit to some higher order (and here is the irony) for the purpose of satisfying the necessities of tonality and sonata procedure, both of which conventionally stand for the quite specifically secular and bourgeois principles of the rational achievement of goals through purposeful striving."[4] The appeal to religious experience, like the chromatic retransition, exposes the irrationality lurking within Mozart's musical commonwealth.

McClary's more thoughtful critics, while granting the importance of her approach, objected to its abstraction. Joseph Kerman confessed him-

Example 17.   Piano Concerto in G, K. 453, Andante, mm. 1–4.

self "more comfortable considering [Mozart's] concertos in their own particular situation—Mozart's situation vis-à-vis his patrons as he worked to establish himself in the musical life of Vienna from 1781 to 1786."[5] Kerman proposed another allegorical reading, yet he sought to mediate musical and social meaning through a literary convention. Mozart's concertos, he suggested, enacted the comedic Myth of Spring from Northrop Frye's *Anatomy of Criticism* (1957). This plot archetype resonated with Mozart's personal and artistic experience and even found expression in his last opera: "In this myth, the individual is incorporated into society and society is transformed. In one Mozartean comedic fiction, Tamino sues and wins entrance to the social order by playing on a magic flute. In seventeen others, Amadeus plays the fortepiano."[6]

The late Harold S. Powers also chafed at McClary's blunt correlation of musical and social structures. He proposed another intermediary, in this case, Ratner's theory of musical topics. According to Powers, topics provided a lexicon that bridged connected musical and social meaning: "Topics are terminological tags naming kinds and manners of music familiar to a particular society of musical consumers. They are verbal equivalents for items in a musical vocabulary. . . . If [Mozart's music] can be interpreted as having 'extramusical' meaning, that meaning is mediated rather than immediate."[7] Powers did not do justice to McClary's reading, which does identify topical referents in K. 453 (Bach's sacred works, operatic vocalism). Nevertheless, both he and Kerman pinpointed an undeniable weakness in her approach—the absence of a semantic theory mediating musical and social meanings.

Kerman and Powers did share one tacit assumption with McClary, a premise that neither seems to have questioned. All three critics took for granted that Mozart's concerto represents the actions and discourse of discrete, self-conscious subjects. This premise reflects the post-Kantian view of the subject that has tacitly or, in the case of Adorno, explicitly informed readings of late eighteenth-century music. In McClary's narrative, the instruments are endowed with reflection, volition, and agency; they strive, have epiphanies, and make leaps of faith. Likewise, in Kerman's mythic reading, the instruments represent human subjects, the novice and initiates who enact the vernal rite. While Powers steered clear of anthropomorphic narratives, his topical reading relies on the metaphor of music as verbal discourse, the expression of subjects capable of using conventional signs. The three critics ask us to hear Mozart's concerto as a representation of individuated, rational subjects.

In practice, this proves a tricky enterprise. If, following Kerman, we seek Mozart himself within K. 453, we find ourselves sifting through multiple personalities. Do the bravura passages represent Mozart Hero wielding his magical powers or Mozart Impresario giving his Viennese audience

Example 18.   K. 453, Allegro, first theme, mm. 1–8.

their fix of brilliant style? Does the enharmonic shortcut to the reprise represent Mozart Bourgeois submitting to social forces or Mozart Composer
indulging in a bit of harmonic *jouissance?* Perhaps the truer comparison
is not with Tamino, but Emanuel Schikaneder—the poet who shapes the
drama, the showman who plays to his public, the director who manages
the stage fire, and, finally, the actor who leaps out to portray the naive
Naturmensch.

Powers's approach poses similar problems. Certainly, the five-bar
motto of the K. 453 Andante submits readily to topical analysis. The stately
tempo and heavy stress on the second beat tag the melody as a sarabande,
while the descending tetrachord bass suggests the operatic *lamento.* The

Example 18.   (continued)

evocation of the sarabande, an expressive solo dance, would seem to align the motto with the concerto soloist. The offbeat accents, straining against the notated meter, might even suggest the willful individual as it struggles vainly against the social order. The descending tetrachord would enhance the sense of an implacable fate bearing down on the individual.[8]

Yet the opening Allegro immediately muddies this interpretation. The buoyant movement begins with Mozart's favorite march rhythm, a dotted motive falling squarely on the downbeat (see example 18). It is also his favorite concerto incipit, featured in three adjacent piano concertos from 1784 (K. 451, 456, and 459); the preceding Concerto in D enlists the martial rhythm in a particularly splendid, festive movement. In K. 453, however, Mozart gave the rhythmic motto a peculiar twist. He did not begin the march with the full ensemble, as in the other concertos, but entrusted the rhythm to the unaccompanied first violins. They play it softly and even embellish the dotted rhythm with a delicate trill. The full orchestra only enters on the downbeat of the second bar, which is accented agogically by a dotted half note. The martial rhythm now functions as an upbeat to the second bar. In effect, Mozart has transformed the march into an *alla breve* gavotte.

The second theme features a similar metrical displacement (see example 19). Following the medial caesura in bar 31, four postcadential measures establish a strong-weak hypermeter. Although the new theme clearly begins on a strong bar, the expressive accent falls on the luscious chromatic sighs in the second and fourth measures. The yearning sighs come straight out of Italian opera (and will return almost verbatim in Cherubino's "Non so più"). As Taruskin has noted, the offbeat sighs also anticipate the opening theme of the Andante, with its sarabande rhythm.[9] The Andante motto, then, would seem to belong to an expressive design that spans both movements, involving the displacement of metrical accent.

This design, however, resists easy interpretation, whether topical or allegorical. The displaced meter and offbeat accents in the Allegro and Andante cut across three separate topics—gavotte, aria, and sarabande. These rhythmic patterns operate beneath the lexical surface, at that "figural" level explored in the previous chapter. Moreover, while the offbeat rhythms might suggest the individual subject struggling against collective society, all three themes originate in the orchestra. In fact, the soloist introduces the first theme in K. 453 that lands emphatically on the downbeat, a martial idea bolstered by virile "horn fifths." Without a doubt, the Concerto in G evokes a poignant sense of subjectivity. But this expressive current runs beneath the surface of individual topics and instrumental agents.

This presents an obvious difficulty for Marxist readings of Mozart. Without stable musical agents who can embody the bourgeois individual or its collective antagonist, dialectical interpretation becomes more than a little problematic. The elusive nature of subjectivity in Mozart, which Michael P. Steinberg has so richly explored, makes it difficult to map class conflicts or other abstract ideas onto his music.[10] It would seem, therefore,

Example 19.   K. 453, Allegro, second theme, mm. 31–43.

that before reconstructing dialectical narratives we need to explore the extent to which Mozart's music actually inscribes discrete agents and how they take shape within the musical structure.

We shall approach this question, perversely enough, through the father of capitalist theory himself, Adam Smith. Smith's philosophy, whether economic, moral, linguistic, or aesthetic, circles persistently around the problem of subjectivity. Indeed, his most original contribution to language theory is a discussion of the first-person pronoun. A knowledgeable music lover, Smith wrote one of the most insightful discussions of instrumental music from Mozart's age. More tellingly, perhaps, he suffused his writings with musical metaphors, which offer us the rare opportunity of reading philosophy musically, rather than the usual converse. Aesthetics and philosophy connect most richly in Smith's theory of the imagination.

·   ·   ·   ·   ·

Smith explored imagination most fully in his early essay on scientific method, "The Principles which Lead and Direct Philosophical Enquiries; Illustrated by the History of Astronomy" (written before 1758). He celebrated the creative, hypothesis-generating activity of scientists, arguing that Ptolemy, Galileo, and Newton relied upon the same imaginative faculty that gave birth to literature, painting, or music. Both science and art, he explained, arose from a common psychological mechanism. According to Smith, the imagination tends toward equilibrium so that mental disturbances, like imbalances of supply and demand, even out over time. Faced with an object it cannot classify or a chain of events it cannot explain, the mind is thrown into confusion. Natural philosophy (science) resolves this unpleasant state, as Smith explained through a musical metaphor: "Philosophy, by representing the invisible chains which bind together all these disjointed objects, endeavours to introduce order into this chaos of jarring and discordant appearances, to allay this tumult of the imagination, and to restore it, when it surveys the great revolutions of the universe, to that tone of tranquility and composure, which is both most agreeable in itself, and most suitable to its nature."[11] Scientific theories thus ensured the harmonious order of the mind, analogously to the Pythagorean *musica mundana*.

Smith carefully distinguished such theoretical systems from the unknowable laws of nature. As the history of astronomy proved, scientific models continually evolved toward greater efficiency, in accordance with the law of mental equilibrium. Smith enlisted another metaphor that pervades his moral, economic, and aesthetic writings: "A system is an imaginary machine invented to connect together in the fancy those different movements and effects which are already in reality performed. The machines that are first invented to perform any particular movement are always the most complex and succeeding artists generally discover that, with fewer wheels, the same effects may be more easily produced."[12] Smith remained skeptical of scientific models, those "mere inventions of the imagination," and even tempered his enthusiasm for Newtonian mechanics by warning readers not to "make use of language expressing the connecting principles of this [system], as if they were the real chains which Nature makes use of to bind together her several operations."[13] Smith did not deny that real laws governed nature. Yet he viewed even Newton's theory as a human device, a machine designed to quiet the restless mind.

Imagination remains central in the first of Smith's two major works, *The Theory of Moral Sentiments* (1759, revised 1790). In his quest for the roots of morality, Smith rejected appeals to a primal state of nature, whether Rousseau's idyllic oblivion or Hobbes's *bellum omnium contra omnes*. Morality, he insisted, arose within society and relied upon the imaginative faculty of sympathy. By sympathy, Smith did not mean simply compassion or empathy, but rather our ability to identify with any emotion suffered by our fellow humans. Unlike Rousseau, Smith did not reduce sympathy to a behavioral reflex, but insisted upon the active role of the imagination. As he pointed out, we suffer vicariously with the dead and insane, even though they remain oblivious to their own misfortune: "We sometimes feel for another, a passion of which he himself seems to be altogether incapable; because, when we put ourselves in his case, that passion arises in our breast from the imagination, though it does not in his from the reality."[14]

The moral imagination, like the scientific, seeks equilibrium. According to Smith, sympathy helps reduce the emotional imbalance between patient and observer that results from suffering. Impelled by the sociable impulses of kindness and compassion, the observer enters vicariously into the patient's distress. Meanwhile, the patient seeks to moderate his emotion through the sterner virtues of self-control and forbearance. Through this reciprocal effort, patient and observer approach that harmony of interests that constitutes moral life: "And hence it is, that to feel much for others and little for ourselves, that to restrain our selfish, and to indulge our benevolent affections, constitutes the perfection of human nature; and can alone produce among mankind that harmony of sentiments and passions in which consists their whole grace and propriety."[15]

Sympathy governed not only interpersonal relations, but also the evolution of personal identity itself. We come to know ourselves only within society, claimed Smith, as we observe the reactions of our fellow humans. We internalize these reactions over time, developing what Smith called variously the "impartial spectator," the "great inmate of the breast," or the "demigod within the breast."[16] This impartial observer both regulates moral behavior and ensures the integrity of the self. Like his teacher David Hume, Smith regarded personal identity as an a posteriori construct, resulting from an aggregate of experiences. The self was thus subject to perceptual distortions that could only be corrected by experience: "The man of to-day is no longer agitated by the same passions which distracted the man of yesterday: and when the paroxysm of emotion, in the same manner as when the paroxysm of distress, is fairly over, we can identify ourselves, as it were, with the ideal man within the breast."[17] Smith's view of the self owes much to Hume's skeptical critique of the Cartesian *cogito* in the *Treatise of Human Nature* (1748): "The identity, which we ascribe to the mind of man, is only a fictitious one, and of a like kind with that which we ascribe to vegetables and animal bodies. It cannot, therefore, have a different origin, but must proceed from a like operation of the imagination upon like objects."[18] Like Hume, Smith regarded personal identity as an emergent construct that could be traced to sensory experience.

Smith also recognized the constitutive role of language in human understanding and identity. His *Considerations Concerning the First Formation of Languages* (published in 1761) derives chiefly from the French sensualists. While he modeled that work primarily upon Gabriel Girard's *Les vrais principes de la langue françoise* (1747), Smith referred explicitly to Rousseau's *Discours sur l'origine et fondements de l'inégalité parmi les hommes* (1755), and implicitly to Condillac, whose *Essai sur l'origine des connoissances humaines* and *Traité des sensations* he owned.[19] Like the French sensualists, Smith portrayed language and thought as interdependent phenomena that evolved in tandem through a process of analysis.

The *Considerations* begins with the familiar scenario of two savages who seek to communicate their basic needs. They begin by inventing proper names; then, by means of the trope of *antonomasia*, they generalize those names, distinguishing between genera and species. Early verbs evolved through the same analytic process. Primitive humans first invented what

Smith called impersonal verbs, which "express in one word a complete event." For instance, *venit* might originally have signified the complex thought "The lion is coming." Over time, primitive speakers generalized its meaning: "When they observed the approach of any other terrible object, they would naturally join the name of that object to the word *venit,* and cry out, *venit ursus, venit lupus.* By degrees the word *venit* would thus come to signify the coming of any terrible object, and not merely the coming of the lion."[20] As grammar developed, the holistic pictures painted by impersonal verbs gave way to "composed" discourse.

The *Considerations* includes a remarkable discussion of personal pronouns. As Smith noted, words like *ego* and *tu* possess curious properties: "Though custom has now rendered them familiar to us, they, both of them, express ideas extremely metaphysical and abstract. The word *I,* for example, is a word of a very particular species. Whatever speaks may denote itself by this personal pronoun. The word *I,* therefore, is a general word, capable of being predicated, as the logicians say, of an infinite variety of objects."[21] Smith anticipated the theory of shifters, later developed by Otto Jespersen, Roman Jakobson, and Emile Benveniste.[22] According to Smith, personal pronouns evolved as humans developed abstract thought. The linguistic self, like the moral self, emerged only gradually through a process of social exchange.

Smith's distance from a post-Kantian viewpoint can be gauged through a comparison with Hegel's *Phenomenology of Spirit* (1807). Hegel also referred to shifters *(I, here, this)* in his opening dialectic of Sense-Certainty. Sensory experience, Hegel explained, initially appears the richest, truest form of knowledge. Yet language undermines this certainty as soon as we try to express our knowledge. Suppose we say, *Here is the tree:* "If I turn round, this truth has vanished and is converted into its opposite: 'No tree is here, but a house instead.' "[23] Likewise, the first-person pronoun plays us false: "I, *this* 'I,' see the tree and assert that 'Here' is a tree; but another 'I' sees the house and maintains that 'Here' is not a tree but a house instead. . . . What does not disappear in all this is the 'I' as universal, whose seeing is neither a seeing of the tree nor of this house, but is a simple seeing."[24] Therefore, language, "which has the divine nature of directly reversing the meaning of what is said," splits apart Sense-Certainty, making way for the higher synthesis of Self Consciousness. Like Smith, Hegel believed in the constitutive role of language. Yet Hegel treated grammar, including shifters, as an innate mental structure. For Smith and his fellow empiricists, the "I," like the unitary self, was not given a priori. It had to be constructed, slowly and laboriously, through experience.

Smith viewed this process ambivalently. He described the growth of pronouns and cases, and the corresponding simplification of inflections, through a favorite metaphor: "All machines are generally, when first invented, extremely complex in their principles, and there is often a particular principle of motion for every particular movement which it is intended they should perform. Succeeding improvers observe, that one principle may be so applied as to produce several of those movements; and thus the machine becomes gradually more and more simple, and produces its effects with fewer wheels, and fewer principles of motion."[25] This process proved a mixed blessing: "The simplification of machines renders them more and more perfect, but this simplification of the rudiments of languages renders them more and more imperfect, and less proper for many of the purposes of language."[26] Modernity purchased rational clarity at the cost of prolixity, monotony, and grammatical rigidity, trading sensual immediacy for intellectual abstraction.

Smith's musical aesthetics rest upon the same psychological theory that informs his scientific, moral, and linguistic thought. His essay "Of the Nature of that Imitation which Takes Place in What are Called the Imitative Arts" (written 1777–88) grants instrumental music a privileged position among the arts. According to Smith, our pleasure in mimesis arises from the discrepancy between sign and object: "That pleasure is founded altogether upon our wonder at seeing an object of one kind represent so well an object of a very different kind, and upon our admiration of the art which surmounts so happily that disparity which Nature had established between them."[27] Like scientific inquiry, aesthetic experience begins with confusion, as the mind confronts the dissimilarity of sign and object. As we grasp the representational technique, however, we experience a restoration of mental tranquility: "The pleasing wonder of ignorance is accompanied with the still more pleasing satisfaction of science. We wonder and are amazed at the effect; and we are pleased ourselves, and happy to find that we can comprehend, in some measure, how that wonderful effect is produced."[28] Pleasure increases in direct proportion to the disparity between sign and object; thus, a landscape affords greater pleasure than a statue because the painter, unlike the sculptor, must translate three-dimensional objects to a plane surface.

Instrumental music stands outside this aesthetic model. Wordless music affects the listener directly, without representing absent objects: "Whatever effect it produces is the immediate effect of that melody and harmony, and not of something else which is signified and suggested by them: they in fact signify and suggest nothing."[29] Or, again: "Whatever we feel from instrumental Music is an original, and not a sympathetic feeling: it is our own gaiety, sedateness, or melancholy; not the reflected disposition of another person."[30] Smith's essay has been hailed as an early manifesto of "absolute music." Yet he did not deny that music imitated nature, merely the claim that it produced its effect indirectly by imitating absent objects. Instead, music represented emotions by replicating patterns of psychological experience. Like morality, economics, or science, the emotions were governed by the principle of equilibrium: "What may be called the natural state of the mind, the state in which we are neither elated nor dejected, the state of sedateness, tranquility and composure, holds a sort of middle place between those two opposite extremes; our thoughts succeed one another more slowly, and with a more distinct connection, than in the one; more quickly, and with a greater variety, than in the other."[31] By replicating these patterns of mental activity, music could index the corresponding emotions and even awaken them in the listener: "But instrumental Music, by a proper arrangement, by a quicker or slower succession of acute and grave, of resembling and contrasting sounds, can not only accommodate itself to the gay, the sedate, or the melancholy mood; but if the mind is so far vacant as not to be disturbed by any disorderly passion, it can, at least for the moment, and to a certain degree, produce every possible modification of each of those moods or dispositions."[32]

Herein lies the privileged role of instrumental music. According to Smith, the imitative arts derived their charm from the equilibrating mechanism of the mind as it confronted the disparity between sign and object. Instrumental music, which featured no such disparity, represented the mechanism itself. As Wilhelm Seidel explained, "What the hearer experiences and what pleases him, according to Smith, is the system of a composition. It reminds him of the systematic nature of every other science."[33] Instrumental music manifested that psychological mechanism which underlies every other sphere of human activity, whether scientific, moral, economic, or artistic—hence, the musical metaphors that run through Smith's writings.

Consider, for example, how Smith described the sympathetic bond between an afflicted man and his observers in *The Theory of Moral Sentiments:* "To see the emotions of their hearts, in every respect, beat time to his own, in the violent and disagreeable passions, constitutes his sole consolation. But he can only hope to obtain this by lowering his passion to that pitch, in which the spectators are capable of going along with him. He must flatten, if I may be allowed to say so, the sharpness of its natural tone, in order to reduce it to harmony and concord with the emotions of those who are about him."[34] Elsewhere Smith characterized the sociable emotions as "soft, clear, and melodious," claiming that they "naturally express themselves in periods which are distinguished by regular pauses."[35] Several decades later, he would echo this second passage almost verbatim in his essay on the imitative arts: "The sentiments and passions which Music can best imitate are those which unite and bind men together in society. . . . They are, if I may say so, all Musical Passions; their natural tones are all clear, distinct, and almost melodious; and they naturally express themselves in a language which is distinguished by pauses at regular, and almost equal intervals; and which, upon that account, can more easily be adapted to the regular returns of the correspondent periods of a tune."[36] Smith's musical metaphors (which show an astute grasp of contemporary style) are not merely ornamental. They reflect his belief that music represents the psychological mechanism that governs every sphere of human activity.

Nowhere did Smith express this belief more clearly than in his account of listening to a concerto: "In the contemplation of that immense variety of agreeable and melodious sounds, arranged and digested, both in their coincidence and in their succession, into so complete and regular a system, the mind in reality enjoys not only a very great sensual, but a very

high intellectual, pleasure, not unlike that which it derives from the contemplation of a great system in any other science."[37] Unlike modern critics, Smith showed no interest in the contest of instruments. It is the harmonious system that fascinates him, not the individual actors. Admittedly,
Smith had in mind a concerto grosso by Corelli or Handel, and not a solo
concerto. Yet his description may prove even more relevant to Mozart's
piano concertos. For Mozart was working within a style that in many ways
eroded the illusion of voice, agency, and subjectivity. The frequent cadences of galant music broke up the rhetorical flow typical of Corelli or
Handel; the rapid play of topics fragmented the Cartesian unity of affect;
and periodicity had established a principle of organization that dissoci-
ated musical material from voice-source. These stylistic changes challenge
the metaphor of music as a dialogue or drama that embodies human subjectivity and agency.

Smith's psychological theory offers an alternative model for interpreting the meaning of Mozart's concertos. The following analysis of the Concerto in B♭, K. 450, probes beneath the surface level of actors, topics, and
plot. We shall treat Mozart's 1784 concerto instead as a Smithian machine,
an equilibrating system in which identity itself takes shape. This analysis by no means aims to replace or supersede narrative readings. Rather,
it explores the conditions that make possible such readings, including
Marxist dialectics, within the semiotic structures of Mozart's music.

. . . . .

Few Mozart concertos profile the performing forces more sharply than K.
450. It is Mozart's first piano concerto with obbligato winds, a novelty that
he advertised in the opening antiphony between woodwind and string
choirs. Meanwhile, the keyboard enjoys some of the most virtuosic writing in his Viennese concertos; as he wrote his father, "I believe that both
concertos [K. 450 and 451] will make you sweat—but the one in B♭ is more
difficult than the one in D."[38] In the Concerto in B♭, Mozart would seem
to have been intent on carving out three distinct personalities.

On closer listening, however, the solid figures begin to run together.
This happens gradually in the second-movement Andante, a theme with

Example 20.   Piano Concerto in B♭, K. 450, Andante, mm. 1–32.

two variations. The entire movement consists of an antiphonal exchange
between orchestra and soloist, who trade repeated eight-bar phrases. The
theme's chorale texture and sarabande rhythm evoke inward reflection,
anticipating the Andante of K. 453 (see example 20). The formal design,
on the other hand, exhibits an almost mechanical rigidity. The periodic
theme divides strictly into eight-, four-, and two-bar phrases, separated
by rests. This mechanical schema creates a peculiar counterpoint with the

subjective, confessional tone of the theme. Mechanism eventually over-comes subjectivity, as the repeating phrases dismantle the surface divi-sion between instrumental "actors."

The boundary between soloist and ensemble goes first. In the first vari-ation, the soloist introduces an arpeggiated countersubject above the strings' opening phrase (mm. 33–64). As the keyboard echoes each eight-bar phrase, this counterpoint passes into the left hand, while the right hand plays the orchestra's melody. The second variation reverses roles entirely (mm. 65–101), with the soloist beginning and the orchestra answering. Ini-tially, this might suggest a shift of power toward the soloist, were it not for the dramatic entrance of the concertante winds. After the opening theme of the Allegro, Mozart's new instrumental choir had receded into the background, and fell silent in the Andante. The sudden infusion of wind timbre in the second variation upstages the soloist, even as the new choir usurps the keyboard's position within the phrase structure. By the end of the movement, Mozart has abstracted the form of the opening di-alogue, breaking down the opposition of strings and keyboard, project-ing the two parts into the soloist's left and right hands, and reconfigur-ing the keyboard within a three-choir texture.

Mozart's treatment of instrumental forces in the Andante recalls the mu-sical dice games of the *ars combinatoria*. He has freely permuted the strings, winds, and keyboard within the phrase structure, shuffling the instru-mental paradigms within the periodic syntagm. Lulled by the regular oscillation of the form, we find ourselves drawn into an abstract ballet of timbres, ornamentation, and harmony. As in one of Mikhail Glinka's "changing-background" variations, the hypnotic repetitions invite the lis-tener to revel in the sensory details—the rippling arpeggios in the first variation, the pungent new timbre of the winds, the plush chromatic trills in mm. 85–86. Ultimately, the contrasting instruments themselves blur into the play of colors and textures. In Smith's terms, the phrase structure func-tions as a machine, a system that harmonizes the disparate elements into a tranquil whole.

The machine metaphor helps make sense of the first movement, which also begins with an antiphonal dialogue (see example 21). The opening theme juxtaposes martial and lyrical ideas, pitting a chromatic motive

Example 21. K. 450, Allegro, first theme, mm. 1–14.

Example 21. (*continued*)

against a triadic fanfare. This is a standard gambit, familiar from the Piano Concertos in E♭, K. 271 and 482. Yet K. 450 reverses the normal order of ideas. The lyrical motive takes the lead, instead of echoing her virile partner. Moreover, the instruments have switched roles. The winds, better suited to triadic flourishes, present the chromatic line, while the softer and more nimble strings play the fanfare. The strings continue to masquerade as brass instruments in mm. 9–13, playing "horn fifths."[39]

Such timbral cross-dressing accounts for much of the musical wit of Mozart and his contemporaries. The "Hunt" Quartet, K. 458, another B♭ work from 1784, presupposes that the listener will recognize hunting horns in the string instruments. Haydn expected his audience to recognize a *trompe de chasse* in the opening theme of Haydn's Symphony no. 6 ("Le matin"), even though it is played by a flute. As Monelle put it, "Haydn seems to ask: do you recognize the character of this tune, in spite of its wrong timbre?"[40] Likewise, the humor of Figaro's "Non più andrai" depends upon our hearing trumpet calls in the vocal line. Such metaphoric listening makes possible Ratner's topics, whose distinctive features are chiefly rhythmic and textural, rather than timbral. Topical semantics would be impossible without this independence between timbre and characteristic material.

The Allegro of K. 450 demonstrates with particular clarity the fluid relationship between voice and material. The shortest first movement in Mozart's mature concertos, the Allegro downplays the drama between piano and orchestra.[41] The primary interest resides, rather, in the textural interaction between piano, strings, and winds. The Concerto in B♭ dramatizes the formation of identity itself, enacting the process by which instruments reclaim their idiomatic material. As in the Concerto in G, this process operates beneath the level of themes, topics, and instrumental agents.

The first theme of K. 450 submits readily to Ratner's topical lexicon, · suggesting perhaps a composite of "sensibility" and "fanfare."[42] Yet before fixing labels, let us explore the semantic structure of the first theme. Mozart has introduced three musical oppositions that will play out across the orchestral ritornello: chromatic/diatonic, upbeat/downbeat, and wind/string. The first motive (mm. 1–2) assimilates the marked terms from all three categories. It saturates the triad with chromatic passing tones, begins on an upbeat, and foregrounds the solo winds. By contrast, the second motive (mm. 2–4) consists almost entirely of harmonic tones, outlines the tonic triad on the strong beats, and is played by the strings. These musical oppositions correlate with, and are organized by, analogous oppositions within late eighteenth-century culture:

Free	Structured
Private	Public
Sensible	Rational
Feminine	Masculine
Chromatic	Triadic
Offbeat	Metrically defined
(Wind)	(String)
(Primary)	(Secondary)

Only the instrumentation and order of ideas (shown in parentheses) invert the logic of this semantic system.

By reversing the expected order of motives, Mozart also created a syntactic tension within the first theme. Fanfares and martial motives normally precede lyrical ones, because they better define the key and meter. While Mozart's chromatic motive does not obscure the tonality, it certainly undercuts the metrical structure. In K. 450, for the first and only time, Mozart began a piano concerto on an upbeat. This places a special burden on the opening motive to clarify the meter. Yet the chromatic motive, with its even stream of eighth notes, implies no clear downbeat, nor does it help that the dissonant E♮ falls on the strong beats. Moreover, the first agogic accent falls on a weak beat (m. 2), which further confuses the meter. The concerto begins with syntactic and semantic imbalances that the musical machinery must restore to equilibrium.

The process begins in the consequent phrase, as the two motives are repeated. The woodwind motive enters half a beat early in m. 4, a metrical adjustment that shifts the accent to a chord tone, E♭. The strings then enter two beats early in m. 6, stating their ornamental flourish twice. The first motive shrinks to a three-note upbeat in the continuation of the sentence (mm. 8–11), becoming a mere pickup to the strings' downbeat "horn-call" motive. These subtle metrical adjustments transfer leadership to the strings, while restoring the winds to their traditional role of harmonic reinforcement. By the time the transition begins in m. 14, every marked feature—upbeat, concertante winds, metrical ambiguity, chromaticism—has been smoothed out of the theme.

The transition solidifies the unmarked structure (mm. 14–25). The strings continue to outline the triad, and their upbeat and final appoggiaturas have vanished. The two-bar phrases divide cleanly into strong-weak pairs that the winds, having settled into a supporting role, emphasize with agogic accents and martial rhythms. Aside from a few passing notes in the bass and a chromatic glimmer in mm. 19–20, the passage consists entirely of harmonic tones.

The transition exemplifies the principle of neutralization, introduced in the previous chapter, according to which a formal context suppresses a marked (or, less commonly, unmarked) trait. Mozart's symphony and concerto transitions typically begin with an elision, which forecloses the possibility of an upbeat. They also arrive *forte* with the full ensemble, which rules out concertante scoring. Moreover, the tonal role of transitions—launching the modulation to the new key—proscribes metrical complexities or chromatic sensibility. The formal context thus neutralizes every marked feature in Mozart's opening theme.

The second theme, however, restores the tensions from the opening bars (see example 22). The marked rhythm of the first theme returns; indeed, not only does the melody begin with an upbeat, but it maintains a syncopated rhythm against the bass line. As in a gavotte, the theme balances two competing meters, the marked (syncopated) grouping in the violins and the unmarked (notated) version in the lower strings. The syncopated melody, with its yearning suspensions and chromatic appoggiatura, most obviously indexes the *empfindsamer Stil* of North German keyboard music. This topic, which returns in the second variation of the Andante, echoes the *sensibilité* of the first theme, with its delicate chromatic opening.

The second theme resolves the rhythmic disequilibrium through a change of topic. As we saw, displaced meter can function as a distinctive feature, or figura, for multiple topics, including both sensibility and learned style. This shared feature allowed Mozart to shift topics with a simple adjustment of the texture. As the winds repeat the syncopated melody, the violins introduce a countersubject in third species—in fact, a countersubject Mozart borrowed from the *alla breve* finale of his preceding concerto, K. 449 (mm. 40–42, shown in example 37a in chapter 6). The new subject creates a Fuxian texture within which the syncopations are now heard as fourth-species suspensions. Syntactically, the new texture reinforces the notated meter, placing a chord tone on every strong beat. Semantically, it provides a new stylistic-historical context for the displaced meter. Within the *stile antico*, the syncopated melody loses its modern connotation of free self-expression. (We might draw a parallel with the minor cadences in Beethoven's Lydian *Heiliger Dankgesang;* within the archaic modality, the minor mode loses its modern correlation with dysphoria.) The repetition of the second theme does not suppress the marked metrical displacement. Rather, it creates a stylistic framework within which the markedness relationship is no longer pertinent.

The closing theme (mm. 45–53) continues to work through the structural conflicts from the opening bars. The instruments are still estranged

Example 22. K. 450, Allegro, second theme, mm. 25–41.

Example 23.   K. 450, Allegro, closing theme, mm. 53–59.

from their characteristic material: the strings play a vigorous proclamatory theme, ending with a fanfare-like flourish. Martial and sensible styles also remain confused. While the new theme reinforces the harmonic and metric structure, it retains the syncopated rhythms and sighing appoggiaturas from the second theme. Only in the quiet sequel do the opening oppositions sort themselves out (see example 23). The antiphonal dialogue from mm. 1–13 returns, with winds and strings trading two-bar phrases. But now the "natural" wind instruments propose a triadic horn call (derived from the end of the closing theme), while the strings answer with a stepwise motive, delicately inflected with accented passing tones.

Mozart has corrected the order of motives, so that the fanfare assumes its proper position before its sensible partner.

And, with this quiet passage, Mozart has finally reunited the instruments with their idiomatic material. The winds reclaim their fanfare, the strings their lyrical melody. As Daniel Leeson and Robert Levin have documented, such passages regularly follow the final structural cadence in Mozart's orchestral ritornellos.[43] They provide a respite from the forward momentum, a calm space amid the drama. Appropriately, the orchestral actors achieve integration in this reflective moment.

The keyboard soloist, ironically, has the least individuated material in the Allegro. From the first entrance, the soloist displays a noticeable poverty of thematic material. In the adjacent concertos, K. 449 and 451, the keyboard enters with the first theme immediately after the ritornello. In K. 450, the soloist slips in on the tail of the closing theme, prolonging the tonic cadence with twelve measures of decorative passagework. This nonthematic material is tonally superfluous, since it neither resolves the end of the ritornello nor prepares the first theme with a half cadence.

Even the soloist's new theme lacks substance. After two measures of a jaunty martial idea, the soloist leaps an octave for a sequence of ornamental flourishes. The antecedent phrase fills in this registral gap with equally vapid scalar passages. After eight bars, the soloist turns the melody over to the orchestra and spins out arpeggios for the remainder of the theme. In K. 449, by contrast, the soloist plays the entire thematic sentence, engaging the orchestra in a lively dialogue. In K. 450, the soloist eschews thematic statements, reverting continually to decorative passagework.

The beginning of the development confirms this pattern. The soloist again slips in on the final orchestral phrase, the lyrical violin melody that concluded the ritornello. Rather than develop the theme, however, the keyboard takes advantage of the scalar melody for another bravura passage. For the first twelve measures, the two hands toss the chromatic scales back and forth in invertible counterpoint. The remainder of the development consists of free passagework in the keyboard, accompanied unobtrusively by the orchestra. There is no hint of that stormy confrontation between soloist and orchestra that distinguishes K. 449. The keyboard remains absorbed in its virtuosic play.

Example 24.   K. 450, Allegro (finale), first theme, mm. 11–13.

Thus, Mozart's soloist, the alleged vessel of bourgeois individuality, proves as elusive as his orchestral antagonists. Unable to sustain a thematic argument or engage the other instruments, the virtuosic soloist remains a cipher. This lack of personality might seem paradoxical in a concerto that flaunts its diverse performing forces. Yet it fits with Mozart's strategy in K. 450, which calls into question the integrity of all the instrumental agents.

The finale provides a comical counterpart to the first movement. The 6/8 Allegro suggests a typical hunting finale, a logical choice for a B♭ con-

Example 25. K. 450, finale, coda, mm. 294–306.

(continued)

certo with obbligato winds. The sonata-rondo theme descends by thirds, however, outlining the subdominant. This inconvenient feature excludes the B♭ horns, the characteristic hunting instruments whose natural overtones outline the tonic triad. As the orchestra repeats the first theme, the horns must content themselves with sustaining a tonic pedal. Not until the end of the ritornello do they finally shine (see example 24). Mozart has appended a triadic horn call, based entirely on the natural overtones. This closing fanfare, which echoes the end of the first-movement ritornello, allows the horns to reclaim their characteristic material. They also join in a second horn call that concludes the theme (mm. 39–42).

Example 25.   (continued)

The horn-call motive disappears in the succeeding statements of the rondo theme, and only returns at the end of movement after the cadenza (see example 25). In a humorous twist, the piano commandeers the motive, denying the horns their rightful music. Nevertheless, in the coda, the horns harmonize a soft call beneath the soloist's arpeggio figuration, mimicking the sound of a distant hunting party. In these closing measures, instrument and idiomatic material at last reunite.

·   ·   ·   ·   ·

In the Concerto in B♭, Mozart did not stage a drama between individuated musical actors. On the contrary, he alienated the instruments from

Example 25. *(continued)*

their idiomatic material and blurred the distinction between the performing forces. The concerto enacts the process by which musical subjects take shape, working out their identity within the labile play of signs. As K. 450 demonstrates with unusual clarity, the musical subject is not given a priori in Mozart's music. It must be constructed within the machinery of the musical syntax, as instruments and material find their proper alignment within the balanced structure of phrasing, form, tonality, and texture.

This puts a crimp in Marxist critiques that would map the bourgeois individual, social forces, or other abstract ideas onto the voices in Mozart's music. Such readings skip a crucial step. They ignore one of the most brilliant and enduring ideas of the Enlightenment—that individual consciousness only emerges within the collective structures of language. This idea could spark new insights into musical ideology in the later eighteenth century, offering an alternative to the post-Kantian outlook that has tended to dominate the discussion.

Ironically, Adam Smith can provide this rejuvenating perspective. This makes sense, since both Smith and Marx owed a common debt to the materialist philosophy of the Enlightenment. The Scottish polymath worked out the implications of the new empiricism in every branch of philosophy, whether political economy, moral philosophy, language theory, or music aesthetics. Perhaps no other major philosopher besides Rousseau located music so fully within the intellectual context of the later eighteenth century. For critics pursuing an ideological understanding of Mozart's music, including those of us who do not embrace Marxism or even materialism, Smith's writings provide an alluring path.

FIVE A Dubious Credo

For over two centuries, Mozart's "Credo" masses have huddled on the margins of scholarship, together with the rest of his Salzburg church music. Only a single article written over fifty years ago has explored the Masses in F and C, K. 192 and 257, in which Mozart treated the opening word of the Credo as a refrain. Critics and biographers have understandably neglected these modest specimens of *Gebrauchsmusik*. As Georg Reichert documented, Mozart's Credo masses belong to an Austrian tradition dating back to Johann Joseph Fux.[1] The formulaic statements of faith indicate no peculiar zeal on the composer's part, nor do they suggest any intimate connection with his outer life such as we find in the "Great" Mass in C Minor or the Requiem.

From the perspective of language theory, however, Mozart's Credo masses command considerable interest. As Otto Jahn noted long ago, the

Credo presents the vocal composer with a grammatical challenge: "A long movement, whose several parts are dependent on one emphatic verb placed at the beginning, cannot be musically rendered in such a way that the connection remains apparent to the hearers."[2] In most eighteenth-century Credo settings, the opening verb vanished altogether and was intoned instead by the celebrant. The written text thus amounts to a mere string of predicates, detached from any subject or verb. Indeed, the Credo resembles the primitive nomenclature imagined by Enlightenment language theory.

The conventions of the Austrian *missa brevis* further eroded any sense of subjective presence. Bruce MacIntyre has noted the "declamatory, parlando choral writing and the almost mechanical alternation of chorus and soloists" in Viennese Credo settings, pointing out that as preparation for the Eucharistic liturgy the movement attracted little musical attention.[3] Mozart faced stiffer constraints in Salzburg, where Archbishop Colloredo had imposed strict time limits on the Mass. Jettisoning word repetitions, text-painting, and expressive vocalism, Mozart typically dispatched the long Credo text in brisk homophonic declamation propelled by energetic ostinatos in the orchestra. Ironically, the one section of the Mass ordinary that features first-person verbs—*credo, confiteor, expecto*—inspired the most impersonal setting of the *missa brevis*.

These perfunctory settings contrast rudely with the Neapolitan "number mass" to which Mozart gladly turned whenever he escaped Colloredo's jurisdiction. In solemn masses like K. 139 ("Waisenhaus-Messe"), K. 167 ("Missa in honorem Sanctissimae Trinitatis"), or the Mass in C Minor, Mozart divided the Credo text into many short movements, each dedicated to expressing a single affect or image. The *missa brevis* compresses these leisurely orations into three movements that move swiftly through the narrative of Christ's incarnation, crucifixion, and resurrection. In operatic terms, the *missa brevis* replaces aria with ensemble, rhetorical expression with dramatic representation. Thrasybulos Georgiades could even compare the Viennese mass to Pergolesi's *La serva padrona*: "The music is not so much concerned with mirroring an affect or even a change of affect. What the composer sets to music is the situation, the action, the events on the stage, the incidents taking place before our eyes, in our presence, here and now."[4]

This theatrical style understandably repelled listeners who expected spiritual uplift from church music. As Friedrich Nicolai complained in 1784: "But now operatic music forces itself everywhere, also in church, and what is worse, the vacuous ["fade"] kind of newfangled Italian operatic music. I knew not with many a Credo or Benedictus whether I was hearing music from an Italian opera buffa or not. . . . Seldom did I hear anything moving or sublime."[5] The new secular style, as Karl Fellerer insisted, did not necessarily signify a decline of piety on the part of Mozart and his fellow composers.[6] Nevertheless, their Mass settings accorded with an aesthetic that discouraged the expression of mystical or metaphysical ideas. Enlightenment poetics no longer prized the Baroque "unity of the arts" described by Jean Hagstrum: "The form of expression— color, line, word—was therefore necessarily less important than its meaning or the experience to which it could lead."[7] On the contrary, Du Bos, Batteux, Baumgarten, Lessing, and Burke focused their attention on the sign itself, analyzing the mechanisms of representation. David Wellbery has explained the ideological motivation behind this scientific poetics: "The desacralization of language is the extrication of language from its place within the ceremonies of religious and absolutist authority and its transformation into a medium of communication and debate among equal subjects."[8]

Certainly, that was Archbishop Colloredo's intention. The archbishop played a key role in the Febronian movement, an offshoot of late Jansenism that aimed to strengthen the Austrian bishops' hand against the papacy. His reforms in Salzburg—the streamlined liturgy, German hymnal, and restrictions on processions, pilgrimages, candles, and statues—were all aimed at weakening Roman authority.[9] Colloredo's lodestar was Lodovico Antonio Muratori, whose influence he had absorbed at the Collegium Germanicum in Rome (Salzburg University also hosted a prominent cadre of Muratorians). The Italian philologist's essay *Della regolata divozione de' cristiani* (1723) went through twenty editions in German translation, eight of them published in Vienna.[10] Muratori disdained the pomp and ostentation of Baroque Catholicism, prescribing instead a simple rational devotion. His dissection of religious symbology recalls the semiotic analyses of his literary contemporaries: "The relics of the saints, in and of themselves, are nothing but earthly material; their images are nothing but an aggregate of colors painted on plate or canvasses, or perhaps gold, silver, marble, wood, or stucco, shaped into statues. That which is matter is not worthy of adoration; and whoever would adore and venerate it commits idolatry."[11] In the same spirit, the Austrian *missa brevis* disenchanted the musical sign, stripping away the magnificent trappings of the Baroque ceremonial mass. In his Salzburg masses, Mozart realized (however glumly) Muratori's ideal of a transparent, self-effacing liturgy.

The Credo mass restores opacity to the religious sign. The insistent refrain, "Credo, credo," revives the mystical dimension suppressed by the Josephine liturgy by foregrounding the expression of belief itself. The result is a fascinating intertextuality. As composers reconstructed the linguistic subject, that self which believes, trusts, and expects, they had to reach beyond the representational paradigm of the *missa brevis*. The Credo mass faces the question posed by the previous chapter: how could composers construct a transcendent subject in a style that in many ways seems designed to eliminate subjective presence? The genre provides a glimpse into the alternative models of language that coexisted in Mozart's age, each with its own intellectual, social, and ideological entailments.

Joseph Haydn's single Credo Mass provides an instructive case study. In the Missa Cellensis, H. XII: 5 ("St. Cecilia"), the words "Credo in unum Deum" return five times during the opening Vivace. The refrain, introduced by the chorus, is echoed by a soprano soloist who sings the remaining refrains alone (see example 26). As in all Credo masses, the refrain functions as a ritornello, anchoring the new keys explored during the modulating episodes; since these episodes correspond to the doctrines of the Creed, the refrains evoke a sense of affirmation, a ringing assent to each new article of faith. Haydn restricted solo singing to the Credo refrains, allowing the soprano to glitter against the foil of the chorus. Her melody grows increasingly florid as the Vivace proceeds, acquiring new ornaments with repetition. In short, Haydn has constructed his Credo subject as a virtuosic soloist from the world of Italian serious opera.

This operatic subject, in turn, encodes social and ideological meanings. The *dramma per musica* enshrined the values of absolutist court culture, in which rhetorical mastery represented political authority, rational control, and aristocratic prestige. This rhetorical model rested upon a Cartesian

Example 26. Haydn, *Missa Cellensis,* H. XII: 5, Credo, mm. 1–5.

duality according to which language and music expressed the static ideas and passions of the soul; thus, Haydn's soprano spins out a single affect across the Vivace, elaborating but never departing from the buoyant mood of the refrain. By interpolating the rhetorical model of opera seria, Haydn was able to transcend the representational aesthetic of the Josephine mass, carving out a position for the metaphysical subject. The "St. Cecilia" Credo creates a multilayered discourse that allows music to represent not only doctrinal content, but also the subjective expression of belief.

Mozart's Credo masses present a more complex picture. The idiosyncratic designs of K. 192 and 257 do not correspond obviously to a linguistic model, like neoclassical rhetoric. Nevertheless, Mozart wove both Credos from a conventional repertoire of musical signs and compositional strategies. This chapter examines the interpolated refrains of K. 192 and 257 and suggests how they might correlate with important strains of eighteenth-century language theory. A concluding analysis of the Credo from the Mass in C, K. 317 ("Coronation"), will provide a counterexample. This

Example 27.   Mass in F, K. 192, Credo, mm. 1–2.

splendid movement, Mozart's finest setting of the Credo, reveals his most characteristic solution to the problem of belief.

.   .   .   .   .

Mozart pursued an archaizing strategy in K. 192. The Mass in F is Mozart's most rigorous exercise in learned counterpoint, his closest approach to Fux's *stylus antiquus*. Originally scored for church trio and *colla parte* trombones, K. 192 places supreme emphasis upon vocal counterpoint. The Kyrie opens with a full fugal exposition followed by a four-part canon at the second, while the Christe culminates in a double canon. Mozart set the Hosanna fugally and saturated the Benedictus with canonic imitation. The Gloria begins and ends with a vocal *cantus firmus* sustained against the orchestra, a texture that runs throughout the movement. For the Credo refrain, Mozart chose his favorite Gregorian melody, famous from the "Jupiter" Symphony, and set it as an *alla breve* chorale (see example 27).

Like Haydn, Mozart constructed his Credo on the formal template of the Italian ritornello. The refrain returns twelve times across the movement, affirming the new keys explored in the episodes. Other composers had used Gregorian melodies in Credo masses; for example, both Fux and Johann Georg Reinhardt derived refrains from the traditional Credo intonation.[12] Yet Mozart departed from these models by developing his chant within the episodes as well as the refrains. Moreover, for the first and only time, he abandoned the traditional fast-slow-fast ternary form and set the entire Credo in a single tempo. In effect, this flattens the dramatic representation of Christ's incarnation, death, and resurrection, even as it enhances the continuous development of the Gregorian motive.

The Credo motto progressively permeates the counterpoint as the movement progresses. The four-note motive invites stretto, as the "Jupiter" finale demonstrates. Mozart began modestly with a two-part stretto at the octave (mm. 27–30, 86–88). The second stretto, expanded to four voices, reveals the further possibility of imitation at the fifth (mm. 36–40, 100–104). Contrapuntal complexity deepens in the "Crucifixus," a four-voice fugue. Mozart reserved his *pièce de résistance* for the "Et vitam venturi," a strict permutation fugue based on the Credo motto and four countersubjects, and final "Amen," a four-part stretto at both octave and fifth (see example 28).

The chant refrain first spills over into the episodes during the "Crucifixus," traditionally the solemn nadir of the Credo. The Gregorian motive serves as the subject of a C-minor fugato, ascending through the four voices. Accompanied by a vigorous bass line, the fugato projects a surging energy unusual for "Crucifixus" settings. The sense of purposeful motion is even more pronounced in the "Confiteor," where the plainchant next enters an episode. The motto now resolves a weighty half cadence and launches the final section of the Credo. Unusually, this cadence serves to restore the tonic from which the "Et incarnatus est" had strayed. Mozart has retooled the ternary shape of the Credo, in which tonic resolution normally arrives with the "Et resurrexit." In K. 192, he set the "Et resurrexit" in the subdominant and deferred resolution to the "Confiteor" (although bar 89 does touch on I, the cadence arrives through $V_{4/3}$ and falls on a weak beat). By postponing tonal closure until the "Confiteor," Mozart has shifted emphasis from the narrated events of Christ's death

Example 28. K. 192, Credo, mm. 118–32.

and resurrection to the believer's first-person response, "I confess." Appropriately, a solo voice now sings the Credo refrain for the first time.

Mozart also mined the harmonic potential of his Gregorian motive. He found four different harmonizations and introduced each in an important formal position—the opening ritornello, the end of the first main textual division ("Et descendit de caelis"), the "Confiteor" reprise, and the final ritornello. Moreover, he exploited the tonal ambiguity of the motive, which

Example 28.   (continued)

can function as either $\hat{1}$–$\hat{2}$–$\hat{4}$–$\hat{3}$ of I or $\hat{5}$–$\hat{6}$–$\hat{1}$–$\hat{7}$ of V. This ambiguity makes the motive ideal for fugal treatment in the "Crucifixus" and "Et vitam venturi," which balance the two versions as subject and answer. When transposed into minor and shorn of its semitone, the motive also becomes modally ambiguous. Thus, the first stretto introduces the motive in D minor and then repeats it untransposed in the relative major, F. The medieval chant also implies a move to the subdominant, with *mi-fa* serving as pivot ($\hat{4}$–3 becomes $\hat{1}$–$\hat{7}$). This tendency is realized progressively in the keys of the refrain (F, C, D minor, G minor, C minor, B♭). Mozart exploited the subdominant tendency most obviously in the second stretto, which rotates the motto downward through the circle of fifths (G-C-F-B♭).

In summary, we might say that Mozart's first Credo mass constructs first-person subjectivity as pure intellectual activity. The K. 192 Credo downplays the representation of external events and foregrounds instead the synthetic power of the mind as it exhausts the contrapuntal and harmonic potential of a simple idea. This introspective procedure recalls the seventeenth century more than the eighteenth, the rationalist *Solitaires* more than the empiricist *Lumières*. Indeed, the learned style was ideally suited to the introspective method of rationalist thought. The highly regulated rhythm, counterpoint, and harmony filter out characteristic gestures, styles, or topics. Cloistered from the external world, the musical mind was cast back upon its own structural resources. While the *stile antico* could itself function as a stylistic index, its strictures inhibited the representational impulse of Enlightenment aesthetics. Indeed, the *stile antico* approaches the ideal of a purely formal language.

Yet Mozart's learned Credo leaves a crucial question unanswered, one that exercised philosophers from Descartes onward: how can the solitary mind make judgments about mind-independent reality? How does autonomous reason interact with the world of sense and experience, that world in which God might become flesh, die, and rise again? Leibniz had recourse to "preestablished harmony," according to which God has synchronized the rational and sensory realms like two clocks. Malebranche appealed to the doctrine of "occasionalism," claiming that sensory stimuli served merely as pretexts for God's production of ideas. The problem also sparked considerable interest in "universal grammar" during the eighteenth century. This branch of Enlightenment language theory can help explain the role the *stile antico* played for Mozart and his contemporaries, not merely as another style to be represented but as an alternative to the representational aesthetic itself.

·   ·   ·   ·   ·

Universal grammar reflected the systematic spirit of rationalism. Works like Herbert of Cherbury's *De Veritate* (1624), the Port-Royal *Grammaire* (1660), James Harris's *Hermes* (1751), and Nicholas Beauzée's *Grammaire générale* (1767) sought to establish the principles governing all human languages. The universal grammarians hoped thereby to discover the underlying structures of human thought, the rational universals from which all human tongues descended. This pre-Babelian knowledge, they hoped, would facilitate the spread of scientific knowledge and promote reconciliation between religious sects.[13]

In this spirit, Leibniz proposed his famous *De arte combinatoria* (1666), which inspired the *ars combinatoria* of eighteenth-century music theory. Leibniz envisioned a language of concepts, a "universal alphabet of human thought." It would allow scientists to generate a priori propositions about the sensory world, just as a composer could generate new minuets by shuffling paradigmatic phrases. Logic would thus transcend its demonstrative function and become an instrument of scientific discovery. Rational introspection, independent of all experience, could yield synthetic judgments about mind-independent reality.

Leibniz amplified this claim in his later writings. All propositions, he claimed, concerned indivisible spiritual substances (monads), which alone conferred unity on the infinitely divisible aggregates of matter.[14] Monads developed spontaneously and in perfect autonomy, in accordance with preestablished harmony.[15] Therefore, Leibniz could claim in his *Discours de métaphysique* (1686) that "the notion of an individual substance includes once and for all everything that can ever happen to it and that, by considering this notion, one can see everything that can truly be said of it."[16] For example, the notion of Julius Caesar includes the fact that he will overthrow the Republic, since "it is the nature of such a perfect notion of a subject to contain everything, so that the predicate is included in the subject."[17] Sufficient reason demanded that such notions be grounded in God's perfect foreknowledge, leading Leibniz to defend the scholastic essences against Locke's nominalism in the *Nouveaux essais sur l'entendement humain* (1703): "For ideas are in God from all eternity, and they are in us, too, before we actually think of them."[18]

Leibniz's linguistic theory would seem to lead us logically to Kant, who distilled the general problem of pure reason in the question, "How are a priori synthetic judgments possible?"[19] Conveniently, Kant's three Critiques span Mozart's Viennese decade, a conjunction explored fruitfully by Marshall Brown, Rose Rosengard Subotnik, Elaine Sisman, and James Webster.[20] Yet the Kantian comparison suffers from a major drawback. Unlike most Enlightenment philosophers, Kant ignored language. Indeed, in his later writings, he explicitly rejected the linguistic turn of eighteenth-century philosophy, taking special aim at Herder.[21] Kant's neglect of language and signs makes him a problematic guide to Mozart, an operatic composer whose entire oeuvre evinces a delight in musical representation.

No such difficulty arises with Thomas Reid, the so-called Scottish Kant. Like Kant, Reid set out to refute David Hume's skeptical empiricism, but he pursued an entirely different strategy. More famous during Mozart's lifetime than Kant, Reid left a profound mark on British, French, and American philosophy, including C. S. Peirce's pragmatism.[22] His "common-sense" philosophy also made a powerful impression in Germany, enough so that Kant felt compelled to rebut Reid's ideas in his 1783 *Prolegomena zu einer jeden zukünftiger Metaphysik*. Unlike Kant, Reid granted language a central role in his epistemology, drawing especially upon the theory of universal grammar.

To refute Hume, Reid attacked an unquestioned axiom of Enlightenment philosophy, the so-called Way of Ideas. Descartes, Locke, Malebranche, Condillac, Berkeley, and Hume all agreed (or so Reid claimed) that the mind can only grasp sensory reality indirectly, through ideas. We do not perceive objects, but only their images within our mind, just as the image of a mountain is reflected in a lake. In Descartes's famous metaphor, the mind was a theater in which ideas represented the events of the outer world. As Terence Cuneo and René van Woudenberg summarized Hume's theory, the human mind was "the Newtonian universe writ small—a theater in which the 'materials' are 'particles' of impressions and ideas governed by the quasi-Newtonian laws of contiguity, resemblance, and causality."[23]

The Way of Ideas, Reid protested, had lured philosophy from the path of common sense and plunged it into solipsism. Because modern thought sundered ideas and reality, Descartes could doubt his own existence, Berkeley could deny the existence of matter, and Hume could question causality and personal identity itself. Yet, demanded Reid, where were these alleged ideas? Where in the brain did these phantoms enact their drama? And even if ideas did exist, would not their intervention merely defer the problem of perception, leaving unanswered the question of how the rational mind receives sensory data?

Reid argued instead for "direct realism," the unmediated perception of sensory objects. As he asserted in the *Inquiry into the Human Mind on the Principles of Common Sense* (1764): "Something which is extended and solid, which may be measured and weighed, is the immediate object of my touch and sight. And this object I take to be matter, and not an idea."[24] Perception was an irreducible faculty of the human mind, like spatiotemporal organization in Kant's Transcendental Aesthetic. Yet whereas Kant treated time and space merely as formal conditions of cognition, Reid claimed that perception afforded direct access to mind-independent reality.

Reid adduced a linguistic proof of direct realism in the *Inquiry* that recalls Berkeley's Divine Language argument: "The signs by which objects are presented to us in perception, are the language of Nature to man; and as, in many respects, it hath great affinity with the language of man to man; so particularly in this, that both are partly natural and original, partly acquired by custom."[25] If perception is the language of nature, argued Reid, then we should expect it to obey the same rules as human language. This assumption rests upon "providential naturalism," the assumption that God has tailored human reason to the design of nature. We are innately inclined to trust the veracity of human language: "There is therefore in the human mind an early anticipation, neither derived from experience, nor from reason, nor from any compact or promise, that our fellow-creatures will use the same signs in language, when they have the same sentiments." In the same way, we trust in natural causality: "If there were not a principle of veracity in the human mind, men's words would not be signs of their thoughts; and if there were no regularity in the course of nature, no one thing could be a natural sign of another."[26]

Reid amplified his linguistic proof in the *Essays on the Intellectual Powers of Man* (1785), adducing arguments from universal grammar. As he pointed out, Hume had reduced thought to a train of ideas and impressions, joined only by mechanical forces of association. Yet human language belies this atomistic model, testifying to deeper structures within the mind: "There are general rules of grammar, the same in all languages. This similarity of structure in all languages shews an uniformity among men in those opinions upon which the structure of language is founded. . . . Language is the express image and picture of human thoughts; and from the picture, we may draw very certain conclusions with regard to the original."[27] For example, adjective dependence proves that supposedly secondary qualities actually inhere in objects: "It is well known, that every adjective in language must belong to some substantive expressed or understood; that is, every quality must belong to some subject."[28] Likewise, the different grammatical voices (or tenses, in Reid's account) attest to the principle of causality: "If there was any nation who did not distinguish between acting and being acted upon, there would in their language be no distinction between active and passive tenses."[29] Universal grammar thus refuted Berkeley's idealism: "The distinction between substances, and the qualities belonging to them; between thought and the being that thinks; between thought, and the objects of thought; is to be found in the structure of all languages: and therefore, systems of philosophy, which abolish those distinctions, wage war with the common sense of mankind."[30]

Reid's appeal to universal grammar resembles Kant's exposition of the Table of Categories, insofar as both thinkers identified a priori categories that govern the human understanding. Yet, whereas Kant bypassed language, Reid recognized its constitutive role in thought. In this sense, he remained within the empiricist camp of Vico, Condillac, and Smith. He held back, however, from their more radical conclusions. Although he acknowledged an innate language of nature, he denied that syntax originated in gestures or that reflection evolved from sensation. For Reid, as for Harris and Beauzée, linguistic structures were hardwired into the brain; they determined our interactions with the sensory world but were not affected by them. Universal grammar thus safeguarded the soul from materialism. It rested, as Ulrich Ricken explained, upon "the assumption of two discrete substances, namely the physical and the intellectual, as well as on the premise of the a priori character of the intellectual, from which the laws of logical thought can be deduced as the self-evident foundation of language."[31]

The *stile antico* played an analogous role in eighteenth-century music. The learned style also preserved the ideal of a universal language, governed by unchanging laws and immune to national differences or fashion. Galant music had adapted itself to the naturalism of Enlightenment aesthetics, evolving structures that could capture the fleeting life of sense and feeling. The *stile antico*, on the other hand, continued to enshrine the ideal of a purely rational language, grounded in universal principles. Of course, as Sisman, Allanbrook, and others have shown, the *stile antico* also served Mozart and his contemporaries as a topic, a stylistic index rich in connotations of the sacred and sublime. Yet as the comparison with universal grammar suggests, the learned style played a deeper role. It provided an escape from the whole system of representation in which topics operate.

The Credo of K. 192 illustrates both functions of the *stile antico*. The plainchant motto and *alla breve* chorale certainly function as topics, introducing a marked "sacredness" into the secularized church style. Mozart's idiosyncratic treatment of the Credo, however, demonstrates the deeper conception of the archaic style, diametrically opposed to topical representation. The continuous form, neglect of text-painting, and exhaustive contrapuntal and harmonic exploration work against an imitative aesthetic. Mozart's design shows little concern with representing Christ's descent, incarnation, crucifixion, or resurrection. On the contrary, as the refrain invades the episodes, it absorbs these sensual images into the abstract development of the Gregorian chant. The Mass in F deploys the *stile antico* not simply as a topic, but as a method of subverting musical representation itself. Like Reid's philosophy, the Mass in F resists an encroaching empiricism that would banish metaphysical experience and confine human knowledge to sensory perception. Mozart's first Credo mass offers a glimpse into the pure structure of the mind and, thereby, into the Divine Mind in whose nature it participates.

.   .   .   .   .

Mozart switched tactics entirely in his second Credo mass. The Mass in C, K. 257 (1776), inaugurated what Alfred Einstein called Mozart's "song masses," in which the composer eschewed learned counterpoint in favor of simple, folklike melody.[32] Mozart set the outer sections of the K. 257 Credo in quick triple time and, following the tradition of the Austrian pastoral mass, cast the "Et incarnatus" as a siciliano. He restricted counterpoint to a modest canon at "sub Pontio Pilato" and barely feinted at a closing fugue. When the Gregorian melody from K. 192 returns in the Sanctus, it strikes a conspicuously solemn note amid the prevailing *Volkstümlichkeit*.

Mozart derived his refrain from another Gregorian melody, isolating the falling third of the Credo chant (see example 29). He could look back on numerous models. Reichert has cited similar Credo refrains by Fux, Marc'Antonio Ziani, Franz Gerhard Pruneder, Matthias Oettl, and Carl Paschmidt.[33] Mozart himself reused the falling-third prototype in his Mass in C Minor, where the motto returns twice in the manner of a Credo mass. Yet he showed no interest in the contrapuntal potential of his plainchant motive in K. 257. As Einstein remarked, "The *Credo* device, to which the Mass owes its name, is not constructed with an eye towards contrapuntal use, as is that of the F major Mass of 1774, K. 192. . . . It is quite simple and has the effect each time of a childlike outcry."[34]

These outcries create a jarring effect within the Credo. In K. 192, Mozart wove the Gregorian motive carefully into the contrapuntal, harmonic, and formal structure. In K. 257, on the other hand, he seems to have been bent on dissociating the Credo refrain from the surrounding movement. The clipped unison motive continually interrupts the rhythmic flow, damping the buoyant energy of the Credo. The internal repetition within the refrain also creates an unsettling effect. The *piano* echo weakens the ringing unison, while the half cadence transforms the assertion into a question—"I believe!" becomes "I believe?" The motto injects a persistent note of uncertainty, undercutting the confident assertions of faith. The effect verges

Example 29.   Mass in C, K. 257, Credo, mm. 1–4.

on comedy when the motive returns before the "Et resurrexit," stopping the resurrection dead in its tracks. Not surprisingly, the 1803 Breitkopf and Härtel edition omitted the Credo refrains altogether, as did a 1785 copy supervised by Mozart's sister.[35]

Mozart tailored the ritornello structure to his quirky refrain. The Credo motto returns twelve times, as in K. 192, but Mozart has reversed its harmonic function. Instead of anchoring the keys explored in the episodes, the ritornello now instigates the modulations, preparing each new key with a half cadence. The repeated "Credo, credo" refrain directs the tonality toward each new key area, as if the believing subject were generating each new predicate. The ritornellos do not seem to affirm the articles of faith, as in K. 192. Rather, they suggest a restless, inquisitive activity—a more faithful representation, perhaps, of the religious experience of Mozart and his educated contemporaries.

The transition to the "Et incarnatus" epitomizes this subjectivist per-

Example 30.   K. 257, Credo, mm. 70–81.

spective (see example 30). Mozart has avoided the expected text-painting on "Et descendit de caelis" ("And descended from heaven"), which Austrian composers almost inevitably illustrated with a descending melody. Indeed, he even set the words to an ascending melody! The focus falls instead on the Credo refrain, whose abrupt cadence on V/vi brings the movement to a sudden halt. A full bar of silence ensues, as if the believer were struck dumb by the mystery of the Incarnation. Rather than depict the object of belief, Mozart has represented its effect upon the believing subject.

The K. 257 Credo does suggest a rapprochement, however, between subject and object. Toward the end of the movement, the "Credo, credo" interjections enter into a more intimate engagement with the surrounding text (see example 31). In bar 198, for the first time, a solo voice sings the refrain. The bass soloist states the refrain four times, exclaiming "Credo, Credo" after each new statement of faith. The refrains now answer the

Example 31. K. 257, Credo, mm. 198–209.

doctrinal assertions, remaining in the same key rather than modulating. In these solo statements, the subject no longer directs the discourse, but responds passively to the ensemble. Moreover, the Credo motto no longer interrupts the momentum; a vigorous new violin line accompanies the staccato refrain, drawing it into the rhythmic flow. In these solo refrains, the skeptical subject seems finally to embrace the creed.

The disruptive refrains of K. 257 recall similar moments in Haydn, like the famous chord in the Andante of the Symphony no. 94 ("Surprise") or the finale coda of the Quartet in E♭, Op. 33, no. 2 ("Joke"). Such passages jolt the listeners out of their comfortable absorption by disrupting the predictable sequence of events. As Mark Evan Bonds explained, "these techniques were perceived to undermine the traditional premise of aesthetic illusion, thereby creating a sense of ironic distance between the work and the listener."[36] Bonds drew convincing parallels between Haydn's whimsical play with conventions and Laurence Sterne's narrative intrusions in *Tristram Shandy* and *A Sentimental Journey*. Another point of comparison, particularly relevant to this chapter, comes from Sterne's devotee and exact contemporary Denis Diderot. Diderot emulated the British author's narrative style in his short stories and novels, which date from the same years as Mozart's Salzburg masses. Unlike Sterne, Diderot left important writings on language and music that can help illuminate the ironic impulse in Haydn and Mozart.

·   ·   ·   ·   ·

Diderot forayed into Sternian irony most overtly in *Ce n'est pas une conte* (*This is Not a Story*, 1770). The whimsical tale breaks through the aesthetic frame by foregrounding the role of the reader. "When one tells a story," begins the narrator, "there has to be someone to listen; and if the story runs to any length, it is rare for the storyteller not sometimes to be interrupted by his listener." Throughout the tale an unidentified listener continually intrudes upon the narration: "—It might be best if I kept my little story for another occasion. —*You mean when I'm not here?* —No, I don't mean that. —*Or you are afraid I will not be as kind to you, in private, as I would be in a crowded drawing room, with someone I didn't know.* —No, that's not the reason."[37] The repartee between author and reader, which runs throughout the tale, emphasizes the arbitrary nature of the narrative.

In his posthumous novel, *Jacques le Fataliste* (1771–78), Diderot used narrative disruptions to explore the problem of scientific determinism. The crafty servant Jacques debates the existence of free will with his master:

JACQUES: I was thinking that all the time you've been talking to me and I've been answering, you were talking without wanting to and I was answering without wanting to.

MASTER: And?

JACQUES: And? That we were therefore a couple of living, thinking machines.

MASTER: But what do you want at this moment?

JACQUES: By God, it doesn't matter what I want. All wanting does is to activate another set of cogs in both our machines.[38]

The novel preserves the illusion of free will by self-consciously playing with literary conventions. After his master delivers a long and eloquent eulogy, Jacques responds: "I've lost my Captain, I'm grief-stricken and you come out, like a parrot, with a slice of funeral oration written by some man or other, or maybe by a woman to another woman who has just lost the man she loved."[39] Elsewhere, the narrator archly comments, "I shall interrupt [his master's tale], for no very good reason except to annoy Jacques by proving that it was not written on high, as he believed, that he would go on being interrupted while his Master never would be."[40] Irony provides a precarious refuge from the determinism of a mechanistic worldview.

The specter of mechanism also haunts Diderot's best-known musical essay, the posthumous *Le neveu de Rameau*. In a familiar passage, the eccentric nephew loses himself in a parody of operatic styles: "He sang thirty tunes on top of each other and all mixed up: Italian, French, tragic, comic, of all sorts and descriptions. . . . Here we have a young girl weeping, and he mimes all her simpering ways, there a priest, king, tyrant, threatening, commanding, flying into a rage, or a slave obeying. He relents, wails, complains, laughs, never losing sight of tone, proportion, meaning of words and character of music."[41] The nephew's virtuosic performance suggests dissociation, as if the signs of emotions had become dislodged from the feeling self. Diderot recommended precisely this manner of imitation in his *Paradoxe sur le comédien:* "What then is true talent? Being familiar with the outward signs of the nature one has assumed, directing one's performance at the sensations of those who hear and see us and deceiving them by the imitation of these signs."[42] Such hollow virtuosity runs counter to doctrine of *sensibilité* that had defined the emerging bourgeois identity. It defies Horace's injunction, famously quoted by C. P. E. Bach, "Si vis me flere, dolendum est/primum ipsi tibi" (If you wish to make me weep, you yourself must first feel sorrow).

The nephew's performance, however disconcerting, bears comparison with Mozart's own style. His music also swerves between contrasting styles, genres, and affects, often with disconcerting abruptness. Diderot might almost have been describing the "Jupiter" Symphony, whose first movement juxtaposes martial grandeur to sentimental lyricism and opera buffa. Mozart's Salzburg masses, in which *stile antico* counterpoint jostles with Italian opera and popular song, epitomize Mozart's indifference to stylistic unity. This motley style drew the censure of north German critics; as one of Haydn's critics complained in 1771: "Now the works of Heiden, Toeschin, Cannabich, Filz, Pugnani, and Campioni are getting the upper hand. One need be only a quasi-connoisseur to notice the emptiness, the strange mixture of comic and serious, of the trifling and the moving, that reigns everywhere."[43] The new south German and Italian music, like the nephew's virtuosic parody, betrayed a gap between outward expression and inward feeling. Such facility struck at the roots of the modern musical subject, what Elizabeth Le Guin has described as "the discrete, individual, feeling self, the newly conceived common man, central player of both democracy and *sensibilité*."[44]

It seems particularly telling that modern critics can identify a "sensibility" topic in late eighteenth-century music. For example, Kofi Agawu analyzed the opening theme of Mozart's String Quintet in C, K. 515, as the juxtaposition of Mannheim rocket and sensibility.[45] For C. P. E. Bach's generation, the ideal of *sensibilité* had governed the entire composition and delivery of a musical oration. For Mozart, it has become a mere representation, a topic to be shuffled with marches, dances, and buffa arias. The authentic feeling self, that self who might profess faith in God, has been absorbed into the play of signs.

Diderot's treatise hints at the precise nature of Mozart's musical mechanism. In another celebrated passage, the nephew prescribes the proper style of operatic verse: "It is the animal cry of passion that should dictate the melodic line, and these moments should tumble out quickly one after the other, phrases must be short and the meaning self-contained, so that the musician can utilize the whole and each part, omitting one word or repeating it, adding a missing word, turning it all ways like a polyp, without destroying it. All this makes lyric poetry in French a much more difficult problem than in languages with inversions which have these natural advantages."[46] While this passage has attracted much commentary, critics have overlooked the importance of the final sentence. With this crucial reference to inversions, Diderot has folded the musical argument into a larger linguistic debate. As we saw in the first chapter, word order became a *point d'appui* for the sensualist philosophers in their campaign against rationalist metaphysics. Condillac, Batteux, Algarotti, and Herder denied that the modern S-V-O order represented an innate mental structure, claiming instead that syntax evolved historically as languages grew more analytical and ceased to rely upon gesture and speech inflection. Diderot had entered the debate in his *Lettre sur les sourds et müets* (1751), where he measured verbal syntax against the order of ideas in sign language for the deaf. As Sophia Rosenfeld explained, Diderot complained that the French language "suffered as well as benefited as a result of its great distance from the prerational, primitive language of gesture. Its gains in cognitive value were matched by a loss of vigor, warmth, affective value, and especially, *enérgie*, as the inherent limitations of verbal language were exacerbated by historical achievements."[47]

In short, Diderot has set forth a language model diametrically opposed to Thomas Reid's universal grammar. Reid found the grounds for the metaphysical self—substance, causality, personal identity—enshrined within the innate structures of language. The nephew dismisses these same structures as artificial constructs, which hinder the truthful representation of nature. In claiming that the "animal cry of passion" should dictate the melody, the nephew appeals to the preverbal logic of natural signs. He wants short and flexible poetic phrases, whose meaning is "self-contained"—that is, like the inflected words of ancient languages, which could circulate freely within the sentence. Diderot idealizes an operatic poetry in which both signs and syntax transparently reflect their bodily origins. And Mozart was ready to set it for him with his supple, dance-based style.

Caught in that sensual music, the subject of K. 257 can only express belief negatively, in silences and gaps. Mozart's second Credo mass preserves, if not a sanctuary for the faithful, at least a haven for agnostics. Fittingly, this space opens within the most mechanistic element of Mozart's musical language, the periodic phrase. The chiming repetitions of "Credo, credo," with their questioning half cadences, create an echo chamber where the subject can reflect upon its own speech. That inner echo keeps alive the possibility of faith in something beyond mere mechanism, perhaps even God.

.   .   .   .   .

Although the Mass in C, K. 317 ("Coronation"), does not qualify as a Credo mass, the opening words do return during the final orchestral ritornello. This brief coda, I shall argue, consummates an ingenious musical and linguistic design. The believing subject of K. 317 does not manifest itself in exhaustive contrapuntal invention, nor does it peek ironically through cracks in the musical facade. Indeed, Mozart has skirted entirely the problematic relationship between subject and object. His solution was to transform the referential Credo into a speech act, an illocutionary statement. The "Coronation" Credo avoids metaphysical propositions altogether by retreating into the self-referential logic of performative speech.

Mozart's design hinges on an unremarkable motive, an idea so banal as to escape notice. The orchestral ritornello is built from a rising pentachord, introduced by the strings and oboes and repeated in rising sequence (see example 32). The motive features an upbeat rhythm whose drive to the cadence complements the upward thrust of the melody. On its third statement, the motive is inverted, with a voice exchange between rising and falling versions. This simple motive permeates the Credo and provides the key to Mozart's play with language function.

Example 32.   Mass in C, K. 317 ("Coronation"), mm. 1–9.

(continued)

Mozart seems to have borrowed his invertible motive from an earlier Mass in C, K. 258 (see example 33). He used the falling version, with the identical rhythm, for the words "Et descendit de caeli" ("And descended from heaven"), and the rising version for "Et resurrexit" ("And rose again"). The motive thus originated as a pictorial icon, the most naive species of text-painting. It plays the same role in the "Coronation" Credo. At the "Et descendit," the soprano and alto spin out the falling version in a canon at the seventh, which the tenor and bass answer with a canon at the fourth (see example 34).

Example 32.   (continued)

Yet the madrigalism of K. 258 plays a more abstract role in the "Coronation" Credo. It already pervades the orchestral ritornello and accompanies the chorus's opening words, long before any mention of Christ's descent and resurrection. The motive here seems to represent the subjective perspective of the faithful as they exclaim "Credo in unum Deum." Rather than depict a specific physical image, the surging melody and sequence evoke a general sense of exaltation, the energetic movement of the soul toward God. (The melody recalls the rhetorical figure of *anabasis,* which theorists prescribed for feelings of exaltation and joy.[48]) The upbeat rhythm reinforces the sense of vigorous affirmation. It propels each two-bar phrase toward the predicate of the statement, which Mozart has repeated for emphasis—"Credo in unum *De*-um, in unum *De*-um." Meanwhile, the horns, trumpets, and kettledrums sound Mozart's favorite march rhythm, enhancing the sense of purposeful motion.

Conveniently, the march rhythm is also a popular pattern for *settenari,* and thus serves perfectly for the opening words.[49] The chorus doubles the brass, intoning the opening words on a single pitch. In effect, Mozart has relegated the chorus to an accompanying role, while locating the thematic

Example 33. Mass in C, K. 258, Credo: a. "Et descendit," mm. 52–57; b. "Et resurrexit," mm. 68–72.

material in the strings and woodwind. (In K. 192 and 257, by contrast, the instruments merely double the voices in the Credo refrains.) A space thus opens between utterance and enunciation: the orchestra's pictorial motive interprets the symbolic meaning of the words, while the chorus's monotone chant depicts the act of speech. This division of labor recalls an opera buffa ensemble, in which a repeated orchestral motive colors the singers' *parlante* declamation. From the outset, K. 317 frames the statement of faith as a dramatic utterance, a representation of speech itself.

Example 34.   K. 317, Credo, mm. 50–57.

Mozart's five-note motive may have originated as a pictorial icon, but, apart from the "Et descendit," its meaning has become abstracted from the images of the Credo. It returns in mm. 36–40, accompanied by the identical monotone chant, but now the chorus sings "Genitum non factum, consubstantialem Patri" (Begotten not made, one in being with the Father). It serves in mm. 72–76 and 114–18 to set the words "Et resurrexit tertia die, secundum Scripturas" (And rose again on the third day, in accordance with the Scriptures) and "Et unam catholicam et apostolicam Eccelesiam" (And in one holy catholic and apostolic Church). The five-note motive might seem to function symbolically following the opening ritornello. The soprano and alto invert the motive in mm. 9–11, teasing out a cascading sequence on the words "Factorem caeli et terrae" (Maker of heaven and earth). The inversion of the opening sequence suggests the duality of earth and heaven, human striving and divine condescension. Yet when the identical sequence returns in mm. 76–78, the descending melody sets the words "Et ascendit in caeli"! Mozart's motive no longer represents the symbolic meanings of the text, but rather the emotional attitude of the speakers.

Even the middle section of the Credo, repository of the most vivid imagery, becomes absorbed into the enunciatory act. Although the movement follows the ternary division typical of the Austrian *missa brevis*, Mozart has elided the Allegro and Adagio sections. The first Allegro breaks off suddenly on b♭", the apex of the orchestral ritornello. Instead of descending stepwise to c", as in the previous ritornellos, the dissonant seventh passes into the sopranos on the words "Et incarnatus est." It returns in the "Crucifixus," reharmonized as $\hat{5}$ of E♭ minor, before finally descending to c'. Even then, Mozart has delayed resolution so that the deferred cadence is elided with the *tempo primo* attack of the ritornello on "Et resurrexit." The Adagio functions as a linear and tonal prolongation that checks, but does not interrupt, the surging energy of the ritornello. Mozart has reduced the middle third of the Credo, with its images of crucifixion, suffering, and burial, to a mere parenthesis within the buoyant delivery of the creed.

Mozart's most telling transformation of the form comes in the final fugue, traditionally set to the words "Et vitam venturi saeculi." Mozart dispensed with an actual fugue and instead repeated the canonic setting of "Et descendit de caelis," now on the single word "Amen." While this reprise makes for a satisfying formal symmetry, it disregards the linear narrative of the Credo with its climactic vision of the Last Judgment. Mozart's design involves another type of abstraction. When the music of "Et descendit" returns at the end of the Credo, the five-note motive sheds entirely its referential function. The canonic passage originated as an icon, depicting a sensual image; it returns as pure song, a joyous canticle paired arbitrarily with the word *Amen*. Mozart has transformed the sign into a performance.

The Amen itself signals this shift in speech function. The Hebrew word belongs to the category of illocutionary statements, or speech acts, which accomplish an action in being spoken. In proclaiming "amen," the believer does not refer to any object, but rather gives assent to the doctrinal statements. Similarly, in confessing "Credo in unum Deum," the faithful do not merely provide information about their personal beliefs; more importantly, they bind themselves to the teaching of the Catholic Church. Both the Credo and Amen belong to John Searle's category of "assertives," speech acts that "commit the speaker (in varying degrees) to something's being the case, to the truth of the expressed proposition."[50] With the reprise of the "Et descendit" canons, both music and language shift from representation to performance.

The coda completes the transformation of reference into speech act, as the opening "Credo in unum Deum" returns (see example 35). Mozart has recalled the original orchestral ritornello, yet he has detached the words from the martial rhythm. The chorus no longer declaims the text in monotone speech-song, nor do they stress the predicate *Deum*. Instead, they join with the instrumental melody for the first time, soaring rapturously to g". As the sopranos descend to the cadence, they state the five-note motive one last time in augmentation. The falling motive now performs the final descent of the $\hat{5}-\hat{4}-\hat{3}-\hat{2}-\hat{1}$ *Urlinie*. As the chorus pronounces "Credo in unum Deum," they enact the final cadence, the musical equivalent of the Amen.

With this triumphant gesture, Mozart crowned his most masterful Credo. It is also his most characteristic. Mozart would return frequently to the *stile antico*, but never with the single-minded rigor of K. 192. His later works display flashes of self-conscious irony reminiscent of K. 257, but that was more Haydn's trademark. The "Coronation" Credo reveals Mozart's particular virtues. The command of dramatic pacing and tonal structure; the balance of oppositions and sense of proportion; the seamless integration of motive and form—all of these qualities look ahead to the concertos, operas, chamber music, and symphonies of his Viennese maturity. In K. 317, as it were, Mozart confessed "I believe" in his own voice.

Yet, ironically, Mozart solved the problem of belief by avoiding it altogether. Faced with the metaphysical claims of the Credo, the "Coronation"

Example 35. Mass in C, K. 317 ("Coronation"), Credo, mm. 145–51.

Mass simply abandons referentiality. In her essay on the Don Juan myth, Shoshana Felman has explored the peculiar nature of illocutionary acts: "When he replies 'I promise' to 'we have to know the truth,' the seducer's strategy is paradoxically to create, in a linguistic space that he himself controls, a dialogue of the deaf. For, by committing speech acts, Don Juan literally escapes the hold of truth. Although he has no intention whatsoever of keeping his promises, the seducer, strictly speaking, does not lie, since he is doing no more than playing on the self-referential property of these performative utterances, and is effectively accomplishing the speech acts that he is naming."[51] In K. 317, the speech act creates another closed space that excludes the troublesome issues of truth, metaphysics, and belief. But no Stone Guest intervenes here to force a more meaningful utterance. As the "Coronation" Credo demonstrates, faith truly requires a miracle in Mozart's music, a transcendent voice that can penetrate the bastions of Enlightenment representation.

SIX Archaic Endings

The first of Herder's *Kritische Wälder* (1769) aims a telling critique at Lessing's *Laokoon*, published three years earlier. The dispute concerns a passage from the *Iliad* in which Apollo hides Hector, pursued by Achilles, beneath a cloud (xx: 441–54). Lessing had interpreted the cloud metaphorically: "In poetic language, this means nothing more than that Achilles was so enraged that he no longer saw his enemy. Achilles saw no real cloud, nor does the entire artifice whereby the gods make themselves invisible consist in a cloud, but rather in their swift departure."[1] Herder attacked this reading as foreign to the Hellenic mind: "No! My Homer is much too sensate to conceive his entire poem through such spiritualized gods and refined allegories."[2] Such a reading, he protested, assumed anachronistically that Homer could distinguish between literal and figurative meaning. Lessing failed to appreciate the primitive vigor of Homer's language, reducing him to "one of those sober poets of our time, who think prosaically and speak poetically, whose *Gradus ad Parnassum* is the magic thesaurus that transforms prosaic thought into a poetic language."[3]

Herder's critique echoes a wider debate over the nature of language. Lessing upheld the rationalist view of language as communication. According to this conservative view, still promoted by Johann Christoph Gottsched, Nicholas Beauzée, or Thomas Reid, words merely served as a conduit between minds, permitting the transfer of ideas. Herder, on the other hand, articulated the empiricist theory of language as cognition. This view, also espoused by Vico, Condillac, and Adam Smith, saw language as an evolutionary tool that allowed humans to think, learn, and attain self-reflection. Marcelo Dascal summarized the debate: "The main underlying question is whether language mirrors the mind only because it serves to convey to others one's language-independent contents or because it also somehow participates in the mental operations involved in the formation of such contents."[4]

The rationalist view assumed a Cartesian dualism of soul and body that underwrote the rhetorical binarisms of *res* and *verba*, matter and manner, prose and poetry. The empiricists temporalized these binarisms, projecting the Cartesian hierarchy into history. They claimed that language began as primitive poetry, rich in sensation and emotion, and evolved toward increasingly abstract prose. Herder could thus argue that the *Iliad* contained neither metaphors nor poetry of any kind: Homer was speaking the everyday language of primitive humanity.

The reference to the *Gradus ad Parnassum* hints at related debates in musical poetics. Herder was not referring to Johann Joseph Fux's counterpoint treatise but its famous namesake, a Latin thesaurus by Paul Aler that went through thirty-nine editions between 1689 and 1770. Aler and Fux both followed the Jesuit rhetorical program, teaching students to elaborate a simple structure *(amplificatio)* according to strict rules *(praecepta)*, borrowing formulae from Classical models *(imitatio)*.[5] Such pedagogy persisted throughout the Enlightenment, not least in composers' lessons in strict counterpoint. Yet it consorts oddly with the new galant style, whose proponents shunned artifice and complexity in favor of a pleasing "natural" simplicity. Long before he submitted to Padre Martini's tutelage,

Mozart cut his teeth on simple minuets, and he schooled his student Thomas Attwood with the same light dance forms.[6] In both method and aim, *style galant* and *stile antico* differ as fundamentally as Homerian verse and formal rhetoric.

By the late eighteenth century, traditional rhetoric had fallen from favor among aesthetic writers, supplanted by the new representational poetics. As the preceding chapters have argued, formal rhetoric also plays a limited role within Mozart's musical thought, serving as a foil to his more normative procedures. The rhetorical tradition by no means disappeared, in either literature or music; it remained an option for both authors and composers. We should resist the temptation, however, to fold these historical practices into a single overarching system. Neoclassical rhetoric and Enlightenment poetics belong to distinct historical moments and enshrine largely antithetical social and intellectual ideals.

The point emerges dramatically in Mozart's *stile antico* finales, such as the "Jupiter" Symphony finale. Warren Kirkendale hailed Mozart's "terza prattica" in these hybrid movements, which triumphantly unite strict counterpoint and free composition.[7] Yet, as I shall argue, these movements expose a rift in eighteenth-century thought that no single system could overcome. An analysis of three works from his early Viennese period will show how Mozart used his "archaic endings" to negotiate these contradictions in his intellectual world. We thus return to the question posed in the first chapter—how do old and new paradigms interact within Mozart's music?—and conclude our study with an essay in Mozartian method.

· · · · ·

Traditional rhetoric accounts quite well for the Cum Sancto Spiritu of the Mass in C Minor, K. 427 (1782). The fugue not only crowns the Gloria, but also serves as finale to *Davide penitente*, Mozart's revision of the Mass as a Lenten cantata (1785). Mozart rigorously developed the first four notes of his subject, exploiting the rich potential for stretto (see example 36). He included two-part stretti at the octave (mm. 35–43); at the eleventh and fifth (60–67, 81–88); at the octave, *al rovescio* (138–54); and in four parts at both octave and fourth (167–75). He also added a countersubject to the

Example 36.   Examples of stretto in Mozart, Mass in C Minor, K. 427, Cum Sancto Spiritu:
a. at the fifth (mm. 81–85); b. at the octave, with new countersubject (mm. 112–16); c. at the
octave, *al rovescio* (mm. 138–43); d. at the fourth and octave, four voices (mm. 167–75).

two-part octave stretto, permuting all three subjects (106–38). The fugue
ends by pitting vocal subject against orchestral countersubject (186–92).

The Cum Sancto Spiritu exemplifies the rhetorical process that Laurence
Dreyfus has traced in J. S. Bach's music.[8] As preparatory sketches attest,
Mozart first worked out the possibilities of his subjects, including stretto,
inversion, and permutation.[9] Following this initial process of *inventio*, he
selected and arranged his materials in the most effective order, or *dispo-*

Example 36. (continued)

sitio. Mozart thus ordered his stretti from simplest to most complex, saving the four-voiced version for the climax; the modulating, mixed-mode stretti at the eleventh and fifth belong in the middle of the fugue; and the striking inversion of the subject serves to signal the return to the tonic. With his materials properly arranged, Mozart could proceed to fill in the counterpoint, the stage of *elocutio.* The process runs smoothly from mind to body, rational invention to sensual elaboration.

This hierarchy correlates with the dualistic ontology of Cartesian rationalism. Bernard Lamy, the leading rhetorician French neoclassicism, thus defined sound and meaning as the "body" and "soul" of words. Lamy expressed the rationalist view of language through a popular pictorial meta-phor: "Because words are the signs that represent the things that occur in our spirits, one might say that they are like a painting of our thoughts, that language is the brush that traces that painting, and that the words in which the discourse is composed are its colors."[10] Kaspar Stieler, a German contemporary, described the oration as "a lively soul in a straight, healthy, and well-shaped body."[11] As James Harris demanded in *Hermes, or A Philosophical Inquiry Concerning Universal Grammar* (1751): "What is conversation between man and man? To the speaker, 'tis to descend from ideas to words; to the hearer, 'tis to ascend from words to ideas."[12]

This view of language presupposed an immutable order of things behind the arbitrary signs of language. As Sidonie Clauss has explained, a dogmatic realism underlay the efforts of Leibniz, Marin Mersenne, John Wilkins, and other proponents of a universal language: "Clearly the presumption that all people share the same thoughts is prerequisite to the invention and institution of a philosophical language whereby they will use uniform signifiers to express universal ideas."[13] This realist view of language enjoyed vigorous influence, and not only among such conservative rhetoricians as Henry Aldrich or John Ward. Even the article on *langage* in the *Encyclopédie* still affirmed that "God himself taught *language* to mankind."[14]

The divine order of ideas reinforced a rigid political and religious hierarchy. The overwhelming Jesuit influence lent Catholic rhetoric a doctrinaire Aristotelian bent, while the Lutheran tradition fostered an equally orthodox *Redekunst* that aimed to incite virtue, strengthen faith, and combat heresy. Rhetoric helped sustain an elaborate system that regulated religion, class, and social conduct and that was governed by the supreme law of *decorum*, or *bienséance*. Claude Favre de Vaugles distilled the conformist aims of courtly rhetoric in his famous remarks on *le bon usage:* "It is the same with usage as with faith, which obliges us to believe simply and blindly, without bringing to bear the natural light of our reason."[15] In eighteenth-century Britain, the Elocutionary Movement reduced rhetoric to a tool of social advancement, helping Scots and Irishmen shed their provincial accents.[16] The authoritarian impulse behind Baroque rhetoric appears most strongly in the overwhelming emphasis on *persuasio*, or moving the affects. This "operational" model, as one writer dubbed it, suggests an obvious and oft-noted affinity with political absolutism.[17]

These connotations fit the Cum Sancto Spirito, a sacred fugue in the grand Hapsburg manner. The purity and authority of the *stile antico* surely dictated the placement of such fugues at end of the Gloria and Credo, where they confer a sense of unity on these sprawling movements. Yet neoclassical rhetoric seems less relevant to Mozart's normal style. Archaic fugues can punctuate his Gloria and Credo movements precisely because they contrast with his usual church style, a motley blend of erudition, opera, and *Volkstümlichkeit*. This playful style more clearly suggests the newer empiricist model traced in the previous chapters. The Piano Concerto in E♭, K. 449, will provide an example of this second paradigm and suggest the role *stile antico* endings play in Mozart's secular music.

·   ·   ·   ·   ·

According to Alan Tyson's paper studies, Mozart abandoned work on K. 449 in 1782 midway through the first movement and only completed the concerto in early 1784, shortly after returning from Salzburg and the premiere of the Mass in C Minor.[18] This may explain the resemblance between the concerto finale and the Cum Sancto Spiritu fugue. The *alla breve* rondo theme begins with a descending version of the fugue subject; the consequent then inverts the interlocking fourths in a fivefold sequence. Mozart treated his learned theme to a series of brilliant variations, and even slipped an additional statement into the sonata-rondo during the first solo episode (mm. 90–97).[19] Each return of the theme inspires fresh ornamentation, culminating in the transformation into a 6/8 gigue during the coda (see example 37).

Mozart eschewed stretto in this finale, concentrating on the more fundamental Fuxian principle of diminution. ("The four re-dressings of the refrain," remarked Arthur Hutchings, "could not have been made by a composer who was not an adept in academic counterpoint."[20]) The process already begins in the soloist's exposition of the theme, which subdivides the quarter notes into eighths. Mozart's *stile antico* refrain lends the finale

Example 37. Examples of diminution in Mozart, Piano Concerto in E♭ Major, K. 449, finale:
a. solo exposition (mm. 33–48); b. coda (mm. 269–76).

Example 37. (continued)

of K. 449 a peculiarly static quality. This arises in part from the four-square cut of the theme, in part from its sequential construction. Above all, it owes to the logical process of *elaboratio* through which Mozart develops his simple invention.

A certain predictability seems mandated by the first movement of K. 449, the most disruptive concerto movement Mozart had ever written. Simon Keefe has detailed the many idiosyncrasies in this movement: the swerve to C minor in mm. 16–17 and, more jarringly, before the soloist's cadenza (mm. 319–20); the second key area within the orchestral exposition (the only such modulation after 1782); and the contretemps between orchestra and soloist during the development.[21] There is, however, a method to this madness. The first movement epitomizes that new manner of development that Charles Rosen discerned in the Classical style: "The material can be made to release its charged force so that the music no longer unfolds, as in the Baroque, but is literally impelled from within."[22] The impulsion comes from the first four bars, where Mozart has planted a far-reaching tonal ambiguity (see example 38). The unison incipit [E♭-C-G] outlines C minor—a false start that is emphatically corrected by the A♭ in measure 3, marked by an offbeat accent and *tutti* trill. Mozart would use the identical gambit in the Concerto in C Minor, K. 491: the first theme begins with an exact inversion of the opening motive of K. 449, and an accented ♯4̂ (F♯) again corrects the false key.

Example 38. K. 449, Allegro Vivace, mm. 1–19.

This initial feint toward C minor in K. 449 explains the immediate modulation to that key in m. 16, as well as the bizarre return before the cadenza. Mozart's motivic work supports this reading. He insistently developed the offbeat trill from measure 3, transforming it into a closing theme, and worrying it for the first two-thirds of the development. Moreover, the modulation to C minor arrives both times through a rising version of the trill motive. The memory of that offbeat A♮—and the tonal conflict it resolved—lingers throughout the movement.

The initial confusion of tonality skews the first theme, which dwells inordinately on cadential gestures. Although the first eight bars form a balanced period, Mozart has repeated the consequent (mm. 9–12) and then reiterated its last two bars twice (13–16). In effect, he has added a cadence to the cadence of a cadence. These "appendices," to use Karol Berger's term, last fully as long as the original period.[23] Allanbrook has identified the opening four bars as a ballroom *riverenza* (bowing music), painting an even stranger picture: the minuet consists of four bars of introduction and twelve bars of cadence, with no theme in between![24] The protracted cadences betray an anxiety to confirm the true key (a reasonable enough concern, as the C-minor modulation immediately proves). Meanwhile, the unbroken variation of the trill motive preserves the memory of the initial rupture, even as the theme buries it beneath a surplus of cadences.

The first theme of K. 449 is thus doubly marked. Mozart has problematized both tonality (hinting at C minor) and function (weighting cadential gestures in an opening theme). In rhetorical terms, K. 449 opens with a disjuncture between *inventio* and *dispositio:* the material does not fit its position as an opening theme. Paradoxically, the opening page exemplifies that process of thematic transformation that Bonds has identified with rhetorical *elaboratio,* as a simple invention (the trill motive) undergoes a continuous series of variations.[25] Yet this process differs fundamentally from the treatment of the rondo finale. Mozart's *stile antico* theme inspired an untroubled series of ornamental diminutions. The first movement, on the other hand, opens with a jarring confusion of keys and metrical accents, which the following period proceeds to unpack. The motivic work suggests less amplification than decompression. If the finale theme invites synthesis, the opening of the concerto demands analysis.

The turn to the *stile antico,* therefore, does not simply introduce a new topic or stylistic register. If anything, the finale lightens the mood. The shift occurs at a deeper level and concerns opposing conceptions of musical development. The finale steps outside the entire methodology of analysis and decomposition, harking back to a more static conception of both reality and art. The break is less drastic, of course, than with the Cum Sancto Spiritu. As in the "Jupiter" finale or the overture to *Die Zauberflöte,* Mozart has accommodated the strict style to the modern sonata form. On the matter of thematic development, however, the outer movements represent different historical strata.[26]

The analytical process of the first movement of K. 449 relies upon the new logic of galant periodicity. Despite its tonal and functional irregularity, the first theme falls into a sixteen-bar hypotactic structure, built up from phrases of two, four, and eight bars; accordingly, Mozart could disrupt key and thematic function without fear of incoherence. Leonard Ratner illuminated this function of periodicity through his discussion of the *ars combinatoria.*[27] Ratner was articulating a classic structuralist model, according to which paradigms (phrases, motives, topics) substitute interchangeably within the functional positions of a syntagm (period).

This aleatoric substitution has nothing in common with the procedures of the *stile antico.* The learned style provided strict rules for transforming musical ideas—diminution, inversion, augmentation, fugue, and so forth. Contrapuntal constraints, as well as the lack of a hypotactic phrase structure, ruled out the facile substitution of melodic paradigms into the musical syntagm. In the case of stretto, canon, and permutation fugues, the distinction between the paradigmatic and syntagmatic axis vanishes altogether: the combinatorial possibilities of the material determine its sequential presentation.

The outer movements of K. 449, then, illustrate diametrically opposed methods of musical development. The first untangles a specific complex of structural and expressive elements; the second elaborates a simple structure according to general rules. The first method is analytic and inductive; the second, synthetic and deductive. The first relies on the "horizontal" axis of phrase structure; the second on the "vertical" axis of texture. Most important, the two methods coexist in the Concerto in E♭. Mozart's *méthode* involves a dialogue between heterogeneous, indeed, contradictory methods.

. . . . .

Enlightenment language theory betrays the same ambivalence toward method. On the one hand, Condillac, Herder, Vico, and Smith all believed that language evolved through analysis and induction. Their treatises enshrine the scientific method of Sir Isaac Newton, which had eclipsed Descartes's speculative "hypotheses." Newton laid out his approach in the *Opticks* (1704), in a passage quoted in the *Encyclopédie* article "Analytique": "As in Mathematicks, so in Natural Philosophy, the Investigation of difficult things by the Method of Analysis, ought ever to precede the Method of Composition. . . . By this way of Analysis, we may proceed from Compounds to Ingredients, and from Motions to the Forces producing them; in general, from Effects to their Causes, and from particular Causes to more general ones, till the argument end in the most general. This is the Method of Analysis."[28] Jean le Rond d'Alembert echoed Newton's prescription in his *Discours préliminaire* to the *Encyclopédie* (1751): "It is not by vague and arbitrary hypotheses that we can hope to know nature; it is by thoughtful study of phenomena, by the comparisons we make among them, by the art of reducing, as much as that may be possible, a large number of phenomena to a single one that can be regarded as their principle."[29] In this spirit, Condillac could declare in his posthumous *Langue des calculs* (1780) that "all language is an analytical method, and every analytical method is a language."[30]

Yet analysis proved a mixed blessing in the evolution of languages. Smith decried the rational mechanization of language that stripped speech of expression, gesture, and sensual immediacy. Vico gloomily traced the descent of languages into a "barbarism of reflection," as rational abstraction distanced language from its healthy origins: "Learned fools took to maligning the truth. And false eloquence arose, prepared to argue opposite sides of a cause with equal force. People now misused eloquence, as did the plebeian tribunes at Rome."[31] Likewise, Rousseau's *Essai sur l'origine des langues* laments the loss of passionate speech, which left behind only the strident rhetoric of modernity: "Since there is nothing to say to people besides *give money*, it is said with placards on street corners or by soldiers in their homes."[32]

Condillac's *Essai sur l'origine des connoissances humaines* concludes with the same bleak diagnosis. Like Vico, Condillac distinguished false eloquence from the natural tropes and figures that characterized primitive speech. Artificial rhetoric emerged as languages, having attained a peak of rational perfection, began to decline: "We find that the epoch of their decadence occurred at the time when they seemed to aspire to the greatest beauties. We see figures and metaphors piling up and overloading the style with ornamentations, to the point where the foundation seems accessory."[33] Language begins to rot at the roots, even as its literature flowers: "We see dawning the reign of subtle and convoluted conceits, of precious antitheses, brilliant paradoxes, frivolous turns of phrase, arcane expressions, needless words, and, in short, the jargon of *beaux esprits* spoiled by a bad metaphysics . . . the same movement that has been a principle of life now becomes the principle of destruction."[34] The life of a language is thus bounded by two rhetorics, the pure poetry of nature and the decadent eloquence of civilization. Paradoxically, the same faculty that allows humans to develop language and reason ends by corrupting speech and thought. At some mysterious point, analysis gives way to synthesis, empirical discovery to metaphysical speculation.

Jacques Derrida probed this aporia in his preface to Condillac's *Essai, L'archéologie du frivole* (1973). Condillac's desire to purge language of metaphysics, Derrida noted, drove him to posit a pure language, derived immediately from nature. But, he queried, "Isn't that in order to make amends through language for language's misdeeds, to push artifice to that limit which leads back to nature?" Both natural speech and artificial rhetoric rely on the surplus value of language, that "frivolity" that exceeds pure representation: "This frivolity does not accidentally befall the sign. Frivolity is its congenital breach. . . . Since its structure of deviation prohibits frivolity from being or having an origin, frivolity defies all archaeology, condemns it, we could say, to frivolity."[35] Derrida's last sentence pinpoints the contradiction within Condillac's argument from origins (as well as Foucault's theory of the Classical episteme), a contradiction that lodges within the nature of language itself.

Eighteenth-century linguists dealt with this contradiction in different ways. Vico concluded the *Scienza nuova* with a vision of an endless *ricorso* whereby new civilizations and languages continually arose from the ashes of the old.[36] Herder's *Fragmente. Über die neuere deutsche Literatur* (1768) also traced the life cycle of languages in which poetry (childhood) led to prose (adulthood) and ended with philosophy (old age). The greatest literature sprang from the middle age, the golden mean betwixt poetry and philosophy: "The most beautiful and the most perfect language are not possible at the same time; the middle ground is indisputably the best place, because both sides can be reached from there."[37] Condillac proposed his own three ages of language in *De l'art d'écrire* (1775), and also located the best literature in the middle age. His *Traité des systêmes* (1749) closes with a vision of the perfect equilibrium: "The imagination should furnish the philosopher with grace without taking anything away from precision, and analysis should give precision to the poet without taking away any grace."[38] Meanwhile, Rousseau fixed the opposition geographically, distinguishing the southern tongues, born of pleasure and passionate expression, from the northern languages, generated by physical needs.[39]

The twin paradigms coexist within the writings of Johann Georg Sulzer, a thinker beholden to both sensualist and rationalist traditions.[40] Sulzer's article entitled "Erfindung" in the *Allgemeine Theorie der schönen Künste* (1771–74) identifies two opposing methods:

> There are two general ways by which inventions are made. Either
> the goal or the intention of the work is established, and one seeks the
> means by which it can be attained; or one already has some material
> or idea, and discovers upon reflection that it might be useful in attain-
> ing a specific goal, which is to say, that it is suited for certain inten-
> tions. The speaker usually proceeds by the first way; he normally has
> a certain goal in mind before he writes his speech, and he seeks a means
> to achieve it. The dramatic poet or the painter usually takes the other
> route. . . . The most important inventions probably do not arise through
> the first deductive manner described above, but rather by the second
> way: the main subject appears only dimly at first to the artist; he recog-
> nizes its importance and takes time to think about its contents so it can
> be set in its proper light. This is how a famous composer told me he
> worked.[41]

Sulzer's ambivalence informs the title of an earlier essay, "Observations sur l'influence réciproque de la raison sur le langage et du langage sur la raison" (1768). On the one hand, Sulzer upheld the traditional role of rhetoric as *persuasio:* "For example, if one failed to convince a man rationally that there is a God, author and sustainer of the natural order, one could make him feel this truth by bringing him to see the resemblance between the course of nature and a vessel steered by a good pilot."[42] On the other hand, Sulzer emphasized the new cognitive understanding of rhetoric: "The progress of reason depends greatly on perfecting the metaphoric part of languages. . . . The human mind contains an infinite number of obscure ideas that place limits on the progress of knowledge. Each felicitous metaphor pushes back those limits by drawing one of those ideas out of obscurity."[43] Significantly, Sulzer did not side with either linguistic model. On the contrary, he claimed that two methods coexisted, deductive and inductive, from which composers could choose. That Mozart relied on both becomes evident from an analysis of *Die Entführung aus dem Serail,* in particular, the great quartet that ends Act 2 (No. 16, "Ach, Belmonte! Ach, mein Leben!").

.   .   .   .   .

The quartet did not originate in Christoph Friedrich Bretzner's *Belmont und Konstanze* (1780), the model for *Die Entführung aus dem Serail.* Mozart's librettist, Gottlieb Stephanie the Younger, concocted it for purely musical reasons. "Although the dramatic pretext for this quartet is slight," explained Thomas Bauman, "Mozart's overall musical architecture demanded such a keystone here at the end of Act II."[44] Stephanie derived the multisectional quartet, Mozart's most elaborate ensemble to date, from a few spoken lines in Bretzner's libretto. Text and music thus enjoy a rare equality in this fabricated ensemble. The quartet provides an ideal laboratory in which to observe Mozart's use of signs, both verbal and musical. As the following analysis will argue, a single semantic structure generates both the dramatic and musical design, at the level of the quartet and of the entire opera.

Let us work backward from the ending. *Die Entführung* concludes with a strophic *vaudeville* (No. 21a, "Nie werd' ich deine Huld verkennen") in which the four lovers thank Pasha Selim for his mercy. Each character joins the ensemble in orderly fashion, repeating the strophic melody and uniting in the moralistic refrain: "Whoever can forget such mercy / Should be regarded with contempt." Only Osmin dissents from the general will. He interrupts the fourth strophe with an angry outburst (mm. 64–94), abandoning F major to reprise his A minor rant from Act 1 (No. 3, "Solche hergelauf'ne Laffen," coda). The lovers close ranks in a *sotto voce* chorus of disapproval ("Nothing is so hateful as revenge"), before reprising the happy refrain. In logical terms, the *vaudeville* exemplifies the method of deduction, or reasoning from general to particular. The same syllogism that pronounces the lovers human excludes Osmin, casting him into outer darkness with Mozart's other discontents—Electra, Don Giovanni, Monostatos, and the Queen of the Night.

Osmin plays an indispensable role in this rationalist utopia. He is the exception who proves the rule, the barbarian who marks the borders of Western civilization. As Matthew Head remarked (quoting from Mozart's own description), "Osmin's 'towering rage' functions as an antithesis through which 'order, moderation and propriety' are defined."[45] The final *vaudeville* might thus be described in terms of the contrast between order and chaos, deduction and exclusion. This ending would seem to vindicate the rationalist worldview, affirming a faith in logic, absolutist authority, and universal moral principles.

Yet *The Abduction from the Seraglio* presents a more complex picture. As the title announces, the opera concerns liberation from enclosure and authority. Mozart himself realized this program musically as he exploded one *Singspiel* convention after another, beginning with the opening number. Bretzner's libretto opened with a spoken monologue for Belmonte, followed by Osmin's strophic *Lied*, "Wer ein Liebchen hat gefunden." On Mozart's insistence, Stephanie fashioned an arietta from Belmonte's monologue (No. 1, "Hier soll ich dich denn finden") and pushed Osmin's *Lied* forward into a second number. Moreover, Mozart had Stephanie rework the *Lied* as an action duet, with Belmonte interrupting after each of Osmin's three strophes.[46] Mozart and Stephanie thus created an intriguing parallel with the final *vaudeville*, in which Osmin will interrupt Belmonte's song.

In "Wer ein Liebchen hat gefunden," however, the song does not withstand the invasion. After Belmonte's third interruption the strophic form dissolves into an amorphous duet, moving through a series of keys and textures, and ending in a different key than the beginning (D major instead of G minor). The scene illustrates the simultaneous penetration of genre and seraglio: Mozart forces open the *Singspiel* tradition, just as Belmonte intrudes himself into Osmin's world. Mozart even allows Belmonte to share in his self-conscious mastery. On the final interruption, as Belmonte cries "Verwünscht seist du samt deinem Liede!" ("To hell with you and your song!"), he mocks Osmin with a scrap of his own tune (see example 39).

Musical constraints thus play an opposite role in *Lied* and *vaudeville*. In the *Lied*, strophic song symbolizes the Oriental rigidity that teleological Western man must explode. In the *vaudeville*, the strophic form represents the civilized order that the Oriental outsider simultaneously threatens and reinforces. Between the first and last numbers, the musical form has assumed a new and contradictory meaning. What accounts for this reversal in the semantic structure?

The answer lies in the dialectic between deductive and inductive methods. The *vaudeville* exemplifies deduction, in which the characters derive their moral judgment from a general law. Osmin's rebellion actually strengthens this law: the moral order both excludes him and is defined by his exclusion. The duet between Belmonte and Osmin, on the other hand, exemplifies induction, whereby the general law is not given a priori but emerges from the specific. Belmonte does not pit himself against the laws of Pasha's world; he simply ignores them and becomes a law unto himself. Similarly, Mozart does not simply bend Osmin's strophic *Lied*, but explodes it from within, absorbing the fragments into a sui generis action ensemble.

The opera thus opens with a dramatic movement from stasis to activity, from the rigidity of the Oriental seraglio (or *Singspiel* genre) to the dynamism of Western man. Here, in a nutshell, is the analytical method of Enlightenment thought, which liberates reason from fixed authority and sets in motion the process of discovery. Belmonte and Mozart both realize the project mapped out by George Berkeley: "The work of science and

Example 39.   Mozart, *Die Entführung aus dem Serail,* "Wer ein Liebchen hat gefunden," mm. 49–54.

speculation is to unravel our prejudices and mistakes, untwisting the closest connexions, distinguishing things that are different, instead of confused and perplexed, giving us distinct views, gradually correcting our judgment, and reducing it to a philosophical exactness."[47] In this spirit, Mozart (and Belmonte) dissects Osmin's song, dissolving the rigid form into the teleological drama.

Such a program harbors obvious dangers, which play out across *Die Entführung.* On the positive side, the autonomous Western individual repeatedly triumphs over compulsion and prejudice—Belmonte risks death in pursuit of love, Konstanze chooses torture over submission, Blonde shatters sexist stereotypes, Belmonte and Pedrillo outwit Osmin. Yet the assault on authority veers toward nihilism. Belmonte enters the seraglio by lying to Selim, while Pedrillo effects the escape by tempting Osmin into breaking his religious vows. Anarchy threatens to devour the Western lovers themselves when Selim discovers Belmonte's identity. Having abandoned objective morality, Belmonte finds himself with no protection but his money, whose exchange value cannot equal Selim's desire for revenge. The opera exposes the perils of Enlightenment rationality, whose restless struggle for autonomy leaves the subject alienated from nature, morality, and itself. ·

The descent into chaos ends when Selim forgives Belmonte, proving himself a better Christian than his Western rival:

> Take your freedom, take Konstanze, sail away to your homeland; tell your father that you were in my power and that I set you free, so that I could tell him that it was a far greater satisfaction to reward grievous injustice with goodness than to repay wrong with wrong.

> (Nimm deine Freiheit, nimm Konstanzen, segle in dein Vaterland, sage deinem Vater, daß du in meiner Gewalt warst, daß ich dich freigelassen, um ihm sagen zu können, es wäre ein weit größer Vergnügen eine erlittene Ungerechtigkeit durch Wohltaten zu vergelten, als Laster mit Lastern tilgen.)

This turning point does more than simply resolve the plot; it transforms the entire system of meaning. Selim's merciful act explodes the opposition of deduction and induction, authority and individualism, by introducing a new mediating term—*universality.* Selim unveils a universal ethic that encompasses all humanity, yet resists deduction from any positive law. To this point, law has regulated positive oppositions (Turk against Christian, male against female, despot against subject) against which the protagonists rebel for positive goals (love, freedom, pleasure). Selim's universal ethic, like Kant's moral law, dictates a formal ethic in place of positive law; it transcends mere egotism by identifying the individual with the general will. Legal authority, once a source of tyranny and oppression, suddenly glows brilliantly as a defense of the individual.

In the same way, Selim's gracious act endows strophic form with a new utopian meaning. The repeating form of the *vaudeville*, with its moralistic refrain, no longer symbolizes blind authority, as in Osmin's *Lied*. It now represents the universal law that unites each individual (solo verses) with the collective will (choral refrain). As for the sins of the Europeans, they can be transferred to a convenient scapegoat, Osmin, who rejects the new order. This mechanism of "self-Othering," as Head termed it, erases the shadows of Enlightenment thought, leaving behind pure radiance.

The same dynamic emerges from the quartet, once the basic terms are discovered. The plot is simple: (1) the four lovers rejoice in their future freedom; (2) Belmonte and Pedrillo pull apart and, after some dithering, ask the women if they have been faithful; (3) Konstanze and Blonde react with hurt and outrage; (4) the men plead for forgiveness and eventually receive pardon; (5) the four vow to love without further suspicions. The quartet begins, like no other Mozart finale, with a complete absence of outer conflict. Nor does it advance the plot. It is an exploration of a state of being—in effect, the analysis of a happy ending. A semantic interpretation must therefore begin by establishing the terms and logic of a Mozartian *lieto fine*.

Like most comedies, *Die Entführung* revolves around a love story. Since meaning operates through difference, a semantic analysis must unpack the oppositions implicit in Mozart's conception of love. The internal dynamics of the quartet—indeed, of all Mozart's mature operas—make best sense in terms of an inherent conflict between *desire* and *autonomy*. Erotic desire everywhere deprives Mozart's characters of autonomy, ensnaring them in jealousy, dependency, imprisonment, or rape. Mozart's most beautiful love duets (aside from seductions) occur only between friends (Pamina and Papageno), female pairs (Fiordiligi and Dorabella, Susanna and the Countess), or with sexless castrati (Idamante and Ilia, Annio and Servilia). A remarkable number of Mozart's greatest arias and scenes— "Martern aller Arten," "Non più andrai," "Non mi dir," "Come scoglio," the entrance of the Stone Guest—concern the renunciation of erotic desire. Belmonte's finest aria, "O wie ängstlich," reduces love to a collection of pathological symptoms, while Konstanze famously chooses torture over sex. The lovers only join in a duet after they have been condemned to death. The old seria conflict between inclination and duty lives on in these tainted erotic imbroglios. The inherent tension between desire and autonomy explains why the Act 2 quartet, after beginning so joyously, degenerates almost immediately into suspicion and alienation.

This deterioration betrays the teleology of Enlightenment thought, which demands that instinct yield to reason, sensation to reflection, feminine emotion to masculine self-control. This trajectory unfolds most clearly in *Die Zauberflöte*. Tamino and Papageno forswear food, drink, and women alike in pursuit of Enlightenment; Pamina herself must be torn from her mother and initiated into the masculine order—"defeminized"—before she is worthy of love. In *Die Entführung*, the spell of the Oriental harem fuses both erotic and racial entanglements. Abduction from the seraglio means, in the deepest sense, liberation from sensuality, nature, and the body. Such a trajectory, by definition, precludes happy romantic endings.

The Enlightenment promised to free humanity from instinctual desire by subjecting nature to rational analysis and judgment. Reason empowered the individual, placing him in a superior relationship to the objects of his desire. In Mozart's operas, this process takes the form of trials designed to test or snare sexually transgressive characters. The judges frequently disguise themselves in order to enhance their control. Thus Ferrando and Guglielmo don exotic costumes to try their lovers' fidelity; Susanna and the Countess trade clothing to entrap the Count; Papagena dresses as an old woman to test Papageno; and Anna, Elvira, and Zerlina mask themselves to catch Giovanni. Not coincidentally, perhaps, Belmonte and Pedrillo slip into imitative counterpoint, redolent of the old church manner, for their inquisition of Konstanze and Blonde.

The interrogation extricates the men from the women's erotic toils, yet it leaves the lovers in hostile camps. In order to attain comedic closure, while still preserving this freedom, the plot must somehow find a way to restore relationship without thereby renouncing freedom. The solution, common to Mozart's operas, is the redefinition of love as Christian charity. The men rejoin the women, just as the Europeans rejoin Selim, through a cleansed, incorporeal love. Like Ilia, the Countess, or Donna Elvira, Konstanze transforms erotic desire into a spiritual love that does not contaminate. The semantic "explosion," in this case, dislodges the coalition of love and power. Charity implies a disinterested concern for the object, an ability to love without control or domination. The quartet restores a higher sense of community, retracing in microcosm the path of the entire opera.

This semantic maneuver helps explain one of the old puzzles of Mozart scholarship, the contradictory plot of *Die Zauberflöte*. The Queen of the Night reverses roles over the course of the opera, beginning as sympathetic victim and ending as murderous villain. A persistent myth even holds that Mozart and Schikaneder changed the plot midway through writing the opera. Yet *Die Zauberflöte* simply manifests the semantic duplicity underlying all of Mozart's operas. The broken narrative records a slippage between systems, that sleight of hand that transforms love from destructive compulsion to disinterested forgiveness, from "Der Hölle Rache" to "In diesen heilgen Hallen." We watch through Tamino's bewildered eyes as the ethical universe rotates on this mysterious axis. *Die Zauberflöte*, more than any other work, demonstrates the contradiction at the heart of Mozart's rational utopias.

The same underlying (il)logic explains Mozart's musical choices in the *Entführung* quartet. Let us begin with the last section of the quartet, another *stile antico* finale. Mozart has prepared the concluding Allegro with an expectant V^7 chord, once again using interlocking fourths. Konstanze and Blonde sing a brief canon based on the rising version of the Cum Sancto Spiritu subject (see example 40). This introduction sets the tone for the Allegro, which takes shape around four separate canons (mm. 259–74, 278–88, 304–14, and 317–28). The opening texture, with *alla breve* voices above rushing violins, anticipates the final chorus of *Don Giovanni* ("Questo è il fin di chi fa mal!"). Yet where the later stretto merely gestures at learned counterpoint, Mozart here works out each canon in all four voices, moving systematically from highest to lowest (see example 41).

Mozart marshaled not only imitation, but also that more fundamental principle of the *Gradus ad Parnassum*, diminution. Stephanie's quatrain falls into amphibrachs, altered only in the final truncated verse:

Es *le*-be | die *Lie*-be!
Nur *sie* sei | uns *Teu*-er,
Nichts *fa*-che | das *Feu*-er
Der *Ei*-fer- | sucht *an*.

Example 40. *Die Entführung aus dem Serail,* Act 2 Quartet, transition to final Allegro, mm. 245–250.

Example 41. *Die Entführung aus dem Serail,* Quartet, final canons: a. first canon (mm. 259–74); b. second canon, identical to the third (mm. 279–90); c. fourth canon (mm. 317–27).

Example 41. *(continued)*

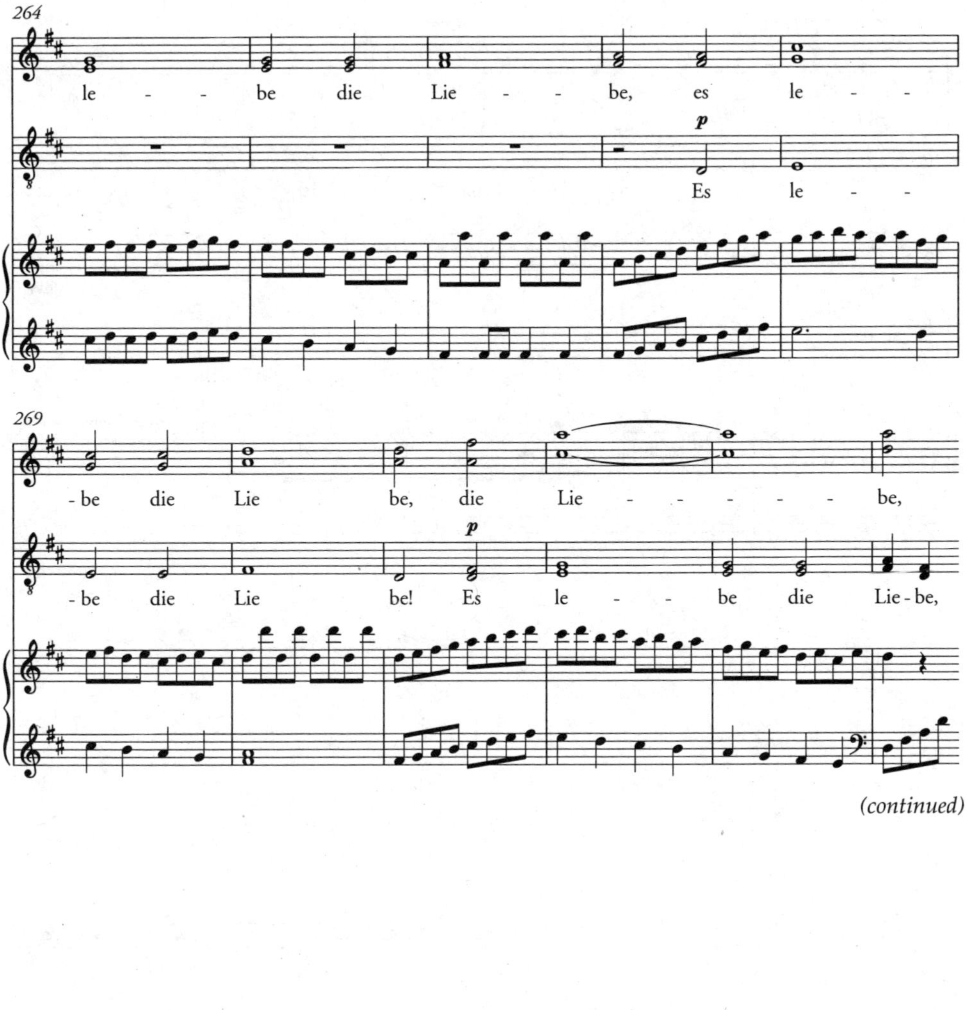

(continued)

Example 41. (continued)

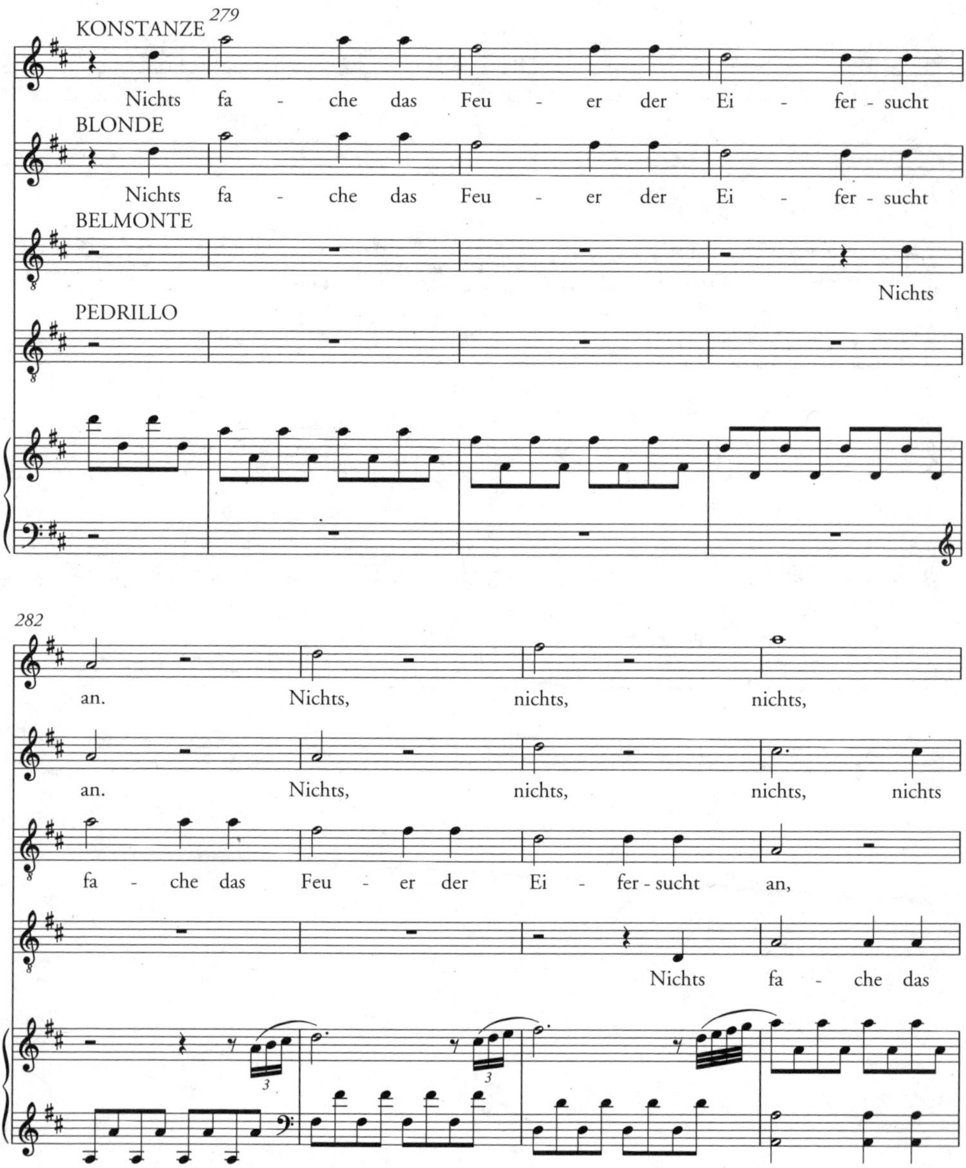

Example 41. *(continued)*

(continued)

Example 41. (continued)

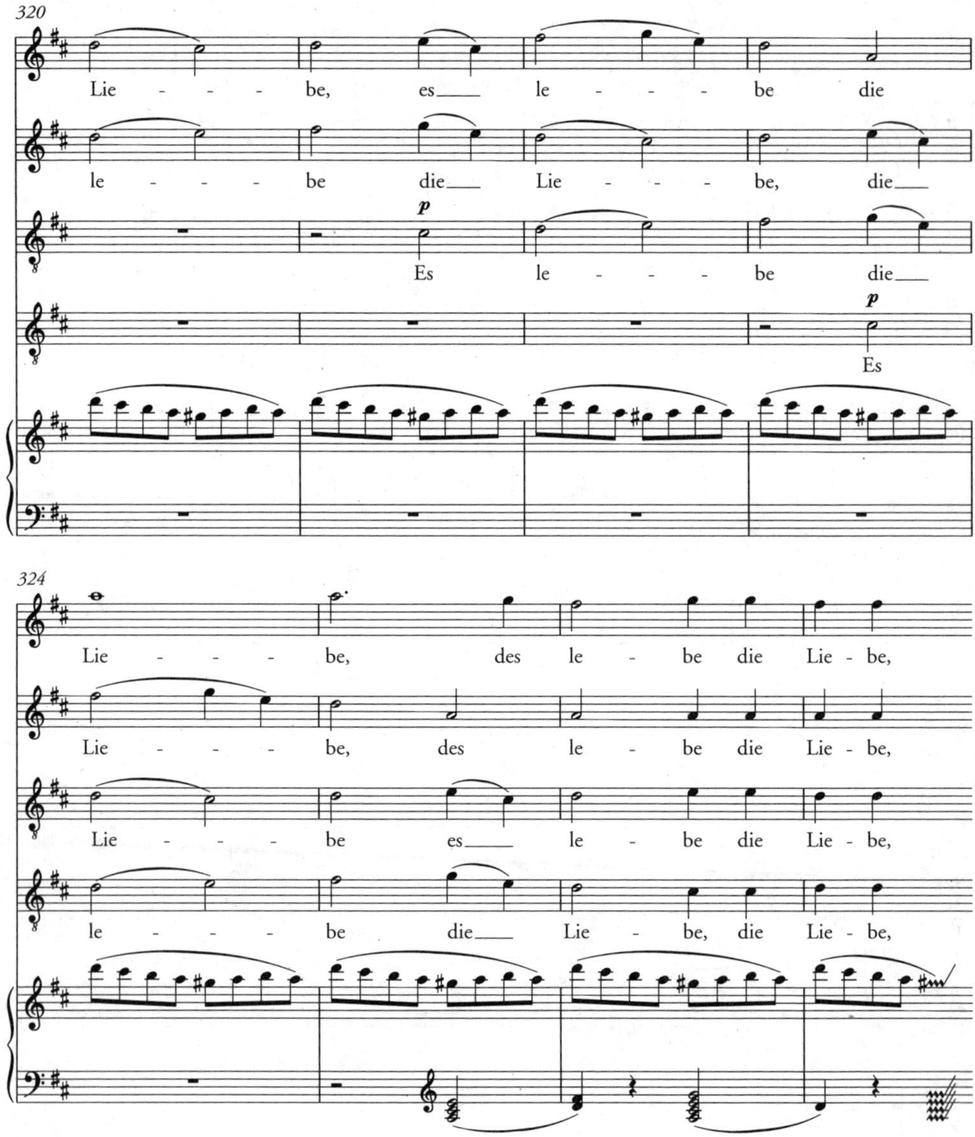

The opening canon faithfully reproduces this poetic meter. As the singers break into homophonic declamation, the amphibrachs continue in a strict 1:2 diminution. Mozart then used this diminished rhythm for the martial second canon (identical to the third), before returning to an ornamented version of the *alla breve* rhythm for the fourth canon. He thus forged a strict rhythmic hierarchy between *stile antico* and *stile moderno,* transforming the *alla breve* subject into a quicker march rhythm. As with the canons, Mozart has followed the deductive procedure of the orator, generating his text by elaborating a simple underlying idea.

The opening Allegro, on the other hand, demonstrates Mozart's more normative procedure (see example 42). Like the finale, the first eight bars juxtapose a triumphal march and a more lyrical motive. Yet these contrasting ideas are not generated through a "vertical" process of rhythmic diminution; they balance one another "horizontally" within the symmetrical period. Another, more pregnant opposition emerges during the opening vocal statement (mm. 9–29), as Konstanze's entries shift to the third beat of the 4/4 meter. Her first two phrases begin on the downbeat. She attacks the next, however, beginning on the third beat, emphasizing the offbeat with a high a" ("*Ist* es möglich? *Welch* Entzücken!"). Her final two phrases ("Nach so vieler Tage Leid") confirm this new placement of the downbeat. By the end of the opening period, Konstanze has transformed the march into a gavotte.

In every way, Konstanze sails into the quartet with remarkable assertion. Her first four phrases begin on a", and she elides Belmonte's interjected phrase after only three bars. This is no helpless damsel, such as Belmonte affects to comfort in the simpering aria preceding the quartet (No. 15, "Wenn der Freude Tränen fließen"). Konstanze arrives aglow with the intensity of "Martern aller Arten," her last turn onstage. She betrays those richer accents that Bauman traced to her Oriental encounters: "The dark side of Selim's complex personality has evoked, in the best traditions of opera, a strong new voice in Konstanze's hitherto melancholic personality."[48] Her opening period is scarcely calculated to assuage masculine insecurities.

The end of the Allegro shifts power still more decisively away from the men (see example 43). After a brief modulation for the servants' duet (mm.

Example 42. *Die Entführung aus dem Serail,* Quartet, mm. 1–22.

Example 42.   (continued)

47–59), the opening march returns to support a jubilant homophonic chorus. From m. 70 to the end of the Allegro, however, every phrase begins on the third beat, transforming the march into a gavotte. When the men beg for forgiveness later in the quartet, they will again adopt the double upbeat of the gavotte. As in Mozart's other operas, the gavotte topic represents the feminine orbit, whose gravity continually captures the masculine march.[49]

Gavotte and march, as we have seen, present marked and unmarked versions of duple meter. Like fourth-species counterpoint, gavotte imposes an alternative metrical grouping, which conflicts with the notated meter: 3 4 | 1 2 vs. | 1 2 3 4 |. Given the Enlightenment mandate for rational clarity, the opening confusion of meters presents an intolerable situation. March and gavotte cannot coexist, any more than tonic and dominant.

The G-minor Andante (mm. 89–140) erases the conflict by switching from compound to simple meter. As the men draw apart to interrogate the women, the meter shifts to 3/8, eliminating the ambiguous grouping of the compound 4/4. The opera contains only one other melody in 3/8, Belmonte's opening arietta, which first appears as the contrasting middle section of the overture (mm. 119–52). In both passages, the 3/8 minuet follows a frenzied Janissary march, and establishes Belmonte as rational Westerner. Moreover, the Turkish music of the overture begins with a gavotte-like double upbeat, which creates a metrical ambiguity similar to that in the opening of the quartet (see example 44). Thus, when Belmonte extricates himself from Konstanze and her Orientalized taint, he revives a musical opposition from the opening pages of the opera.

Example 43. Die Entführung aus dem Serail, Quartet, mm. 81–92.

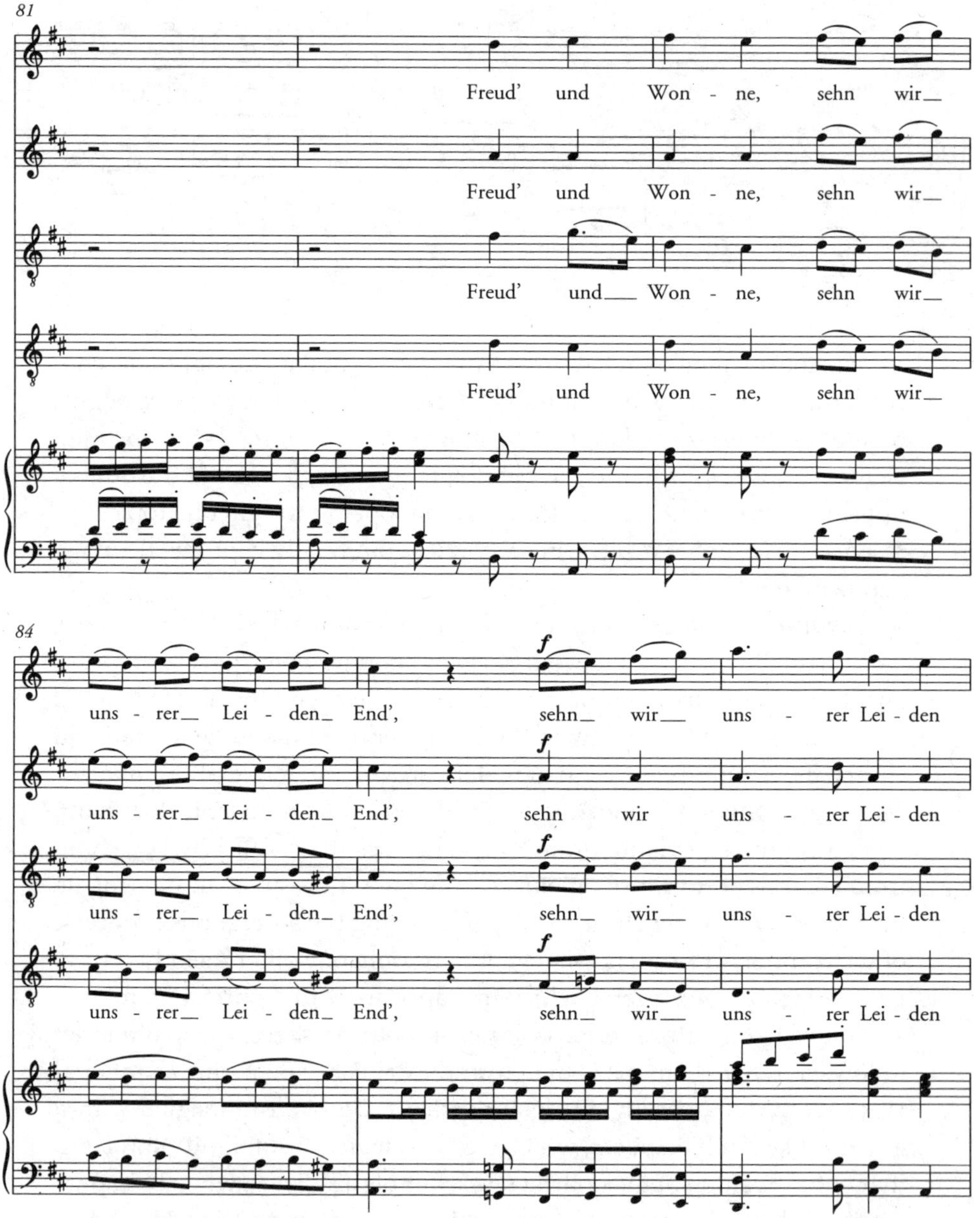

Example 43. (continued)

The metrical grouping remains clear throughout the following 4/4 section, as the men question the women (Andante-Allegro assai-Adagio, mm. 143–92). The topics progress from imitative counterpoint to march to French overture, without ever contesting the meter. Although Belmonte and Pedrillo begin the E♭ Andante in imitation, with competing accents on first and third beats, the servant's accents never challenge the master's downbeat. As they distance themselves from the women, the men restore the metrical hierarchy threatened by the gavotte.

Example 44.   Die Entführung aus dem Serail, Overture: a. Presto, mm. 1–4; b. Andante, mm. 119–28.

The men are impelled by an Enlightenment teleology that demands order, simplicity, and clarity. Yet while this analytic method produces fine science, it makes for poor comic endings. The men purchase rational autonomy at the price of love. The quartet poses the same question as the overall opera: how can the alienated individual recover a sense of wholeness without falling back into bondage and blind obedience?

Mozart again solved the problem by exploding the semantic system. Specifically, he introduced a new way of combining topics that escapes both the confusion of metrical displacement and the rigidity of simple meter. The turning point comes in the beautiful A-major Andantino (mm. 193–208), in which the men admit their error. Their text is actually rather cynical:

When women take offense
That we think them unfaithful,

Then they are truly faithful,
Free from all reproach.

(Sobald sich Weiber kränken,
Daß wir sie untreu denken,
Dann sind sie wahrhaft treu,
Von allem Vorwurf frei.)

Mozart ennobled this doggerel with a hymn, combining two familiar topics (see example 45). The 6/8 meter and lilting rhythms index the pastoral *siciliano;* at the same time, the four-part chorale texture and suspensions evoke the *stile antico.* Here is a marriage of topics that suggests one of Robert Hatten's tropes, what we might call the "pastoral-religious." Unlike march and gavotte, however, these two topics do not present conflicting metrical groupings. The pastoral dance diminishes the underlying chorale, enlivening the *alla breve* with triplet subdivisions. Unlike march and gavotte, which differ according to horizontal groupings of the meter, chorale and *siciliano* are defined through vertical features of the texture (four-part chords, triple subdivision), and can thus coexist simultaneously without threatening the sequential logic of the meter.[50] With this secular hymn, Mozart has rewritten the rules of his musical utopia.

The following Allegretto (mm. 208–57) presents both methods simultaneously (see example 46). With their gavotte rhythm, the men remain stuck in the confused horizontal grouping of the opening Allegro. The dual time signatures, however, demonstrate the new vertical method of the Andantino. As Belmonte and Pedrillo plead in 4/4, Blonde fulminates in 12/8, subdividing the beat into triplets. Gavotte and gigue coexist peacefully, united by the Fuxian technique of diminution. The new method triumphs in the final Allegro, with its four-part canons and diminution of the poetic rhythm.

The Andantino divides the quartet into two roughly equal sections (192 and 175 bars, respectively). On one side lies confusion, accusation, and alienation; on the other, understanding, forgiveness, and reconciliation. No one paradigm is responsible for this redemptive drama, either dramatically or musically. Mozart's community survives precisely because he is inconsistent, because he steps out of one system and into an-

Example 45.   Die Entführung aus dem Serail, Quartet, mm. 193–96.

other. His glowing utopia exposes a fundamental schism in Enlightenment thought.

Of course, Mozart does his best to hide this rip in the fabric. The quartet ends with a ritual exorcism of jealousy and divisiveness: "Let nothing ignite the flames of jealousy!" The characters reiterate the word *nichts* eight times—paradoxically reifying the very negation they long to abolish. The same paradox haunts all of Mozart's opera finales. Every transcendent ending has its rite of annihilation, that moment in which the citizens of the new order hurl the madwoman, the Oriental, the dispossessed matriarch, or the libertine into the abyss. *Le nozze di Figaro* ends by banishing madness itself, as if reason could somehow leap away from its own shadow. But irrationality is not simply an obstacle in Mozart's path. It is the spell by which he conjures up his transcendent visions. He builds his utopias on a contradiction.

.   .   .   .   .

Mozart composed the Mass in C Minor, the Concerto in E♭, and *Die Entführung aus dem Serail* during his first few years in Vienna. He had just made the most disruptive move of his life, trading feudal security for the vicissitudes of the marketplace. Not surprisingly, Mozart returned over and over to the sounds of his youth, echoing the strains of the Salzburg Cathedral. This music reaches beyond the Enlightenment to an age still steeped in tradition, authority, and popular piety. As Mozart labored to build a new consensus in the concert halls and theaters of Vienna, he reached back again and again. Planted at strategic points in his Viennese

Example 46. *Die Entführung aus dem Serail*, Quartet, mm. 214–18.

works, his *stile antico* finales helped create the secular ritual that became bourgeois musical life.

These utopian endings suggest the direction for a new sociological critique of Mozart's music. Susan McClary and Norbert Elias have blazed a trail, but they were relying on rough maps. Abstractions like "negative dialectics" and the "civilizing process" illuminate only the most general connections between music and society. Thanks to the recent studies of musical rhetoric and semantics, however, a fine-grained model is available. We can now analyze the meanings of Mozart's music with unprecedented insight and precision. Yet too often these studies seem more concerned with constructing unified theories than with examining the complex, often contradictory way that rhetoric and signs function within eighteenth-century thought. Such theories, however beguiling, leave little freedom for the play of dialogical tensions within the art work.

Reconnecting analysis and history will mean investigating how eighteenth-century thinkers themselves discussed signs and language. Thinkers like Vico, Herder, Condillac, and Sulzer did not insist on monolithic systems of meaning. On the contrary, they acknowledged the irreducible contradictions in their intellectual world. Mozart also experienced dissonances he could resolve only by switching from one system to another. This is intertextuality in Julia Kristeva's original sense: "*The passage from one sign system to another.*"[52] In such a dialogic semiosis, "heterogeneity is not sublimated but is instead opened up within the symbolic that it puts in process/on trial. There it meets the historical process underway in society, brought to light by historical materialism."[53] For Frederic Jameson, too, such "transcodings" provided the missing link between structural and historical analysis by exposing the social forces at work within texts.[54] A historical semiotics of music can help us hear those forces within the music of Mozart and his contemporaries. We simply need to pick up the conversation where it left off two hundred years ago.

Epilogue

How does the history of Enlightenment semiotics end? Music historians have a clear enough answer, or so recent studies suggest. Around 1800, it is claimed, expression supplanted imitation as the dominant aesthetic paradigm in music and the other arts; in M. H. Abrams's famous metaphor, the artwork changed from mirror to lamp.[1] Instrumental music, previously dismissed as a pleasant but meaningless diversion, became the paragon of the arts precisely because it lacked referential determinacy. No longer tasked with imitating human passions or primitive cries, music was free to soar into the ineffable realm of spirit and express the Absolute.[2]

This narrative has posed a conundrum. In fact, autonomous instrumental music did flourish during the late eighteenth century, even as aesthetic writers clung to a mimetic theory of art. If the age of Enlightenment valued music only so far as it imitated nature, what explains the magnificent harvest of string quartets, symphonies, concertos, and sonatas? Maria Mika Maniates has summarized the problem: "The writers of the later 18th century do recognize that musical meaning must be liberated from the arbitrary demands of imitative aesthetics and that absolute music must find philosophical understanding. But no philosopher of this period crystallizes a vocabulary adequate to deal with the idea of embodied or innate musical meaning."[3] In other words, the late eighteenth century did not understand its own music. Haydn and Mozart had outstripped contemporary aesthetics, pioneering music whose full appreciation awaited Romantic writers like Wilhelm Heinrich Wackenroder, Ludwig Tieck, Jean-Paul Richter, and E. T. A. Hoffmann.

Yet, as this book has argued, eighteenth-century sign theory makes ample sense of the new instrumental repertory. From the standpoint of Enlightenment semiotics, untexted music posed no contradiction to a mimetic theory of art. The missing link is the rich conception of the natural sign. Within an aesthetic that measured the arts by their proximity to nature, the art of tones actually ranked higher than literature. Like painting, dance, and sculpture, music spoke the innate language of nature, unspoiled by the corrupting influence of arbitrary signs. Only as Enlightenment naturalism gave way to the Romantic-idealist cult of Spirit did the conflict arise between music and mimesis. When E. T. A. Hoffmann claimed that music conveyed "a higher significance than feeble words, confined to the expression of banal earthly pleasures, can communicate," he was not merely announcing a new metaphysics of music.[4] He was articulating a new understanding of signs, language, and human reason.

It can hardly be a coincidence that the first great instrumental repertory in Western music emerged in tandem with the first philosophy that fully valorized music—neither as the handmaid of rhetoric, nor as a Pythagorean abstraction, but as a holistic physical, emotional, and cognitive activity. Haydn, Mozart, and their fellow composers did not create absolute music by fleeing language. Instead, they refined those parameters shared by both music and language—gesture, inflection, prosody, phrase structure. In the Enlightenment imagination, these were the pure origins of speech, before the arbitrary sign liberated humanity to begin its bittersweet journey toward civilization.

It would seem that the eighteenth century did understand its own music. Enlightenment sign theory explains perfectly well how Mozart could move between opera and concerto, mass and symphony, cantata and string quartet. There is no need to project nineteenth-century aesthetics back onto his age. We would do better to ask how the cosmopolitan tradition of Condillac, Vico, Herder, Smith, and Reid continued to inform the new century. The end of this path lies mostly hidden, overgrown with Hegelian and Romantic narratives. It remains to explore how long the rich tradition of Enlightenment semiotics survived, and what forces ultimately brought about its demise. That would be a story worth telling.

Notes

INTRODUCTION

1. Alphonse Costadau, *Traité des signes*, ed. Odile Le Guem-Forel (Berne, Switzerland: Peter Lang, 1983), 1: 9.

2. Alexander Gottlieb Baumgarten, *Theoretische Ästhetik. Die grundlegenden Abschnitte aus der "Aesthetica,"* trans. Hans Rudolf Schweizer (Hamburg: Felix Meiner Verlag, 1983), 10.

3. Important studies include Hans Aarsleff, *From Locke to Saussure: Essays on the Study of Language and Intellectual History* (Minneapolis: University of Minnesota Press, 1982); Lia Formigari, *Signs, Science and Politics: Philosophies of Language in Europe 1700–1830*, trans. William Dodd (Amsterdam and Philadelphia: John Benjamins, 1993); Sylvain Auroux, *La sémiotique des encyclopédistes. Essai d'épistémologie historique des sciences du langage* (Paris: Payot, 1979); Ulrich Ricken, *Linguistics, Anthropology, and Philosophy in the French Enlightenment: Language Theory and Ideology*, trans. Robert E. Norton (London: Routledge, 1994); Marcelo Dascal, *Leibniz, Language, Signs, and Thought: A Collection of Essays* (Amsterdam and Philadelphia: John Benjamins, 1987); and Stephen K. Land, *The Philosophy of Lan-*

guage in Britain: Major Theories from Hobbes to Thomas Reid (New York: AMS Press, 1986).

4.   David E. Wellbery, *Lessing's "Laocoon": Semiotics and Aesthetics in the Age of Reason* (Cambridge: Cambridge University Press, 1984).

5.   See, for example, Laurence Dreyfus, *Bach and the Patterns of Invention* (Cambridge, MA: Harvard University Press, 1994); Karl Braunschweig, "The Metaphor of Music as a Language in the Enlightenment: Towards a Cultural History of Eighteenth-Century Music Theory," Ph.D. diss., University of Michigan, 1997; Michael Spitzer, *Metaphor and Musical Thought* (Chicago: University of Chicago Press, 2004); Matthew Riley, *Musical Listening in the German Enlightenment: Attention, Wonder, and Astonishment* (Aldershot, UK, and Burlington, VT: Ashgate, 2004); and Downing Thomas, *Music and the Origins of Language: Theories from the French Enlightenment* (Cambridge: Cambridge University Press, 1995).

6.   Studies of late eighteenth-century music and rhetoric include Leonard G. Ratner, *Classic Music: Expression, Form, and Style* (New York: Schirmer Books, 1980); Wye Jamison Allanbrook, *Rhythmic Gesture in Mozart: "Le nozze di Figaro" and "Don Giovanni"* (Chicago: University of Chicago Press, 1983); Mark Evan Bonds, *Wordless Rhetoric: Musical Form and the Metaphor of the Oration* (Cambridge, MA: Harvard University Press, 1991); George Barth, *The Pianist as Orator: Beethoven and the Transformation of Keyboard Style* (Ithaca, NY: Cornell University Press, 1992); Elaine Sisman, *Haydn and the Classical Variation* (Cambridge, MA: Harvard University Press, 1993); and Sisman, "Learned Style and the Rhetoric of the Sublime in the 'Jupiter' Symphony," in *Wolfgang Amadé Mozart: Essays on His Life and His Music*, ed. Stanley Sadie (Oxford: Clarendon Press, 1996), 213–38; Tom Beghin, "Haydn as Orator: A Rhetorical Analysis of His Keyboard Sonata in D Major, Hob. XVI: 42," in *Haydn and His World*, ed. Elaine Sisman (Princeton, NJ: Princeton University Press, 1997), 201–54; John Irving, *Mozart's Piano Sonatas: Contexts, Sources, Style* (Cambridge: Cambridge University Press, 1997), 111–61; James Webster, *Haydn's "Farewell" Symphony and the Idea of Classical Style: Through-Composition and Cyclic Integration in His Instrumental Music* (Cambridge: Cambridge University Press, 1991), 123–73; Elisabeth Le Guin, *Boccherini's Body: An Essay in Carnal Musicology* (Berkeley and Los Angeles: University of California Press, 2006); Matthew Head, *Orientalism, Masquerade, and Mozart's Turkish Music* (London: Royal Music Association, 2000); and the essays in *Communication in Eighteenth-Century Music*, ed. Danuta Mirka and Kofi Agawu (Cambridge: Cambridge University Press, 2008).

7.   Important semiotic studies include V. Kofi Agawu, *Playing with Signs: A Semiotic Interpretation of Classic Music* (Princeton, NJ: Princeton University Press, 1991); Raymond Monelle, *The Sense of Music: Semiotic Essays* (Princeton, NJ: Princeton University Press, 2000); and Monelle, *The Musical Topic: Hunt, Military, and Pastoral* (Bloomington and Indianapolis: Indiana University Press, 2006); Robert S. Hatten, *Musical Meaning in Beethoven: Markedness, Correlation, and Interpretation*

(Bloomington: Indiana University Press, 1994); and Hatten, *Interpreting Musical Gestures, Topics, and Tropes: Mozart, Beethoven, Schubert* (Bloomington: Indiana University Press, 2004); David Lidov, "The Allegretto of Beethoven's Seventh," in *Is Language a Music? Writings on Musical Form and Signification* (Bloomington: Indiana University Press, 2005), 41–58; and Michael Spitzer, "Inside Beethoven's 'Magic Square': The Structural Semantics of Op. 132," in *Les Universaux en Musique,* ed. Costin Miereanu and Xavier Hascher, Actes du 4e Congrès International sur la signification musicale (Paris: Publications de la Sorbonne, 1999), 87–125; and Spitzer, *Metaphor and Musical Thought.*

8.   See Nicholas Till, *Mozart and the Enlightenment: Truth, Virtue, and Beauty in Mozart's Operas* (New York: W. W. Norton, 1993); Volkmar Braunbehrens, *Mozart in Vienna, 1781–1791,* trans. Timothy Bell (New York: Grove Weidenfeld, 1990); and Robert W. Gutman, *Mozart: A Cultural Biography* (New York: Harcourt, Brace, 1999).

9.   See Edmund Goehring, *Three Modes of Perception in Mozart: The Philosophical, Pastoral, and Comic in Così fan tutte* (Cambridge: Cambridge University Press, 2004).

10.   Leopold Mozart, *A Treatise on the Fundamental Principles of Violin Playing,* 2d ed., trans. Editha Knocker, (Oxford: Oxford University Press, 1985), 25.

11.   Till, *Mozart and the Enlightenment,* 23.

12.   See the commentary in Mozart, *Briefe und Aufzeichnungen. Gesamtausgabe hrsg. von der Internationalen Stiftung Mozarteum, Salzburg,* vol. 6, *Kommentar III/IV, 1780–1857,* ed. Wilhelm A. Bauer and Otto Erich Deutsch (Kassel, Germany: Bärenreiter, 1971), 351.

13.   Moses Mendelssohn, *Phädon, or On the Immortality of the Soul,* trans. Patricia Noble (New York: Peter Lang, 2007), 128.

14.   See Bonds, *Wordless Rhetoric*; and Spitzer, *Metaphor and Musical Thought.*

15.   Franz Szabo, *Kaunitz and Enlightened Absolutism, 1753–1780* (New York: Cambridge University Press, 1994), 34.

16.   Karl Graf von Zinzendorf, *Aus den Jugendtagebüchern: 1747, 1752, bis 1763,* ed. Maria Breunlich and Marieluise Mader, based on work by Hans Wagner (Vienna: Böhlau Verlag, 1997), 297.

17.   Mozart, *Briefe und Aufzeichnungen,* 2: 332.

18.   Georg Knepler, *Wolfgang Amadé Mozart,* trans. J. Bradford Robinson (Cambridge: Cambridge University Press, 1994), 42.

19.   See Szabo, *Kaunitz and Enlightened Absolutism,* 34.

20.   Mikhail Bakhtin, *The Dialogic Imagination: Four Essays by M. M. Bakhtin,* trans. Caryl Emerson and Michael Holquist (Austin: University of Texas Press, 1981), 365.

21.   Auroux, *La sémiotique des encyclopédistes,* 66.

22.   Louis Hjelmslev, *Prolegomena to a Theory of Language,* trans. Francis J. Whitfield (Madison: University of Wisconsin Press, 1961), 47–60.

23. *The Collected Papers of Charles Sanders Peirce,* vol. 2, ed. Charles Hartstone and Paul Weiss (Cambridge, MA: Harvard University Press, 1932), 228.

24. David Lidov, *Elements of Semiotics* (New York: St. Martin's Press, 1999), 107.

25. Ratner, *Classic Music,* 27; Heartz, *Music in European Capitals: The Galant Style, 1720–1780* (New York: W. W. Norton, 2003), 1008.

CHAPTER 1

1. Julian Rushton, "Mozart's Art of Rhetoric: Understanding an Opera Seria Aria ('Deh se piacer mi vuoi' from *La clemenza di Tito*)," *Contemporary Music Review* 17, no. 3 (1998): 16.

2. For an analysis of the anapestic rhythms in *Figaro,* see my "Unveiling Cherubino," *Eighteenth-Century Music* 4, no. 1 (2007): 129–38.

3. Will Crutchfield, "The Prosodic Appoggiatura in the Music of Mozart and His Contemporaries," *Journal of the American Musicological Society* 42, no. 2 (1989): 229–74. But see also Frederick Neumann, "A New Look at Mozart's Prosodic Appoggiatura," in *Perspectives on Mozart Performance,* ed. R. Larry Todd and Peter Williams (Cambridge: Cambridge University Press, 1991), 94–116.

4. See Monelle, *Sense of Music,* 17–18, 66–80.

5. For a discussion of Italian prosody, as well as a nuanced reading of "Non so più," see James Webster's important article "The Analysis of Mozart's Arias," in *Mozart Studies,* ed. Cliff Eisen (Oxford: Clarendon Press, 1991), 133–40, 173–79.

6. See Otto Erich Deutsch, *Mozart: A Documentary Biography,* trans. Eric Blom, Peter Branscombe, and Jeremy Noble (Stanford, CA: Stanford University Press, 1965), 98.

7. Wye Jamison Allanbrook, "Comic Issues in Mozart's Piano Concertos," in *Mozart's Piano Concertos: Text, Context, Interpretation,* ed. Neal Zaslaw (Ann Arbor: University of Michigan Press, 1996), 75.

8. James Robert Tull, "B. V. Asaf'ev's 'Musical Form as a Process': Translation and Commentary, Volume III" (Ph.D. diss., Ohio State University, 1976), 735.

9. Donald Francis Tovey, *Essays in Musical Analysis,* vol. 1, *Symphonies* (London: Oxford University Press, 1972), 193.

10. Spitzer, "Inside Beethoven's 'Magic Square,' 122.

11. For Condillac's European influence, see Aarsleff, *From Locke to Saussure,* 146–209, 335–55; Formigari, *Signs, Science, and Politics,* 113–47; Claudio Marazzini, *Storia e coscienza della lingua in Italia dall'umanesimo al romanticismo* (Turin, Italy: Rosenberg and Sellier, 1989), esp. 225–31; Raffaele Spongano, *La poetica del sensismo e la poesia del Parini* (Bologna, Italy: Patron, 1964); and Walter Moser, "Jean-Georges Sulzer, continuateur de la pensée sensualiste dans l'Académie de Berlin," *Modern Language Notes* 84, no. 6 (1969): 931–41.

12. René Descartes, *The Principles of Philosophy,* in *The Philosophical Works of*

Descartes, trans. Elizabeth S. Haldane and G. R. T. Ross (Cambridge: Cambridge University Press, 1973), 1: 255.

13. John Locke, *An Essay Concerning Human Understanding,* ed. John W. Yolton (London: David Campbell, 1961), 48.

14. Ibid., 248.

15. Ibid., 415. On Locke's Gallic reception, see John Yolton, *Locke and French Materialism* (Oxford: Clarendon Press, 1991).

16. See Condillac, *Essai sur l'origine des connoissances humaines,* in *Oeuvres philosophiques de Condillac,* ed. Georges le Roy (Paris: Presses Universitaires de France, 1949), 1: 10–28. Condillac also summarized this process in the introduction to his *Cours d'études,* in *Oeuvres philosophiques,* 1: 412–15.

17. Condillac, *Essai,* 5.

18. Ibid., 21. Antoine de Rivarol echoed Condillac in his prize-winning essay for the Berlin Academy of 1785, *L'universalité de la langue française,* ed. Jean Dutourd (Paris, 1991), 44: "Chose étrange! si l'homme n'eut pas créé des signes, ses idées simples et fugitives, germant et mourant tour à tour, n'auraient pas laissé plus de traces dans son cerveau que les flots d'un ruisseau qui passé n'en laissent dans ses yeux."

19. Condillac, *Essai,* 22.

20. Johann Jacob Breitinger, *Critische Dichtkunst* (Zurich: Conrad Brell, 1740; repr., Stuttgart, Germany: J. B. Metzlersche Verlagsbuchhandlung, 1966), 67.

21. Denis Diderot, *Conversations on "The Natural Son,"* in *Selected Writings on Art and Literature,* trans. Geoffrey Bremner (London: Penguin Books, 1994), 66.

22. Giuseppe Parini, "Discorso sopra la poesia," in *Prose,* ed. Egidio Bellorini (Bari, Italy: G. Laterza, 1913), 1: 127.

23. Parini, "Ristretto delle lezioni di belle lettere," in *Prose,* vol. 1, *Lezioni. Elementi di retorica,* ed. Silvia Morgana e Paolo Bartesaghi (Milan, Italy: Edizioni Universitarie di Lettere Economia Diritto, 2003), 293. On Parini's French influences, see Mario Cerruti, "Parini e il sensismo" in *L'amabil rito: società e cultura nella Milano di Parini,* vol. 1, ed. Gennaro Barbarisi et al. (Milan, Italy: Cisalpino, 2000), 583–87; and Spongano, *La poetica del sensismo.*

24. See Hans Adler, "Fundus Animae—der Grund der Seele: Zur Gnoseologie des. Dunklen in der Aufklärung," *Deutsche Vierteljahrschrift für Literaturwissenschaft und Geistesgeschichte* 62 (1988): 197–220.

25. Alexander Gottlieb Baumgarten, *Reflections on Poetry: Meditationes philosophicae de nonnullis ad poema pertimentibus,* trans. Karl Aschenbrenner and William B. Holtner (Berkeley and Los Angeles: University of California Press, 1954), 43.

26. Alexander Gottlieb Baumgarten, *Theoretische Ästhetik. Die grundlegenden Abschnitte aus der "Aesthetica,"* trans. Hans Rudolf Schweizer (Hamburg: Felix Meiner Verlag, 1983), 10.

27. Condillac, *Logique/Logic,* trans. W. R. Albury (New York: Abaris Books, 1980), 59.

28. Condillac, *Essai*, 80.

29. David E. Wellbery, *Lessing's "Laocoon": Semiotics and Aesthetics in the Age of Reason* (Cambridge: Cambridge University Press, 1984), 33.

30. Alfred Heuss, "The Minor Second in Mozart's G minor Symphony," in *Mozart: Symphony in G Minor*, K. 550, ed. Nathan Broder (New York: W. W. Norton, 1976), 83–98.

31. For a musical interpretation of the Peircian trichotomies, see Naomi Cumming, *The Sonic Self: Musical Subjectivity and Signification* (Bloomington and Indianapolis: Indiana University Press, 2000), 80–104; and Thomas Turino, "Signs of Imagination, Identity, and Experience: A Peircian Semiotic Theory for Music," *Ethnomusicology* 43, no. 2 (1999): 221–55.

32. Heuss, "Minor Second," 89.

33. See Ratner, *Classic Music*, 51–52; Robert O. Gjerdingen, *A Classic Turn of Phrase: Music and the Psychology of Convention* (Philadelphia: University of Pennsylvania Press, 1988); Spitzer, *Metaphor and Musical Thought*, 46–49.

34. James Hepokoski and Warren Darcy discuss this cadence, or "essential expositional closure," in *Elements of Sonata Theory: Norms, Types, and Deformations in the Late-Eighteenth-Century Sonata* (Oxford: Oxford University Press, 2006), 117–49.

35. Leo Treitler, *Music and the Historical Imagination* (Cambridge, MA: Harvard University Press, 1990), 187.

36. See Ratner, *Classic Music*, 33–47; Bonds, *Wordless Rhetoric*, 68–80.

37. Beghin, "Haydn as Orator," 201–54; Sisman, *Haydn*; Barth, *Pianist as Orator*.

38. Dénes Bartha, "On Beethoven's Thematic Structure," *Musical Quarterly* 56, no. 4 (1970), 778; reprinted in *The Creative World of Beethoven*, ed. Paul Henry Lang (New York: W. W. Norton, 1971), 257–76.

39. Spitzer, *Metaphor and Musical Thought*, 219.

40. See Riley, *Musical Listening*, esp. 121–71.

41. Condillac, *Essai*, 61.

42. Ibid., 61, 103. Condillac's theory foreshadows the cognitive semantics of George Lakoff and Mark Johnson, who traced the origin of human knowledge to metaphoric transformations of basic kinesthetic schemas. See Lakoff and Johnson, *Metaphors We Live By* (Chicago: University of Chicago Press, 1980); and Mark Johnson, *The Body in the Mind: The Bodily Basis of Meaning, Imagination, and Reason* (Chicago: University of Chicago Press, 1987).

43. Condillac, *Essai*, 63, 68.

44. Ibid., 80.

45. See Condillac, *Essai*, 73–78.

46. Thomas, *Music and the Origins of Language*, 68.

47. Sophia Rosenfeld, *A Revolution in Language: The Problem of Signs in Late Eighteenth-Century France* (Stanford, CA: Stanford University Press, 2001), 85.

48.   Condillac, *Essai*, 157.

49.   Ricken, *Linguistics, Anthropology, and Philosophy*, 119.

50.   The authoritative study remains Ricken, *Grammaire et philosophie au siècle des lumières. Controverses sur l'ordre naturel et la clarté du français* (Arras, France: Publications de l'université de Lille, 1978). See also Auroux, *La sémiotique des encyclopédistes*, 191–212; and Aldo Scaglione, *The Theory of German Word Order from the Renaissance to the Present* (Minneapolis: University of Minnesota Press, 1981), 51–79.

51.   Bernard Lamy, *La rhétorique ou l'art de parler*, ed. Benoît Timmermans (Paris: Presses Universitaires de France, 1998), 103.

52.   Abbé Du Bos, *Réflexions critiques sur la poésie et sur la peinture*, 7th ed. (Paris: Chez Pissot, 1770; reprint, Genève-Paris: Slatkine, 1982), 89.

53.   Noam Chomsky, *Cartesian Linguistics: A Chapter in the History of Rationalist Thought* (New York: Harper & Row, 1966). See also Chomsky, *Topics in the Theory of Generative Grammar* (The Hague and Paris: Mouton, 1966), 11–16; and Chomsky, *Aspects of the Theory of Syntax* (Cambridge, MA: MIT Press, 1965), 3–9, 47–59.

54.   Johann Gottfried Herder, *Werke*, vol. 1, *Herder und der Sturm und Drang, 1764–1774*, ed. Wolfgang Pross (Munich: Carl Hanser Verlag, 1984), 111.

55.   Melchiore Cesarotti, *Saggio sulla filosofia delle lingue*, ed. Ugo Perolino (Pescara, Italy: Edizioni Campus, 2001), 50.

56.   Francesco Algarotti, "Saggio sopra la lingua francese," in *Saggi*, ed. Giovanni da Pozzo (Bari, Italy: Giuseppe Laterza e Figli, 1963), 253.

57.   Rousseau, "Lettre sur la musique françoise," in *Écrits sur la musique* (Paris: Éditions Pourrat, 1833; reprint, Paris: Stock, 1979), 272.

58.   François J. Chastellux, *Essai sur l'union de la poésie et de la musique* (Paris: La Haye, 1765), 16–17. Quoted in Ratner, *Classic Music*, 35.

59.   See Daniel Heartz, "Thomas Attwood's Lessons in Composition with Mozart," *Proceedings of the Royal Musical Association* 100 (1973–74), 175–83; Hans Heinrich Eggebrecht, *Versuch über die Wiener Klassik. Beihefte zum Archiv für Musikwissenschaft* 12 (1972), 24–25; and Konrad Küster, "The Minuet as a Teaching Medium," in *Mozart: A Musical Biography*, trans. Mary Whittal (Oxford: Clarendon Press, 1996), 1–9.

60.   See Sisman, *Haydn*, 101, 107.

61.   For a sensible overview of the relationship between rhetoric and music in early eighteenth-century music, see Bettina Varwig, "One More Time: Bach and Seventeenth-Century Traditions of Rhetoric," *Eighteenth-Century Music* 5, no. 2 (2008): 179–208.

62.   On the authenticity of this posthumous work, see the afterward to Mozart, *Muskalisches Würfelspiel. Eine Anleitung Walzer und Schleifer mit zwei Würfeln zu komponieren*, ed. Karl Heinz Taubert (Mainz, Germany: Schott, 1990), 8.

63.   Ratner, "*Ars Combinatoria:* Chance and Choice in Eighteenth-Century

Music," in *Studies in Eighteenth-Century Music: A Tribute to Karl Geiringer on His Seventieth Birthday,* ed. H. C. Robbins Landon, with Roger E. Chapman (New York: Oxford University Press, 1970), 359.

64.   See Leonard Bernstein, *The Unanswered Question: Six Talks at Harvard* (Cambridge, MA: Harvard University Press, 1976), 86–115. Fred Lerdahl and Ray Jackendoff elaborated Bernstein's argument (and his Chomskian approach) in *A Generative Theory of Tonal Music* (Cambridge, MA: MIT Press, 1983), 22–30.

65.   On the problematic boundary between musical syntax and semantics, see Raymond Monelle, *Linguistics and Semiotics in Music* (London: Harwood Academic Publishers, 1992), 237–42.

66.   Recent studies include Hatten, *Interpreting Musical Gestures,* and the collected essays in Anthony Gritten and Elaine King, eds., *Music and Gesture* (Aldershot, UK, and Burlington, VT: Ashgate, 2006).

67.   Monelle, *Linguistics and Semiotics,* 129.

68.   Ratner, *Classic Music,* 26, 30.

CHAPTER 2

1.   For a survey of this tradition, see Bernard Williams,, "Don Giovanni as an Idea," in Julian Rushton, *W. A. Mozart: "Don Giovanni"* (New York: Cambridge University Press, 1981), 81–91.

2.   See Bettina Brandl-Risi, "Der Pygmalion-Mythos im Musiktheater—Verzeichnis der Werke," in *Pygmalion. Die Geschichte des Mythos in der abendländischen Kultur,* ed. Mathias Mayer and Gerhard Neumann (Freiburg, Germany: Rombach, 1997), 665–733.

3.   François Hemsterhuis, *Lettre sur les désirs* (Paris, 1770), 11; quoted in Alex Potts, *The Sculptural Imagination: Figurative, Modernist, Minimalist* (New Haven, CT: Yale University Press, 2000), 36.

4.   Johann Gottfried Herder, *Plastik,* in *Werke,* vol. 4, ed. Jürgen Brummack and Martin Bollacher (Frankfurt am Main: Deutscher Klassiker Verlag, 1994), 313. Inka Mülder-Bach has argued that the living statue celebrated a moment in Enlightenment representation when the subject could sympathetically unite with, yet still remain distinct from, the artistic object; see Mülder-Bach, *Im Zeichen Pygmalions. Das Modell der Statue und die Entdeckung der "Darstellung" im 18. Jahrhundert* (Munich: W. Fink, 1998). See also Oskar Bätschmann, "Pygmalion als Betrachter: Die Rezeption von Plastik und Malerei in der zweiten Hälften des 18. Jahrhunderts," in *Der Betrachter ist im Bild: Kunstwissenschaft und Rezeptionsästhetik,* ed. Wolfgang Kemp (Berlin: Reimer, 1992), 183–224. For specifically musical discussions of living statues, see Elisabeth Le Guin, *Boccherini's Body: An Essay in Carnal Musicology* (Berkeley and Los Angeles: University of California Press, 2006), 7–11; Daniel

Chua, *Absolute Music and the Construction of Meaning* (Cambridge: Cambridge University Press, 1999), 109–11; and Malcolm Baker, "Odzooks! A Man of Stone: Earth, Heaven, and Hell in Eighteenth-Century Tomb Sculpture," in *"Don Giovanni": Myths of Seduction and Betrayal*, ed. Jonathan Miller (New York: Schocken Books, 1990), 62–69.

5. *Generale vom 9. Februar 1784* (Allgemeines Verwaltungsarchiv, Wien, Altes Kultusarchiv 11 Gen 120/5/1784); cited in Hans Hollerweger, *Die Reform des Gottesdienstes zur Zeit des Josephinismus in Österreich*, vol. 1 (Regensburg, Germany: Verlag Friedrich Pustet, 1976), 485.

6. Jean-Jacques Rousseau, *Pygmalion, scène lyrique*, in *Oeuvres complètes de Jean-Jacques Rousseau*, ed. Henri Coulet et al. (Paris: Gallimard, 1959), 2: 1230.

7. Jean-Jacques Rousseau, *Émile, or On Education*, trans. Allan Bloom (New York: Basic Books, 1979), 64.

8. Condillac, *Traité des sensations*, in *Oeuvres philosophiques de Condillac*, ed. Georges le Roy (Paris: Presses Universitaires de France, 1947), 1: 264.

9. Johann Gottlieb Herder, "Zum Sinn des Gefühls" (1769), in *Werke*, ed. Martin Bollacher et al., 4: 236.

10. Immanuel Kant, *Critique of Practical Reason*, trans. Lewis White Beck (Indianapolis: Liberal Arts Press, 1956), 14. Ernst Cassirer viewed the debate over touch and vision as the nexus of Enlightenment epistemology and psychology, the "general theoretical problem in which all the threads of the study unite." Cassirer, *The Philosophy of the Enlightenment*, trans. Fritz C. A. Koelln and James P. Pettegrove (Princeton, NJ: Princeton University Press, 1951), 108. For a broader historical view of touch, see Ulrike Zeuch, *Umkehr der Sinneshierarchie. Herder und die Aufwertung des Tastsinns seit der frühen Neuzeit* (Tübingen, Germany: Max Niemeyer Verlag, 2000).

11. Edward Forman has stressed the importance of taking hands in *Don Giovanni* in "Don Juan before Da Ponte," in *W. A. Mozart: "Don Giovanni,"* ed. Julian Rushton (New York: Cambridge University Press, 1981), 27–44. Kristi Brown-Montesano has traced the origins of Giovanni's "manine" strategy in *Understanding the Women of Mozart's Operas* (Berkeley and Los Angeles: University of California Press, 2007), 61–65.

12. See Margaret Atherton, *Berkeley's Revolution in Vision* (Ithaca, NY: Cornell University Press, 1990), 34–57.

13. George Berkeley, *Philosophical Works Including the Works on Vision*, ed. Michael R. Ayers (London: Rowman & Littlefield, 2000), 45, 49.

14. Ibid., 60.

15. Ibid., 114–15. For a nuanced discussion of Berkeley's critique of abstract ideas, see George Pappas, *Berkeley's Thought* (Ithaca, NY: Cornell University Press, 2000), 23–79.

16. Berkeley, *Philosophical Works*, 105–6.

17. Ibid., 114.

18. See Colin Murray Turbayne, *The Myth of Metaphor* (New Haven, CT: Yale University Press, 1962). See also A. David Kline, "Berkeley's Divine Language Argument," in *Essays on the Philosophy of George Berkeley*, ed. Ernest Sosa (Dordrecht, Netherlands: D. Reidel, 1987), 129–42; and William McGowan, "Berkeley's Doctrine of Signs," in *Berkeley: Critical and Interpretive Essays*, ed. Colin Turbayne (Minneapolis: University of Minnesota Press, 1982), 231–46.

19. Berkeley, *Philosophical Works*, 63.

20. See Wellbery, *Lessing's "Laocoon,"* 24–30; and Victor Anthony Rudowski, "The Theory of Signs in the Eighteenth Century," in *Language and the History of Thought*, ed. Nancy Struever (Rochester, NY: University of Rochester Press, 1995), 83–90.

21. See Ricken, *Linguistics, Anthropology, and Philosophy*, 160–73.

22. Du Bos, *Réflexions critiques*, 124.

23. Ibid., 53.

24. Jean-Georges Noverre, *Lettres sur la danse et sur les ballets* (1760; facsimile reprint, New York: Broude Brothers, 1967), 270; quoted in Le Guin, *Boccherini's Body*, 137.

25. Quoted in Karl Geiringer, *Haydn: A Critical Life in Music*, in collaboration with Irene Geiringer (Berkeley and Los Angeles: University of California Press, 1982), 98–99.

26. See Mary Sue Morrow, *German Music Criticism in the Late Eighteenth Century. Aesthetic Issues in Instrumental Music* (Cambridge: Cambridge University Press, 1997); John Neubauer, *The Emancipation of Music from Language: Departure from Mimesis in Eighteenth-Century Aesthetics* (New Haven, CT: Yale University Press, 1986); Bellamy Hosler, *Changing Views of Instrumental Music in 18th-Century Germany* (Ann Arbor, MI: UMI Research Press, 1981); Bonds, *Wordless Rhetoric;* and Maria Rika Maniates, "*Sonate, que me veux-tu?*" The Enigma of French Musical Aesthetics in the 18th Century," *Current Musicology* 9 (1969): 117–40.

27. Although frequently accused of materialism, Condillac actually embraced Malebranche's doctrine of occasionalism, whereby the senses merely provide the occasion for God's production of ideas. His mechanistic model applied solely to fallen humanity. See Condillac, *L'origine des connoissances humanies*, 6–8.

28. Condillac, *Logique,* 333. On Condillac's linguistic conception of science, see Nicolas Rousseau, *Connaissance et langage chéz Condillac* (Geneva: Librairie, 1986), 300–332.

29. As he confessed to Maupertuis in a letter of 25 June 1752, "Je me suis trompé et j'ai trop donné aux signes." *Oeuvres philosophiques*, 2: 536. See Henry Joly, "Condillac et la critique de l'âge de raison," in *Condillac et les problèmes du langage*, ed. Jean Sgard (Geneva: Slatkine, 1982), 7–25.

30. Condillac, *Traité des sensations*, in *Oeuvres philosophiques*, 1: 239.

31. Ibid., 1: 224.

32. Ibid., 1: 256.

33. Ibid., 1: 275.

34. See Aarsleff, "Condillac's Speechless Statue," in *From Locke to Saussure*, 210–24.

35. Condillac, *L'origine des connoissances humanies*, 103.

36. Condillac, *Logique*, 215, 213.

37. Condillac sought to inculcate this practice through a writing exercise he prepared for the prince of Parma. The philosopher would lead his young pupil to a closed window, open the shutters briefly, and then have him write an analysis of the scene he had glimpsed. In this way, the prince would learn to submit a visual tableau to the successive form of verbal discourse. See Aarsleff, *From Locke to Saussure*, 30.

38. Condillac, *Logique*, 219.

39. Condillac, *Grammaire*, in *Oeuvres philosophiques*, 1: 429.

40. Herder, "Zum Sinn des Gefühls," *Werke*, ed. Bollacher, 4: 237. On Herder and pantheism, see Frederick C. Beiser, *Enlightenment, Revolution, and Romanticism: The Genesis of Modern German Political Thought, 1790–1800* (Cambridge, MA: Harvard University Press, 1992), 204–5, 242–44.

41. Johann Gottfried Herder, *Ausgewählte Werke in Einzelausgaben. Scriften zur Literatur 2/1*, ed. Regine Otto (Berlin: Aufbau, 1990), 128–36, 150–53. See James Harris, *Three Treatises: The First Concerning Art; the Second Concerning Music, Painting, and Poetry; the Third Concerning Happiness* (London: H. Woodfall, 1744), 33–36.

42. On the French connection, see Raymond Immerwahr, "Diderot, Herder and the Dichotomy of Touch and Sight," *Seminar* 14 (1978): 84–96.

43. Herder, *Ausgewählte Werke*, 496.

44. Ibid., 525, 523, 556.

45. Johann Gottfried Herder, *Sculpture: Some Observations on Shape and Form from Pygmalion's Creative Dream*, trans. Jason Gaiger (Chicago: University of Chicago Press, 2002), 45.

46. Herder, *Ausgewählte Werke*, 2/1: 515.

47. Ibid., 2/1: 606.

48. Herder, *Werke in zehn Bänden. Frühe Schriften, 1764–1772*, ed. Ulrich Gaier (Frankfurt am Main: Deutscher Klassiker Verlag, 1985), 713.

49. Ibid., 722.

50. Ibid., 746.

51. Ibid., 724.

52. Ibid., 733. For Condillac's influence on Herder, see Manet van Montfrans, "An Orange on a Pine Tree: French Thought in Herder's Linguistic Theory," in *Yearbook of European Studies* 7 (1994): 55–76; and Jörn Stückenrath, "Der junge

Herder als Sprach—und Literaturtheoretiker—ein Erbe des französischen Aufk-lärers Condillac?" in *Sturm und Drang. Ein literaturwissenschaftliches Studienbuch*, ed. Walter Hinck (Kronberg, Germany: Athanäum, 1978): 81–96.

53. Charles Taylor, "The Importance of Herder," in *Philosophical Arguments* (Cambridge, MA: Harvard University Press, 1995), 93. For a balanced assessment of Herder's critique of Condillac, see Kurt Mueller-Vollmer, "From Sign to Sig-nification: The Herder-Humboldt Controversy," in *Johann Gottfried Herder: Language, History, and the Enlightenment*, ed. Wulf Koepke (Columbia, SC: Camden House, 1990), 9–24.

54. Herder, *Werke*, vol. 8, 364–70.

55. Ibid., 677, 779. "Was hier abgerissen gesagt wird, haben *Du Bos, Goguet, Condillac* und wie viele andre historisch sowohl, als philosophisch erläutert; der Anfang der menschlichen Rede in Tönen, Gebärden, im Ausdruck der Empfin-dungen und Gedanken durch Bilder und Zeichen konnte nicht anders al seine Art roher Poesie sein, und istnoch bei allen Naturvölkern der Erde" (779). Robert E. Norton has emphasized Herder's allegiance to Enlightenment empiricism in *Herder and the European Enlightenment* (Ithaca, NY: Cornell University Press, 1991).

56. See David Hume, *A Treatise of Human Nature*, ed. L. A. Selby-Bigge (New York: Oxford University Press, 1980), 251–63.

57. Mary Hunter, *The Culture of Opera Buffa in Mozart's Vienna: A Poetics of En-tertainment* (Princeton, NJ: Princeton University Press, 1999), 127.

58. Da Ponte originally wrote "È un certo antidoto" for verse 9, then changed *antidoto* to *balsamo*, with its less than subtle allusions to feminine physiology; see Lorenzo da Ponte, *Il Don Giovanni*, ed. Giovanna Gronda (Turin, Italy: Einaudi, 1995), 57. I am grateful to Bruce Alan Brown for pointing out this change.

59. See Mauro Calcagno, " 'Imitar col canto chi parla': Monteverdi and the Creation of a Language for Musical Theater," *Journal of the American Musicologi-cal Society* 55 (2002): 383–431. Calcagno's primary authority is Karl Bühler, *Sprachtheorie. Die Darstellungsfunktion der Sprache* (Jena, Germany, 1934).

60. On the implicit gesturality of settecento opera, see Reinhold Strohm, *Dramma per musica: Italian Opera Seria of the Eighteenth Century* (New Haven, CT: Yale University Press, 1997), 224–27.

61. Monelle, *Sense of Music*, 17–19.

62. See Meredith Little and Natalie Jenne, *Dance and the Music of J. S. Bach*, ex-panded edition (Bloomington: Indiana University Press, 2001), 134.

63. See Head, *Mozart's Turkish Music* (London: Royal Music Association, 2000), 67–89.

64. Lawrence M. Zbikowski, "Dance Topoi, Sonic Analogues and Musical Grammar: Communicating with Music in the Eighteenth Century," in *Communi-cation in Eighteenth-Century Music*, ed. Danuta Mirka and Kofi Agawu (Cambridge: Cambridge University Press, 2008), 285.

65. Friedrich Lippmann, "Der italienische Vers und der musikalische Rhyth-

mus. Zum Verhältnis von Vers und Musik in der italienischen Oper des 19. Jahrhunderts, mit einem Rückblick auf die 2. Hälfte des 18. Jahrhunderts" (2. Teil), *Analecta musicologica* 12 (1973): 283–86, 294–96. See also Heartz, *Music in European Capitals,* 554–55. A *verso sdrucciolo* ends with two unaccented syllables.

66. Condillac, *L'origine des connoissances humanies,* 103.

67. Allanbrook, *Rhythmic Gesture in Mozart.*

68. See Bonds, *Wordless Rhetoric,* 90–118; and Varwig, "One More Time."

69. Condillac, *L'origine des connoissances humanies,* 98.

70. Herder, fourth *Wäldchen,* in *Ausgewählte Werke,* 55.

71. Jessica Waldoff, *Recognition in Mozart's Operas* (New York: Oxford University Press, 2006), 178.

72. Daniel Heartz, *Mozart's Operas,* ed. Thomas Bauman (Berkeley and Los Angeles: University of California Press, 1990), 169–70.

73. Lippmann, "Der italienische Vers," 2. Teil, 334–35, 374.

74. Allanbrook has explored the semantics of this scene in *Rhythmic Gesture in Mozart,* 292–301.

75. Condillac, *L'origine des connoissances humanies,* 63, 68.

76. Marshall Brown has noted the echoes of Zerlina's "Sentilo battere!" ("Vedrai carino," mm. 61–63, 67–71) in the dotted rhythm and octave descent of the Commendatore's "Pentiti!"—itself an echo of his challenge to Giovanni before the dual, "Battiti!" Brown, *The Tooth That Nibbles the Soul: Essays on Music and Poetry* (Seattle and London: University of Washington Press, 2010), 252–61.

77. Paul de Man, *Allegories of Reading: Figural Language in Rousseau, Nietzsche, Rilke, and Proust* (New Haven, CT: Yale University Press, 1979), 187.

78. Rousseau, *Oeuvres complètes,* 2: 1231.

79. The most famous Romantic interpretation comes in E. T. A. Hoffmann's short story *Don Juan* (1813). See Ivan Nagel for the Commendatore as representative of the spatial art of the absolutist Baroque in *Autonomy and Mercy: Reflections on Mozart's Operas,* trans. Marion Faber and Ivan Nagel (Cambridge, MA: Harvard University Press, 1991), esp. 41–46 and 59–62; this reading is seconded by Michael P. Steinberg in *Listening to Reason: Culture, Subjectivity, and Nineteenth-Century Music* (Princeton, NJ: Princeton University Press, 2004), 23–39. Notable Freudian interpretations include Peter Gay, "The Father's Revenge," in *Don Giovanni: Myths of Seduction and Betrayal,* ed. Jonathan Miller (New York: Schocken Books, 1990), 70–80; and, of course, Peter Shaffer's play *Amadeus* (1981).

CHAPTER 3

1. Locke, *Human Understanding,* 274.

2. See W. R. Albury, "The Order of Ideas: Condillac's Method of Analysis as a Political Instrument in the French Revolution," in *The Politics and Rhetoric of Sci-*

entific Method, ed. John A. Schuster and Richard R. Yeo (Dordrecht, Netherlands: D. Reidel, 1986): 203–25; and Winfried Busse and Jürgen Trabant, eds., *Les Idéologues. Sémiotique, theories et politiques linguistiques pendant la Révolution francaise* (Amsterdam and Philadelphia: John Benjamins, 1986). *Idéologie* was suppressed under Napoleon, who dissolved the Écoles normales and drove Condillac's followers underground.

3. Leonard G. Ratner, *Music: The Listener's Art* (New York: McGraw-Hill, 1957), 164–77.

4. Allanbrook, "Comic Issues," 75.

5. Michel Paul Gui de Chabanon, *De la musique considerée en elle-même et dans ses rapports avec la parole,* 2d ed. (Paris: Pissot et fils, 1785); quoted in Allanbrook, *Rhythmic Gesture in Mozart,* 6.

6. Heinrich Christoph Koch, "Instrumentalmusik," in *Musikalische Lexicon* (Frankfurt am Main: August Hermann, 1802); quoted in Allanbrook, " 'Ear-Tickling Nonsense': A New Context for Musical Expression in Mozart's 'Haydn' Quartets," *St. John's Review* 38 (1988): 11.

7. Allanbrook, *Rhythmic Gesture in Mozart,* 3.

8. Ratner, *Music: The Listener's Art,* 2d ed. (New York: McGraw-Hill, 1966), 214.

9. Ratner, *Classic Music,* 9.

10. Ratner, "Topical Content in Mozart's Keyboard Sonatas," *Early Music* 19 (November 1991): 615.

11. Elaine Sisman, "Genre, Gesture, and Meaning in Mozart's 'Prague' Symphony," *Mozart Studies* 2, ed. Cliff Eisen (Oxford: Clarendon Press, 1997), 29; Jonathan Bellman, "The Hungarian Gypsies and the Poetics of Exclusion," in *The Exotic in Western Music,* ed. Jonathan Bellman (Boston: Northeastern University Press, 1998), 101.

12. Agawu, *Playing with Signs.*

13. Monelle, *Sense of Music,* 17.

14. Monelle, *Musical Topic,* 272.

15. David Lidov, *Is Language a Music?* 105–6.

16. See Hatten, *Interpreting Musical Gestures,* and Hatten, *Musical Meaning in Beethoven.*

17. Aristotle, *The "Art" of Rhetoric,* trans. John Henry Freese (Cambridge, MA: Harvard University Press, 1926), 304–5; Cicero, *De Inventione. De Optimo Genere Oratorum. Topica,* trans. H. M. Hubbell (Cambridge, MA: Harvard University Press, 1960), 408–9; Quintilian, *Institutio Oratoria,* trans. H. E. Butler (Cambridge, MA: Harvard University Press, 1921), 4: 252–53.

18. Adam Smith, *Lectures on Rhetoric and Belles Lettres,* ed. J. C. Bryce (Oxford: Clarendon Press, 1983), 174.

19. Johann David Heinichen, *Der General-Bass in der Composition* (Dresden, Germany: 1728; reprint, Hildesheim, Germany: Georg Olms Verlag, 1969), 30.

20. Johann Mattheson, *Der vollkommene Capellmeister,* trans. and ed. Ernest C.

Harriss (Ann Arbor, MI: UMI Research Press, 1981), 285–99. See Ratner, "*Ars Combinatoria*," 343–63

21. See Dreyfus, *Patterns of Invention.*

22. Mattheson, *Der vollkommene Capellmeister*, 285.

23. Antoine Arnauld and Pierre Nicole, *Logic, or The Art of Thinking*, trans. and ed. Jill Vance Buroker (Cambridge and New York: Cambridge University Press, 1996), 182–83.

24. Lamy, *L'art de parler*, 453.

25. Quoted in Peter France, *Rhetoric and Truth in France: Descartes to Diderot* (Oxford: Clarendon Press, 1972), 23.

26. François Fénelon de Salignac, *Dialogues Concerning Eloquence*, trans. William Stevenson (Glasgow: Robert and Andrew Foulis, 1750), 47.

27. "Mit einem Schein von Gründlichhkeit, zu vernünfteln, oder wortreich zu schwatzen." Immanuel Kant, *Kritik der reinen Vernunft* [B] in *Werke*, ed. Wilhelm Weischedel (Wiesbaden, Germany: Insel-Verlag, 1956), 2: 291.

28. Peter A. Hoyt, "Rhetoric and Music," *Grove Music Online* ed. L. Macy (Accessed 25 February 2007), http://www.grovemusic.com.

29. Monelle, *Sense of Music*, 17.

30. Ratner, *Listener's Art* (1957), p. 176.

31. Webster, *Haydn's "Farewell" Symphony*, 125.

32. Harold S. Powers, "Reading Mozart's Music: Text and Topic, Syntax and Sense," *Current Musicology* 57 (1995): 28.

33. William Caplin wrote, "Though Ratner and his followers seem to suggest that topic theory is rooted in the listening habits of composers and their audiences of the eighteenth and early nineteenth centuries, such an implicit claim has yet to be entirely established." Caplin, "On the Relation of Musical Topoi to Formal Function," *Eighteenth-Century Music* 2, no. 1 (2005): 113. See also Monelle, *Sense of Music*, 24–33.

34. Thomas Turino, "Signs of Imagination," 228.

35. Heartz, *Mozart's Operas*, 146.

36. Allanbrook, *Rhythmic Gesture in Mozart*, 75–77.

37. Heartz has noted similarities between the countess's arias and the Agnus Dei of the Masses in C, K. 317 and 337, in *Haydn, Mozart, and the Viennese School, 1740–1780* (New York: W. W. Norton, 1995), 664, 669.

38. Agawu, *Playing with Signs*, 20.

39. Caplin, "Musical Topoi," 124.

40. Isaiah Berlin, *Vico and Herder: Two Studies in the History of Ideas* (New York: Vintage Books, 1977), 9.

41. Lamy, *L'art de parler*, 35.

42. Dietrich Bartel, *Musica Poetica: Musical-Rhetorical Figures in German Baroque Music* (Lincoln: University of Nebraska Press, 1997), 89.

43. Alessandro Giuliani, "Vico's Rhetorical Philosophy and the New Rheto-

ric," trans. Salvatore Rotella, in *Giambattista Vico's Science of Humanity,* ed. Giorgio Tagliacozzo and Donald Phillip Verene (Baltimore and London: Johns Hopkins University Press, 1976), 35.

44. Giambattista Vico, *On the Study Methods of Our Time,* trans. Elio Gianturco (New York: Bobbs-Merrill, 1965), 14.

45. Ibid., 32.

46. Giambattista Vico, *On the Most Ancient Wisdom of the Italians Unearthed from the Origins of the Latin Language,* trans. L. M. Palmer (Ithaca, NY: Cornell University Press, 1988), 101.

47. Michael Mooney, *Vico in the Tradition of Rhetoric* (Princeton, NJ: Princeton University Press, 1985), 24.

48. Giambattista Vico, *The First New Science,* ed. and trans. Leon Pompa. (New York: Cambridge University Press, 2002), 175.

49. Giambattista Vico, *New Science,* trans. David Marsh, 3rd ed. (London: Penguin Books, 1999), 136.

50. Ibid., 191.

51. Ibid., 203.

52. For a valuable explanation of Vico's "sensory" topics, see Leon Pompa, *Vico: A Study of the "New Science"* (Cambridge: Cambridge University Press, 1990), 190–97. Hayden White has analyzed Vico's discussion of tropes in *Tropics of Discourse: Essays in Cultural Criticism* (Baltimore and London: Johns Hopkins University Press, 1978), 197–217.

53. Donald Phillip Verene, *Vico's Science of Imagination* (Ithaca, NY: Cornell University Press, 1981), 171. In his own writings on traditional rhetoric, Vico referred to the Aristotelian topics of "definitions, parts, etymology, genus, species, etc." *The Art of Rhetoric (Institutines Oratoriae, 1711–1741),* trans. and ed. Giorgio A. Pinton and Arthur W. Shippee (Amsterdam and Atlanta, GA: Rodopi, 1996), 31–34.

54. Vico, *New Science,* 146.

55. Gianfranco Cantelli, "Myth and Language in Vico," in *Giambattista Vico's Science of Humanity,* 53.

56. Naomi Cumming, *The Sonic Self: Musical Subjectivity and Signification* (Bloomington and Indianapolis: Indiana University Press, 2000), 73–74.

57. Ibid., 74.

58. Vico, *New Science,* 96, 186. For Vico, as Gary Tomlinson has shown, song transcended the evolutionary schema of Enlightenment anthropology, forming an unchanging link between primitive and modern cultures: "Song looms as a rare shared experience of prerational and rational ages. Or, to put the matter another way, song offers itself as an archetypal instance of the persistence of the primitive imagination in the modern psyche." Tomlinson, "Music and Culture: Vico's Songs: Detours at the Origins of (Ethno) Musicology," *Musical Quarterly* 83, no. 3 (1999): 358.

59. Monelle, *Sense of Music,* 33–38; Monelle, *Musical Topic,* 8–10.

60. Hatten, *Interpreting Musical Gestures*, 55–58.

61. Spitzer, "Inside Beethoven's 'Magic Square.'"

62. See Louis Hjelmslev, *Prolegomena to a Theory of Language,* trans. Francis J. Whitfield (Madison: University of Wisconsin Press, 1961), 47–60.

63. Ibid., 46.

64. Bojan Bujić, "When Is a Musette Not a Musettte? A Response to Robert S. Hatten," *Muzikološki zbornik* 42, no. 1 (2006): 165–69.

65. David Lidov, "Mind and Body in Music," in *Is Language a Music?* 157.

66. Hatten, *Musical Meaning in Beethoven*, 38.

67. See Michael Shapiro, *The Sense of Grammar: Language as Semeiotic* (Bloomington: Indiana University Press, 1983), esp. 15–21.

68. Ibid., 37, 64, 118, 292.

69. Edwin L. Battistella, *Markedness: The Evaluative Superstructure of Language* (Albany: State University of New York, 1990), 9; quoted in Hatten, *Musical Meaning in Beethoven, 37.*

70. Battistella, *The Logic of Markedness* (Oxford and New York: Oxford University Press, 1996), 64. See also Michael Shapiro, *Asymmetry: An Inquiry into the Linguistic Structure of Poetry* (Amsterdam: North Holland Publishing, 1976), 3–55.

71. Hepokoski and Darcy, *Elements of Sonata Theory*, 132–33.

72. Hatten provides a different analysis of the Picardy third, emphasizing stylistic growth, in *Musical Meaning in Beethoven*, 39–43.

73. See Lippmann, "Der Italienische Vers," 386–406. For a more detailed account of *decasillabi* in *Figaro,* see my "Unveiling Cherubino." See also Roger Parker, *Leonora's Last Act: Essays in Verdian Discourse* (Princeton, NJ: Princeton University Press, 1997), 30–32.

74. Cherubino's association with *decasillabi,* both in his own aria and in Figaro's "Non più andrai," perhaps owes to the allegorical meaning that Allanbrook ascribed to the page: "The pastoral diction and musette of 'Non so più' place Cherubino squarely in the Arcadian tradition; as Eros he presides over the couples in the opera—the indigenous deity of pastoral love." *Rhythmic Gesture in Mozart,* 97.

75. The *sdruccciolo* ("Guarda un po', mio caro Figaro"), with its additional accent, is a standard variant of the normal *verso piano* and does not affect the syllable count.

76. Henning Andersen, "Diphthongization," *Language* 48 (1972): 45, n. 23; quoted in Shapiro, *Sense of Grammar,* 94.

CHAPTER 4

1. See Susan McClary, "A Musical Dialectic from the Enlightenment: Mozart's *Piano Concerto in G Major, K. 453,* Movement 2," *Cultural Critique* 4 (Autumn 1986):

129–68; Richard Taruskin, *The Oxford History of Western Music* (New York : Oxford University Press, 2005), 2: 620–22.

2. McClary, "Musical Dialectic," 138.

3. Ibid., 159.

4. Ibid.

5. Joseph Kerman, "Mozart's Piano Concertos and Their Audience," in *On Mozart*, ed. James M. Morris (New York: Woodrow Wilson Center Press, 1994), 161.

6. Ibid., 162.

7. Powers, "Reading Mozart's Music," 29, 23.

8. See Ellen Rosand, "The Descending Tetrachord: An Emblem of Lament," *Musical Quarterly* 65, no. 3 (1979): 346–359; Peter Williams, *The Chromatic Fourth During Four Centuries of Music* (Oxford: Oxford University Press, 1997).

9. Taruskin, *Oxford History of Western Music*, 2: 614.

10. Michael P. Steinberg, *Listening to Reason: Culture, Subjectivity, and Nine-teenth-Century Music* (Princeton, NJ: Princeton University Press, 2004), 18–58.

11. Adam Smith, *Essays on Philosophical Studies*, ed. W. P. D. Wightman and J. C. Bryce (Oxford: Clarendon Press, 1990), 45–46.

12. Ibid., 66.

13. Ibid., 105.

14. Adam Smith, *The Theory of Moral Sentiments*, ed. Knud Haakonssen (Cambridge: Cambridge University Press, 2002), 15.

15. Ibid., 30.

16. The definitive study of Smith's construct remains D. D. Raphael, *The Impartial Spectator: Adam Smith's Moral Philosophy;* rev. ed. (Oxford: Clarendon Press, 2007).

17. Raphael, *Impartial Spectator*, 183.

18. Hume, *Treatise of Human Nature*, 259.

19. See Adam Smith, *Lectures on Rhetoric*, 23–25, 203–5. For Smith's position within eighteenth-century language theory, see Marcelo Dascal, "Adam Smith's Theory of Language," in *The Cambridge Companion to Adam Smith*, ed. Knud Haakonssen (Cambridge: Cambridge University Press, 2006), 80–87; and Christopher Berry, "Adam Smith's *Considerations* on Language," in *Adam Smith*, ed. Knud Haakonssen (Aldershot Hants, UK, and Brookfield, VT: Ashgate, 1998), 532–34.

20. Smith, *Considerations Concerning the First Formation of Languages*, in *Lectures on Rhetoric*, 216.

21. Ibid., 218.

22. See Otto Jesperson, *Language: Its Nature, Development, and Origin* (London: Allen & Unwin, 1922), 123; Roman Jakobson, "Shifters and Verbal Categories," in *On Language*, ed. Linda R. Waugh and Monique Monville-Burston (Cambridge, MA: Harvard University Press, 1990), 386–92; and Émile Benveniste "The Nature of Pronouns," in *Problems in General Linguistics*, trans. Mary Elizabeth Meek (Coral Gables, FL: University of Miami Press, 1971), 217–22.

23. Georg Wilhelm Friedrich Hegel, *Phenomenology of Spirit*, trans. A. V. Miller (Oxford: Oxford University Press, 1977), 60–61.

24. Ibid., 62.

25. Smith, *Considerations*, 223.

26. Ibid., 224.

27. Smith, *Essays on Philosophical Subjects*, 185.

28. Ibid., 185.

29. Ibid., 205–6.

30. Ibid., 198.

31. Ibid., 197.

32. Ibid., 197.

33. Wilhelm Seidel, "Essay von Adam Smith über die Musik. Eine Einführung," *Musiktheorie* 15, no. 3 (2000): 195–204. As Nikolaus de Palézieux explained, "In der sinnlichen Wirkung obsiegt die vokale, in der Befriedigung des Intellekts die instrumentale Musik. Und: die letztere Gattung vermag den Geist vollständig zu beanspruchen, sie wird der Wissenschaft gleichgesetz, erscheint mithin als intellektuells Organon." Palézieux, *Die Lehre vom Ausdruck in der englischen Musikästhetik des 18. Jahrhunderts* (Hamburg: Verlag der Musikalienhandlung Karl Dieter Wagner, 1981), 178. See also Wilhelm Seidel, "Zählt die Musik zu den imitative Künsten? Zur Revision der Nachahmungsästhetik durch Adam Smith," in *Die Sprache der Musik. Festschrift Klaus Wolfgang Niemöller zum 60. Geburtstag am 21. Juli 1989*, ed. Jobst Peter Fricke, with Bram Gätjen and Manuel Gervink (Regensburg, Germany: Gustav Bosse Verlag, 1989), 495–511.

34. Smith, *Theory of Moral Sentiments*, 27.

35. Ibid., 45.

36. Smith, *Essays on Philosophical Subjects*, 192.

37. Ibid., 204–5.

38. "Ich halte sie beyde für Concerten, welche schwizen machen.—Doch hat in der schwürrigkeit das ex B den Vorzug vor dem ex D." Mozart, *Briefe und Aufzeichnungen*, 3: 315. Mario Mercado has explained the technical challenges of K. 450 in *The Evolution of Mozart's Pianistic Style* (Carbondale: Southern Illinois University Press, 1992), 83: "Striking are the extensive passages for the left hand that show the same degree of difficulty as those for the right hand, as well as passages in the last movement . . . calling for an especially adroit cross-hand technique in patterns of unusual rhythmic complexity."

39. David Lidov has summarized the traditional roles of the wind and string choirs in his essay "The Allegretto of Beethoven's Seventh," in *Is Language a Music?* 50: "Though strings can be forceful and winds—at least in solo lines—can be lyrical, the affinities exploited here are more ready to hand; the strings having an advantage in flexibility, the winds in power."

40. Monelle, *Musical Topic*, 3.

41. Daniel Leeson and Robert Levin give precise statistics on the length and

proportion of all Mozart's concerto first movements in "On the Authenticity of K. Anh. C 14.01 (297 b), a Symphonia Concertante for Four Winds and Orchestra," in *Mozart-Jahrbuch 1976/77* (Kassel, Germany: Bärenreiter, 1978), 70–96.

42. Mozart used the 3-4-4♯-5 cell frequently in *arie d'affetto,* such as Belmonte's B-major aria, "Wenn der Freude Tränen fliessen" *(Die Entführung aus dem Serail)* or Ferrando's "Un'aura amorosa" *(Così fan tutte).* The identical cell also begins Tamino's ode to his flute, "Wie stark ist nicht dein Zauberton!" (Act 1 finale, *Die Zauberflöte*).

43. See Leeson and Levin, "Authenticity," 90.

CHAPTER 5

1. Georg Reichert, "Mozarts Credo-Messen und ihre Vorläufer," in *Mozart-Jahrbuch 1955* (Salzburg, Austria: Salzburg Drückerei, 1955), 117–44.

2. Otto Jahn, *Life of Mozart,* vol. 1, trans. Pauline D. Townsend (London: Novello, Ewer & Co., 1882), 247.

3. Bruce C. MacIntyre, *The Viennese Concerted Mass of the Early Classic Period* (Ann Arbor: University of Michigan Research Press, 1984), 319.

4. Thrasybulos Georgiades, *Music and Language: The Rise of Western Music as Exemplified in Settings of the Mass,* trans. Marie Louise Göllner (Cambridge: Cambridge University Press, 1982), 84.

5. Friedrich Nicolai, *Beschreibung einer Reise durch Deutschland und die Schweiz,* vol. 1 (Berlin: Stettin, 1784); quoted in Heartz, *Haydn, Mozart, and the Viennese School,* 16–17.

6. Karl Fellerer, *Die Kirchenmusik W. A. Mozarts* (Laaber: Laaber-Verlag, 1985), 147–96.

7. Jean H. Hagstrum, *The Sister Arts: The Tradition of English Literary Pictorialism and English Poetry from Dryden to Gray* (Chicago: University of Chicago Press, 1958), 101.

8. Wellbery, *Lessing's "Laocoon,"* 36.

9. See Fellerer, *Die Kirchenmusik,* 31–46; and Reinhard G. Pauly, "The Reforms of Church Music under Joseph II," *The Musical Quarterly* 43 (1957): 372–82.

10. See T. C. W. Blanning, *Joseph II* (London and New York: Longman, 1994), 40–55, esp. 43–44.

11. Lodovico Antonio Muratori, *Della regolata divozione de' cristiani,* in *Dal Muratori al Cesarotti,* ed. Giorgo Falco and Fiorenzo Forti (Milan: Riccardo Ricciardi Editore, 1960), 1: 952.

12. See Reichert, "Mozarts Credo-Messen," 121–22.

13. See David F. Cram and Jaap Maat, "Universal Language Schemes in the 17th Century," in *History of the Language Sciences. Geschichte der Sprachwissen-*

schaften. Histoire des sciences du langage, vol. 1, ed. Sylvain Auroux, E. F. K. Koerner, Hans-Josef Niederehe, and Kees Versteegh (Berlin and New York: De Gruyter Mouton, 2000), 1030–43.

14.   Leibniz, *De ipsa natura,* §11, and *Système nouveau de la nature et de la communication des substances, aussi bien que de l'union qu'il y a entre l'âme et le corps.* See Gottfried Wilhelm Leibniz, *Philosophical Essays,* ed. Roger Ariew and Daniel Garber (Indianapolis: Hacket, 1989), 160–61, 138–45.

15.   *Monadologie,* §7, 11. Leibniz, *Philosophical Essays,* 213–14.

16.   Ibid., 44.

17.   Ibid., 45.

18.   Gottfried Wilhelm Leibniz, *New Essays on Human Understanding,* trans. Peter Remnant and Jonathan Bennett (Cambridge: Cambridge University Press, 1996), 300. For Leibniz's dispute with Locke, see Aarsleff, *From Locke to Saussure,* 42–83.

19.   Immanuel Kant, *Critique of Pure Reason,* trans. Norman Kemp Smith (New York: St. Martin's Press, 1965), 55.

20.   See Marshall Brown, "Mozart and After: The Revolution in Musical Consciousness," *Critical Inquiry* 7 (1981): 689–706; Rose Rosengard Subotnik, "Evidence of a Critical Worldview in Mozart's Last Three Symphonies," in *Developing Variations: Style and Ideology in Western Music* (Minneapolis: University of Minnesota Press, 1991), 98–111; Sisman, "Learned Style,"; and Sisman, *Mozart: The "Jupiter" Symphony* (Cambridge: Cambridge University Press, 1993), 9–20. James Webster has extended the Kantian reading to the period 1780–1815, which he provocatively dubbed "the age of the Kantian sublime in music." Webster, "Between Enlightenment and Romanticism in Music History: 'First Viennese Modernism' and the Delayed Nineteenth Century," *19th-Century Music* 25, no. 2/3 (Autumn 2001—Spring 2002), 126.

21.   See Katie Terezakis, *The Immanent Word: The Turn to Language in German Philosophy, 1759–1801* (New York and London: Routledge, 2007), 125–55; Hans Irmscher, "Die geschichtsphilosophische Kontroverse zwischen Kant und Herder," in *Hamann-Kant-Herder.* Acta des vierten Internationalen Hamann-Kolloquiums im Herder-Institut zu Marburg/Lahn 1985, ed. Bernhard Gajek (Frankfurt am Main: Verlag Peter Lang, 1987), 111–92; and Dimitrios Markis, "Das Problem der Sprache bei Kant," in *Dimensionen der Sprache in der Philosophie des Deutschen Idealismus,* ed. Brigitte Scheer and Günter Wohlfart (Würzburg, Germany: Königshausen & Neumann, 1982), 110–54.

22.   See Benjamin W. Redekop, "Reid's Influence in Britain, Germany, France, and America," in *The Cambridge Companion to Thomas Reid,* ed. Terence Cuneo and René van Woudenberg (Cambridge: Cambridge University Press, 2004), 313–36; Manfred Kuehn, *Scottish Common Sense in Germany, 1768–1800: A Contribution to the History of Critical Philosophy* (Kingston: McGill-Queen's University Press, 1987);

and Kuehn, "The Early Reception of Reid, Oswald and Beattie in Germany, 1768–1800," *Journal of the History of Philosophy* 21 (October 1983): 479–96.

23. Terence Cuneo and René van Woudenberg, introduction to *The Cambridge Companion to Thomas Reid*, ed. Terence Cuneo and René van Woudenberg (Cambridge: Cambridge University Press, 2004), 6.

24. Thomas Reid, *An Inquiry into the Human Mind on the Principles of Common Sense*, ed. Derek R. Brookes (Edinburgh: Edinburgh University Press, 1997), 154.

25. Ibid., 43, 171.

26. Ibid., 193, 197.

27. Reid, *Essays on the Intellectual Powers of Man* (Cambridge, MA: MIT Press, 1969), 26.

28. Ibid., 277.

29. Ibid., 26–27.

30. Ibid., 612.

31. Ulrich Ricken, *Linguistics, Anthropology, and Philosophy*, 25.

32. Alfred Einstein, *Mozart: His Character, His Work*, trans. Arthur Mendel and Nathan Broder (London: Oxford University Press, 1945), 339.

33. Reichert, "Mozarts Credo-Messen," 122–23, 137.

34. Einstein, *Mozart*, 339.

35. See *Neue Mozart-Ausgabe*, Ser. I, Abt. 1/1, 3, ed. Walter Senn (Kassel, Germany: Bärenreiter, 1980), xiv–xv. Daniel Heartz has noted that the final notes of the Credo motto (G-A) appear in reverse, turning Cre-do . . . De-um into Cre-do . . . um-De. Heartz detected "another example of an intended impertinence from the composer who could not stop inverting the letters of his own name and indulging in many other verbal pranks." Heartz, *Haydn, Mozart, and the Viennese School*, 658.

36. Mark Evan Bonds, "Haydn, Laurence Sterne, and the Origins of Musical Irony," *Journal of the American Musicological Society* 44, no. 1 (1991): 57. For another view of Haydn's irony, see Daniel Chua, *Absolute Music*, 209–17.

37. Denis Diderot, *"This Is Not a Story" and Other Stories*, trans. P. N. Furbank (Columbia: University of Missouri Press, 1991), 17.

38. Diderot, *Jacques the Fatalist*, trans. David Coward (Oxford: Oxford University Press, 1999), 220.

39. Ibid., 42.

40. Ibid., 208.

41. Diderot, *"Rameau's Nephew" and "D'Alembert's Dream,"* trans. L. W. Tancock (Middlesex, UK: Penguin Books, 1971), p. 102.

42. Diderot, *Selected Writings on Art and Literature*, trans. Geoffrey Bremner (London: Penguin Books, 1994), 101.

43. Johann Christoph Stockman, *Critischer Entwurf einer auserlesenen Bibliothek für Liebhaber der Philosophie und schönen Wissenschaften. Zum Gebrauch akademischer*

Vorlesungen, vierte verbesserte und viel vermehrte Auflage (Berlin, 1771); quoted in Heartz, *Haydn, Mozart, and the Viennese School,* 349.

44. Le Guin, *Boccherini's Body,* 136.

45. Agawu, *Playing with Signs,* 86–91.

46. Diderot, *"Rameau's Nephew,"* 105.

47. Rosenfeld, *Revolution in Language,* 47.

48. See Dietrich Bartel, *Musica Poetica: Musical-Rhetorical Figures in German Baroque Music* (Lincoln: University of Nebraska Press, 1997).

49. See Lippmann, "Der italienische Vers," 327–30, 356–57.

50. John Searle, *Expression and Meaning: Studies in the Theory of Speech Acts* (Cambridge: Cambridge University Press, 1973), 13.

51. Shoshana Felman, *The Literary Speech Act: Don Juan with J. L. Austin, or Seduction in Two Languages,* trans. Catherine Porter (Ithaca, NY: Cornell University Press, 1983), 53.

CHAPTER 6

1. Gotthold Ephraim Lessing, *Laokoon, oder Über die Grenzen der Malerei und Poesie,* in *Werke,* vol. 6, *Kunsttheoretische und kunsthistorische Schriften,* ed. Albert von Schirnding (Munich: C. Hanser, 1974), 94.

2. Herder, *Werke,* vol. 2: *Schriften zur Ästhetik und Literatur, 1767–1781,* ed. Gunter E. Grimm (1993), 171.

3. Ibid., 163.

4. Dascal, "Adam Smith's Theory of Language," 81.

5. See Karl Braunschweig, "Gradus ad Parnassum: A Jesuit Music Treatise," *In Theory Only* 7, no. 8 (1994): 35–38.

6. See Heartz, "Thomas Attwood's Lessons"; and Eggebrecht, *Versuch über die Wiener Klassik.*

7. Warren Kirkendale, *Fugue and Fugato in Rococco and Classical Chamber Music,* trans. Margaret Bent and Warren Kirkendale(Durham, NC: Duke University Press, 1979), 181.

8. See Dreyfus, *Patterns of Invention,* 1–32.

9. See appendix 1 to the NMA edition, I: 1/1/v, ed. Monika Holl and Karl-Heinz Köhler (Kassel, Germany: Bärenreiter, 1983), 169–70.

10. Bernard Lamy, *L'art de parler,* 35. For a discussion of the pictorial tradition in relation to music, see my "Beethoven and the *Ut Pictura Poësis* Tradition," *Beethoven Forum* 12, no. 2 (2005): 113–49.

11. Kaspar Stieler, *Teutsche Sekretariat-Kunst* (Nuremburg, Germany: J. Hofmann, 1673), 1: 234; quoted in Joachim Dyck, *Ticht-Kunst. Deutsche Barockpoetik und rhetorische Tradition* (Tübingen, Germany: M. Niemeyer, 1991), 66.

12.   James Harris, *Hermes, or A Philosophical Inquiry Concerning Language and Philosophical Grammar* (London: H. Woodfall, 1751), 399.

13.   Sidonie Clauss, "John Wilkins's Essay Toward a Real Character: Its Place in the Seventeenth-Century Episteme," in *Language and the History of Thought*, ed. Nancy Struever (Rochester, NY: University of Rochester Press, 1995), 42.

14.   Nicolas Beauzée, "Langage," in *Encyclopédie ou Dictionnaire raisonné des sciences, des arts et des métiers*, ed. Jean le Rond d'Alembert and Denis Diderot (Stuttgart-Bad, Cannstatt, Germany: Frommann, 1967), 9: 242.

15.   Claude Favre de Vaugles, *La Préface des "Remarques sur la langue Françoise* [1646]," ed. Zygmont Marzys (Geneva: Droz, 1984), 50. As Rémy Saisselin has explained, "It is through the notion of decorum that the aesthetic and the ethical join or meet in the *ancien régime,* and one may say that bienséance in the realm of social behavior is nothing less than the principle of imitation outside the realm of art." Saisselin, *The Rule of Reason and the Ruses of the Heart: A Philosophical Dictionary of Classical French Criticism, Critics, and Aesthetic Issues* (Cleveland: Press of Case Western Reserve University, 1970), 48.

16.   See W. S. Howells, *Eighteenth-Century British Logic and Rhetoric* (Princeton, NJ: Princeton University Press, 1971), 144–256.

17.   Thomas M. Conley, *Rhetoric in the European Tradition* (New York: Longman, 1990), 152.

18.   Alan Tyson, *Mozart: Studies of the Autograph Scores* (Cambridge, MA: Harvard University Press, 1987), 19, 153–56. The autograph, which vanished during World War II, resurfaced in the Biblioteka Jagiellonska, Kraków, after the publication of the NMA edition (1975). Mozart had actually used the interlocking-fourth motive earlier in *Idomeneo* (1781) for the gavotte of the Cretan women, a theme he later recycled in the finale of the Concerto in C, K. 503. The chronological proximity of K. 427 and 449, however, together with the Fuxian quality of the concerto theme, make the Cum Sancto Spirtus the likelier source.

19.   See John Irving, *Mozart's Piano Concertos* (Burlington, VT: Ashgate, 2003), 79–80. On the importance of variation in the finale of K. 449, see Charles Rosen, *The Classical Style: Haydn, Mozart, and Beethoven* (New York: Viking Press, 1972), 219; and David Grayson, *Mozart: Piano Concerto No. 20 in D Minor, K. 466, and Piano Concerto No. 21 in C Major, K. 467* (Cambridge: Cambridge University Press, 1998), 73.

20.   Arthur Hutchings, *A Companion to Mozart's Piano Concertos* (Oxford: Oxford University Press, 1948), 87.

21.   See Simon Keefe, " 'An entirely special manner': Mozart's Piano Concerto No. 144 in E flat, K. 449, and the Stylistic Implications of Confrontation," *Music and Letters* 82, no. 4 (2001), 559–81; and Keefe, *Mozart's Piano Concertos: Dramatic Dialogue in the Age of Enlightenment* (Rochester, NY: Boydell Press, 2001), 64–65.

22.   Rosen, *Classical Style,* 120.

23.   Karol Berger, "The First-Movement Punctuation Form in Mozart's Piano

Concertos," in *Mozart's Piano Concertos: Text, Context, Interpretation*, ed. Neal Zaslaw (Ann Arbor: University of Michigan Press, 1996), 244–46.

24. Allanbrook, "Comic Issues," 82.

25. See Bonds, *Wordless Rhetoric*, 90–118.

26. The outer movements of K. 449 would seem to exemplify Karol Berger's dichotomy between Mozart's late eighteenth-century conception of music as a linear, unidirectional process, and the essentially atemporal, cyclical conception of Bach's era; *Bach's Cycle, Mozart's Arrow: An Essay on the Origins of Musical Modernity* (Berkeley: 2007).

27. See Ratner, "*Ars combinatoria.*"

28. Isaac Newton, *Opticks, or A Treatise of the Reflections, Refractions, Inflections and Colours of Light* (New York: Dover, 1952), 404–5.

29. Jean le Rond d'Alembert, *Preliminary Discourse to the Encyclopedia of Diderot*, trans. Richard N. Schwab (Indianapolis and New York: Bobbs-Merrill, 1963), 22.

30. Condillac, *Oeuvres philosophiques*, 2: 419.

31. Vico, *New Science*, 488.

32. Jean-Jacques Rousseau, *Essay on the Origin of Languages and Writings Related to Music*, trans. John T. Scott (Hanover, NH, and London: University Press of New England, 1998), 68, 72.

33. Ibid., 184.

34. Ibid., 102.

35. Ibid., 118–19.

36. See Vico, *New Science*, 483–91.

37. Ibid., 194.

38. See *De l'art d'écrire* in Condillac, *Oeuvres philosophiques*, 1: 604–5; quote from *Traité des systêmes* in *Oeuvres philosophiques*, 1: 205.

39. See Rousseau, *Origin of Languages*, 304–17 (chaps. 8–11).

40. See Moser, "Jean-Georges Sulzer," 931–41.

41. Nancy Kovaleff Baker and Thomas Christensen, trans., *Aesthetics and the Art of Musical Composition in the German Enlightenment: Selected Writings of Johann Georg Sulzer and Heinrich Christoph Koch* (Cambridge: Cambridge University Press, 1995), 61.

42. Johann George Sulzer, "Observations sur l'influence réciproque de la raison sur le langage et du langage sur la raison," in *Histoire de l'académie royale des sciences et des belles lettres de Berlin: avec les mémoires pour la même année, tirez des registres de cette Académie*, vol. 23 (Berlin: Ambroise Haude, 1768), 431–32.

43. Ibid., 430–31.

44. Thomas Bauman, *W. A. Mozart: "Die Entführung aus dem Serail,"* (Cambridge: Cambridge University Press, 1987), 52. On the genesis of the quartet, see pp. 21, 50–52.

45.   Head, *Mozart's Turkish Music*, 3.

46.   See Bauman, *"Die Entführung,"* 12–17; and Mozart's letter of 26 September 1781 in Emily Anderson, trans., *The Letters of Mozart and His Family* (London: Macmillan, 1985), 768–70.

47.   George Berkeley, "The Theory of Vision Vindicated and Explained," in *Philosophical Works*, 291.

48.   Ibid., 82.

49.   Heartz discusses this opposition in *Mozart's Operas*, 145–46.

50.   The ballroom scene of *Don Giovanni* demonstrates both mechanisms: the 3/4 minuet and 2/4 contredanse combine syntagmatically, as alternate groupings within the larger period; the 3/4 minuet and 6/8 *Teutsche* combine paradigmatically, as duple and triple diminutions of the individual measure.

51.   Susan McClary, "Musical Dialectic"; Norbert Elias, *Mozart: Portrait of a Genius*, trans. Edmund Jephcott (Berkeley and Los Angeles: University of California Press, 1993).

52.   Julia Kristeva, *Revolution in Poetic Language*, trans. Margaret Waller (New York: Columbia University Press, 1984), 59.

53.   Ibid., 191.

54.   Fredric Jameson, *The Prison-House of Language: A Critical Account of Structuralism and Russian Formalism* (Princeton, NJ: Princeton University Press, 1972), 214–16.

EPILOGUE

1.   See M. H. Abrams, *The Mirror and the Lamp: Romantic Theory and the Critical Tradition* (New York: Oxford University Press, 1953).

2.   See Mary Sue Morrow, *German Music Criticism in the Late Eighteenth Century: Aesthetic Issues in Instrumental Music* (Cambridge: Cambridge University Press, 1997); Carl Dahlhaus, *The Idea of Absolute Music*, trans. Roger Lustig (Chicago: University of Chicago Press, 1989); Neubauer, *Emancipation of Music*; and Bellamy Hosler, *Changing Views of Instrumental Music in 18th-Century Germany* (Ann Arbor, MI: UMI Research Press, 1981).

3.   Maniates, *"Sonate, que me veux-tu?"* 136.

4.   E. T. A. Hoffmann, *E. T. A. Hoffmann's Musical Writings*, trans. Martyn Clark, ed. David Charlton (Cambridge: Cambridge University Press, 1989), 96, 102.

Bibliography

Aarsleff, Hans. *From Locke to Saussure: Essays on the Study of Language and Intellectual History.* Minneapolis: University of Minnesota Press, 1982.

———. "The History of Linguistics and Professor Chomsky." *Language* 46, no. 3 (1970): 570–85.

Abert, Hermann. "The G minor Symphony." In *Mozart: Symphony in G Minor, K. 550,* ed. Nathan Broder, 69–82. New York: W. W. Norton, 1976.

Adler, Hans. "Fundus Animae—der Grund der Seele: Zur Gnoseologie des Dunklen in der Aufklärung." *Deutsche Vierteljahrschrift für Literaturwissenschaft und Geistesgeschichte* 62 (1988): 197–220.

Agawu, V. Kofi. *Playing with Signs: A Semiotic Interpretation of Classic Music.* Princeton, NJ: Princeton University Press, 1991.

Albury, W. R. "The Order of Ideas: Condillac's Method of Analysis as a Political Instrument in the French Revolution." In *The Politics and Rhetoric of Scientific Method,* ed. John A. Schuster and Richard R. Yeo, 203–25. Dordrecht, Netherlands: D. Reidel, 1986.

Algarotti, Francesco. *Saggi.* Ed. Giovanni da Pozzo. Bari, Italy: Giuseppe Laterza e Figli, 1963.

Allanbrook, Wye Jamison. "Comic Issues in Mozart's Piano Concertos." In
    Mozart's Piano Concertos: Text, Context, Interpretation, ed. Neal Zaslaw, 75–
    106. Ann Arbor: University of Michigan Press, 1996.
———. " 'Ear-Tickling Nonsense': A New Context for Musical Expression
    in Mozart's 'Haydn' Quartets." *St. John's Review* 38 (1988): 1–24.
———. *Rhythmic Gesture in Mozart: "Le nozze di Figaro" and "Don Giovanni."*
    Chicago: University of Chicago Press, 1983.
———. "Two Threads through the Labyrinth: Topic and Process in the First
    Movements of K. 332 and K. 333." In *Convention in Eighteenth- and Nineteenth-
    Century Music: Essays in Honor of Leonard G. Ratner*, ed. Wye Jamison Allan-
    brook, Janet M. Levy, and William P. Mahrt, 125–71. Stuyvesant, NY: Pen-
    dragon, 1992.
Andersen, Henning. "Diphthongization." *Language* 48 (1972): 11–50.
Anderson, Emily, trans. *The Letters of Mozart and His Family.* London: Macmillan,
    1985.
Aristotle. *The "Art" of Rhetoric.* Trans. John Henry Freese. Cambridge, MA:
    Harvard University Press, 1926.
Atherton, Margaret. *Berkeley's Revolution in Vision.* Ithaca, NY: Cornell Univer-
    sity Press, 1990.
Auroux, Sylvain. *La sémiotique des encyclopédistes. Essai d'épistémologie historique
    des sciences du langage.* Paris: Payot, 1979.
Baker, Malcolm. "Odzooks! A Man of Stone: Earth, Heaven, and Hell in
    Eighteenth-Century Tomb Sculpture." In *"Don Giovanni": Myths of Seduction
    and Betrayal*, ed. Jonathan Miller, 62–69. New York: Schocken Books, 1990.
Baker, Nancy Kovaleff, and Thomas Christensen, trans. *Aesthetics and the Art
    of Musical Composition in the German Enlightenment: Selected Writings of Johann
    Georg Sulzer and Heinrich Christoph Koch.* Cambridge: Cambridge University
    Press, 1995.
Bartel, Dietrich. *Musica Poetica: Musical-Rhetorical Figures in German Baroque
    Music* (Lincoln: University of Nebraska Press, 1997).
Barth, George. *The Pianist as Orator: Beethoven and the Transformation of Keyboard
    Style.* Ithaca, NY: Cornell University Press, 1992.
Bartha, Dénes. "On Beethoven's Thematic Structure." *Musical Quarterly* 56, no. 4
    (1970): 759–78. Reprinted in *The Creative World of Beethoven*, ed. Paul Henry
    Lang (New York: W. W. Norton, 1971), 257–76.
Bätschmann, Oskar. "Pygmalion als Betrachter: Die Rezeption von Plastik und
    Malerei in der zweiten Hälften des 18. Jahrhunderts." In *Der Betrachter ist im
    Bild: Kunstwissenschaft und Rezeptionsästhetik*, ed. Wolfgang Kemp, 183–224.
    Berlin: Reimer, 1992.
Battistella, Edwin L. *The Logic of Markedness.* Oxford and New York: Oxford Uni-
    versity Press, 1996.

———. *Markedness: The Evaluative Superstructure of Language.* Albany: State University of New York Press, 1990.

Bauman, Thomas. *W. A. Mozart: "Die Entführung aus dem Serail."* Cambridge: Cambridge University Press, 1987.

Baumgarten, Alexander Gottlieb. *Reflections on Poetry: Meditationes philosophicae de nonnullis ad poema pertimentibus.* Trans. Karl Aschenbrenner and William B. Holtner. Berkeley and Los Angeles: University of California Press, 1954.

———. *Theoretische Ästhetik. Die grundlegenden Abschnitte aus der "Aesthetica."* Trans. Hans Rudolf Schweizer. Hamburg: Felix Meiner Verlag, 1983.

Beauzée, Nicolas. "Langage." In *Encyclopédie ou Dictionnaire raisonné des sciences, des arts et des métiers,* ed. Jean le Rond d'Alembert and Denis Diderot. 29 vols. Stuttgart-Bad, Cannstatt, Germany: Frommann, 1967.

Beghin, Tom. "Haydn as Orator: A Rhetorical Analysis of His Keyboard Sonata in D Major, Hob. XVI: 42." In *Haydn and His World,* ed. Elaine Sisman, 201–54. Princeton, NJ: Princeton University Press, 1997.

Beiser, Frederick C. *Enlightenment, Revolution, and Romanticism: The Genesis of Modern German Political Thought, 1790–1800.* Cambridge, MA: Harvard University Press, 1992.

Bellman, Jonathan. "The Hungarian Gypsies and the Poetics of Exclusion." In *The Exotic in Western Music,* ed. Jonathan Bellman, 74–103. Boston: Northeastern University Press, 1998.

Benveniste, Émile. *Problems in General Linguistics.* Trans. Mary Elizabeth Meek. Coral Gables, FL: University of Miami Press, 1971.

Berger, Karol. *Bach's Cycle, Mozart's Arrow: An Essay on the Origins of Musical Modernity.* Berkeley: University of California Press, 2007.

———. "The First-Movement Punctuation Form in Mozart's Piano Concertos." In *Mozart's Piano Concertos: Text, Context, Interpretation,* ed. Neal Zaslaw, 239–60. Ann Arbor: University of Michigan Press, 1996.

Berkeley, George. *Philosophical Works Including the Works on Vision.* Ed. Michael R. Ayers. London: Rowman & Littlefield, 2000.

Berlin, Isaiah. *Vico and Herder: Two Studies in the History of Ideas.* New York: Vintage Books, 1977.

Bernstein, Leonard. *The Unanswered Question: Six Talks at Harvard.* Cambridge, MA: Harvard University Press, 1976.

Berry, Christopher. "Adam Smith's *Considerations* on Language." In *Adam Smith,* ed. Knud Haakonssen, 532–34. Aldershot Hants, UK, and Brookfield, VT: Ashgate, 1998.

Blanning, T. C. W. *Joseph II.* London and New York: Longman, 1994.

Bonds, Mark Evan. "Haydn, Laurence Sterne, and the Origins of Musical Irony." *Journal of the American Musicological Society* 44, no. 1 (1991): 57–91.

———. *Wordless Rhetoric: Musical Form and the Metaphor of the Oration*. Cambridge, MA: Harvard University Press, 1991.

Brandl-Risi, Bettina. "Der Pygmalion-Mythos im Musiktheater—Verzeichnis der Werke." In *Pygmalion. Die Geschichte des Mythos in der abendländischen Kultur*, ed. Mathias Mayer and Gerhard Neumann, 665–733. Freiburg, Germany: Rombach, 1997.

Braunbehrens, Volkmar. *Mozart in Vienna, 1781–1791*. Trans. Timothy Bell. New York: Grove Weidenfeld, 1990.

Braunschweig, Karl. "Gradus ad Parnassum: A Jesuit Music Treatise." *In Theory Only* 7, no. 8 (1994): 35–58.

———. "The Metaphor of Music as a Language in the Enlightenment: Towards a Cultural History of Eighteenth-Century Music Theory." Ph.D. diss., University of Michigan, 1997.

Breitinger, Johann Jacob. *Critische Dichtkunst*. Zurich: Conrad Brell, 1740. Reprint, Stuttgart, Germany: J. B. Metzlersche Verlagsbuchhandlung, 1966.

Broadie, Alexander. "Sympathy and the Impartial Spectator." In *The Cambridge Companion to Adam Smith*, ed. Knud Haakonssen, 158–88. Cambridge: Cambridge University Press, 2006.

Brown, Marshall. *The Tooth That Nibbles the Soul: Essays on Music and Poetry*. Seattle and London: University of Washington Press, 2010.

Brown-Montesano, Kristi. *Understanding the Women of Mozart's Operas*. Berkeley and Los Angeles: University of California Press, 2007.

Bucciarelli, Melania. *Italian Opera and European Theater, 1680–1720. Plots, Performers, Dramaturgies*. Turnhout, Belgium: Brepols, 2000.

Bujić, Bojan. "When Is a Musette Not a Musettte? A Response to Robert S. Hatten." *Muzikološki zbornik* 42, no. 1 (2006): 165–69.

Busse, Winfried, and Jürgen Trabant, eds. *Les Idéologues. Sémiotique, theories et politiques linguistiques pendant la Révolution francaise*. Philadelphia: John Benjamins, 1986.

Calcagno, Mauro. " 'Imitar col canto chi parla': Monteverdi and the Creation of a Language for Musical Theater." *Journal of the American Musicological Society* 55 (2002): 383–431.

Cantelli, Gianfranco. "Myth and Language in Vico." In *Giambattista Vico's Science of Humanity*, ed. Giorgio Tagliacozza and Donald Phillip Verene, 47–63. Baltimore: Johns Hopkins University Press, 1976.

Caplin, William. "On the Relation of Musical Topoi to Formal Function." *Eighteenth-Century Music* 2, no. 1 (2005): 113–24.

Cassirer, Ernst. *The Philosophy of the Enlightenment*. Trans. Fritz C. A. Koelln and James P. Pettegrove. Princeton, NJ: Princeton University Press, 1951.

Cerruti, Mario. "Parini e il sensismo." In *L'amabil rito: società e cultura nella*

Milano di Parini, vol. 1, ed. Gennaro Barbarisi et al., 583–88. Milan, Italy: Cisalpino, 2000.

Cesarotti, Melchiore. *Saggio sulla filosofia delle lingue.* Ed. Ugo Perolino. Pescara, Italy: Edizioni Campus, 2001.

Chabanon, Michel Paul Gui de. *De la musique considerée en elle-même et dans ses rapports avec la parole.* 2d ed. Paris: Pissot et fils, 1785.

Chappell, Vere. "Locke's Theory of Ideas." In *The Cambridge Companion to Locke,* ed. Vere Chappell, 26–55. Cambridge: Cambridge University Press, 1994.

Chastellux, François J. *Essai sur l'union de la poésie et de la musique.* Paris: La Haye, 1765.

Chomsky, Noam. *Aspects of the Theory of Syntax.* Cambridge, MA: MIT Press, 1965.

———. *Cartesian Linguistics: A Chapter in the History of Rationalist Thought.* New York: Harper & Row, 1966.

———. *Knowledge of Language: Its Nature, Origin, and Use.* New York: Praeger, 1986.

———. *Topics in the Theory of Generative Grammar.* The Hague and Paris: Mouton, 1966.

Chua, Daniel. *Absolute Music and the Construction of Meaning.* Cambridge: Cambridge University Press, 1999.

Cicero, Marcus Tullio. *De Inventione. De Optimo Genere Oratorum. Topica.* Trans. H. M. Hubbell. Cambridge, MA: Harvard University Press, 1960.

Clauss, Sidonie. "John Wilkins's Essay Toward a Real Character: Its Place in the Seventeenth-Century Episteme." In *Language and the History of Thought,* ed. Nancy Struever, 27–49. Rochester, NY: University of Rochester Press, 1995.

Condillac, Etienne Bonnot de. *Logique/Logic.* Trans. W. R. Albury. New York: Abaris Books, 1980.

———. *Oeuvres philosophiques de Condillac.* Ed. Georges le Roy. 3 vols. Paris: Presses Universitaires de France, 1947–51.

Conley, Thomas M. *Rhetoric in the European Tradition.* New York: Longman, 1990.

Cram, David F., and Jaap Maat. "Universal Language Schemes in the 17th Century." In *History of the Language Sciences. Geschichte der Sprachwissenschaften. Histoire des sciences du langage,* vol. 1, ed. Sylvain Auroux, E. F. K. Koerner, Hans-Josef Niederehe, Kees Versteegh, 1030–43. Berlin and New York: De Gruyter Mouton, 2000.

Crutchfield, Will. "The Prosodic Appoggiatura in the Music of Mozart and His Contemporaries." *Journal of the American Musicological Society* 42, no. 2 (1989): 229–74.

Cumming, Naomi. *The Sonic Self: Musical Subjectivity and Signification.* Bloomington and Indianapolis: Indiana University Press, 2000.

Cuneo, Terence, and René van Woudenberg. Introduction to *The Cambridge Companion to Thomas Reid*, ed. Terence Cuneo and René van Woudenberg, 1–30. Cambridge: Cambridge University Press, 2004.

Dahlhaus, Carl. "Romantische Musikästhetik und Wiener Klassik." *Archiv für Musikwissenschaft* 29 (1972): 167–81.

d'Alembert, Jean le Rond. *Preliminary Discourse to the Encyclopedia of Diderot.* Trans. Richard N. Schwab. Indianapolis and New York: Bobbs-Merrill, 1963.

Da Ponte, Lorenzo. *Il Don Giovanni.* Ed. Giovanna Gronda. Turin, Italy: Einaudi, 1995.

Dascal, Marcelo. "Adam Smith's Theory of Language." In *The Cambridge Companion to Adam Smith*, ed. Knud Haakonssen, 80–87. Cambridge: Cambridge University Press, 2006.

———. *Leibniz, Language, Signs, and Thought: A Collection of Essays.* Amsterdam and Philadelphia: John Benjamins, 1987.

Derrida, Jacques. *The Archaeology of the Frivolous: Reading Condillac.* Trans. John P. Leavey Jr. Pittsburgh: Duquesne University Press, 1980.

Descartes, René. *The Philosophical Works of Descartes.* Trans. Elizabeth S. Haldane and G. R. T. Ross. 2 vols. Cambridge: Cambridge University Press, 1973.

Deutsch, Otto Erich. *Mozart: A Documentary Biography.* Trans. Eric Blom, Peter Branscombe, and Jeremy Noble. Stanford, CA: Stanford University Press, 1965.

Diderot, Denis. *Jacques the Fatalist.* Trans. David Coward. Oxford: Oxford University Press, 1999.

———. *Oeuvres completes.* Ed. Herbert Dieckmann, Jean Fabre, and Jacques Proust, with Jean Varloot. 10 vols. Paris: Hermann, 1975–78.

———. *"Rameau's Nephew" and "D'Alembert's Dream."* Trans. L. W. Tancock. Middlesex, UK: Penguin Books, 1966.

———. *Selected Writings on Art and Literature.* Trans. Geoffrey Bremner. London: Penguin Books, 1994.

———. *"This Is Not a Story" and Other Stories.* Trans. P. N. Furbank. Columbia: University of Missouri Press, 1991.

Dreyfus, Laurence. *Bach and the Patterns of Invention.* Cambridge, MA: Harvard University Press, 1994.

Du Bos, Abbé. *Réflexions critiques sur la poésie et sur la peinture.* 7th ed. Paris: Chez Pissot, 1770. Reprint, Genève-Paris: Slatkine, 1982.

Dyck, Joachim. *Ticht-Kunst. Deutsche Barockpoetik und rhetorische Tradition.* Tübingen, Germany: M. Niemeyer, 1991.

Eggebrecht, Hans Heinrich. *Versuch über die Wiener Klassik. Beihefte zum Archiv für Musikwissenschaft* 12 (1972): 24–25.

Einstein, Alfred. *Mozart: His Character, His Work.* Trans. Arthur Mendel and Nathan Broder. London: Oxford University Press, 1945.

Elias, Norbert. *Mozart: Portrait of a Genius*. Trans. Edmund Jephcott. Berkeley and Los Angeles: University of California Press, 1993.

Fellerer, Karl. *Die Kirchenmusik W. A. Mozarts*. Laaber, Germany: Laaber-Verlag, 1985.

Felman, Shoshana. *The Literary Speech Act: Don Juan with J. L. Austin, or Seduction in Two Languages*. Trans. Catherine Porter. Ithaca, NY: Cornell University Press, 1983.

Fénelon, François de Salignac. *Dialogues Concerning Eloquence*. Trans. William Stevenson. Glasgow: Robert and Andrew Foulis, 1750.

Ferrara, Paul Albert. "Gregory Caloprese and the Subjugation of the Body in Metastasio's *Drammi per music*." *Italica* 73, no. 1 (1996): 11–23.

Formigari, Lia. *Signs, Science, and Politics: Philosophies of Language in Europe, 1700–1830*. Trans. William Dodd. Amsterdam and Philadelphia: John Benjamins, 1993.

Foucault, Michel. *The Order of Things*. New York: Vintage, 1973.

Fux, Johann-Joseph. *The Study of Counterpoint from Johann Joseph Fux's Gradus ad Parnassum*. Trans. Alfred Mann. New York: W. W. Norton, 1971.

Gaier, Ulrich. *Herders Sprachphilosophie und Erkenntniskritik*. Stuttgart-Bad Cannstatt, Germany: Fromman-Holzboog, 1988.

Gardt, Andreas. *Geschichte der Sprachwissenschaft in Deutschland. Vom Mittelalter bis ins 20*. Jahrhundert. Berlin: Walter de Gruyter, 1999.

Geiringer, Karl. *Haydn: A Critical Life in Music*. In collaboration with Irene Geiringer. Berkeley and Los Angeles: University of California Press, 1982.

Georgiades, Thrasybulos. *Music and Language: The Rise of Western Music as Exemplified in Settings of the Mass*. Trans. Marie Louise Göllner. Cambridge: Cambridge University Press, 1982.

Giuliani, Alessandro. "Vico's Rhetorical Philosophy and the New Rhetoric," trans. Salvatore Rotella. In *Giambattista Vico's Science of Humanity*, ed. Giorgio Tagliacozzo and Donald Phillip Verene, 31–46. Baltimore and London: Johns Hopkins University Press, 1976.

Gjerdingen, Robert O. *A Classic Turn of Phrase: Music and the Psychology of Convention*. Philadelphia: University of Pennsylvania Press, 1988.

Goehring, Edmund. *Three Modes of Perception in Mozart: The Philosophical, Pastoral, and Comic in Così fan tutte*. Cambridge: Cambridge University Press, 2004.

Grayson, David. *Mozart: Piano Concerto No. 20 in D Minor, K. 466, and Piano Concerto No. 21 in C Major, K. 467*. Cambridge: Cambridge University Press, 1998.

Greimas, Algirdas Julien. *Structural Semantics: An Attempt at a Method*. Trans. Daniele McDowell, Ronald Schleifer, and Alan Velie. Lincoln and London: University of Nebraska Press, 1983.

Griswold, Charles L., Jr. *Adam Smith and the Virtues of Enlightenment*. Cambridge: Cambridge University Press, 1999.

Gritten, Anthony, and Elaine King, eds. *Music and Gesture.* Aldershot, UK, and Burlington, VT: Ashgate, 2006.

Gutman, Robert W. *Mozart: A Cultural Biography.* New York: Harcourt Brace, 1999.

Haakonssen, Knud, and Donald Winch. "The Legacy of Adam Smith." In *The Cambridge Companion to Adam Smith,* ed. Knud Haakonssen, 366–94. Cambridge: Cambridge University Press, 2006.

Hagstrum, Jean H. *The Sister Arts: The Tradition of English Literary Pictorialism and English Poetry from Dryden to Gray.* Chicago: University of Chicago Press, 1958.

Harris, James. *Hermes, or A Philosophical Inquiry Concerning Language and Philosophical Grammar.* London: H. Woodfall, 1751.

———. *Three Treatises: The First Concerning Art; the Second Concerning Music, Painting, and Poetry; the Third Concerning Happiness.* London: H. Woodfall, 1744.

Hatten, Robert S. *Interpreting Musical Gestures, Topics, and Tropes: Mozart, Beethoven, Schubert.* Bloomington: Indiana University Press, 2004.

———. *Musical Meaning in Beethoven: Markedness, Correlation, and Interpretation.* Bloomington: Indiana University Press, 1994.

Head, Matthew. *Orientalism, Masquerade, and Mozart's Turkish Music.* London: Royal Music Association, 2000.

Heartz, Daniel. *Haydn, Mozart, and the Viennese School, 1740–1780.* New York: W. W. Norton, 1995.

———. *Mozart's Operas.* Ed. Thomas Bauman. Berkeley and Los Angeles: University of California Press, 1990.

———. *Music in European Capitals: The Galant Style, 1720–1780.* New York: W. W. Norton, 2003.

———. "Thomas Attwood's Lessons in Composition with Mozart." *Proceedings of the Royal Musical Association* 100 (1973–74): 175–83.

Hegel, Georg Wilhelm Friedrich. *Phenomenology of Spirit.* Trans. A. V. Miller. Oxford: Oxford University Press, 1977.

Heinichen, Johann David. *Der General-Bass in der Composition.* Dresden, Germany: 1728. Reprint, Hildesheim, Germany: Georg Olms Verlag, 1969.

Hepokoski, James, and Warren Darcy. *Elements of Sonata Theory: Norms, Types, and Deformations in the Late-Eighteenth-Century Sonata.* Oxford: Oxford University Press, 2006.

Herder, Johann Gottfried. *Ausgewählte Werke in Einzelausgaben. Scriften zur Literatur 2/1.* Ed. Regine Otto. 3 vols. Berlin: Aufbau, 1990.

———. *Sculpture: Some Observations on Shape and Form from Pygmalion's Creative Dream.* Trans. Jason Gaiger. Chicago: University of Chicago Press, 2002.

———. *Werke.* Ed. Jürgen Brummack and Martin Bollacher. 10 vols. Frankfurt am Main: Deutscher Klassiker Verlag, 1985–2000.

———. *Werke*. Ed. Wolfgang Pross. 3 vols. Munich: Carl Hanser Verlag, 1984.

Heuss, Alfred. "The Minor Second in Mozart's G Minor Symphony." In *Mozart: Symphony in G Minor, K. 550*, ed. Nathan Broder, 83–98. New York: W. W. Norton, 1976.

Hjelmslev, Louis. *Prolegomena to a Theory of Language*. Trans. Francis J. Whitfield Madison: University of Wisconsin Press, 1961.

Hobbes, Thomas. *Leviathan*. Ed. Edwin Curley. Indianapolis: Hackett, 1994.

Hollerweger, Hans. *Die Reform des Gottesdienstes zur Zeit des Josephinismus in Österreich*. Regensburg, Germany: Verlag Friedrich Pustet, 1976.

Howells, W. S. *Eighteenth-Century British Logic and Rhetoric*. Princeton, NJ: Princeton University Press, 1971.

Hoyt, Peter A. "Rhetoric and Music." *Grove Music Online*, ed. L. Macy. Accessed 25 February 2007. http://www.grovemusic.com.

Hume, David. *A Treatise of Human Nature*. Ed. L. A. Selby-Bigge. New York: Oxford University Press, 1980.

Hunter, Mary. *The Culture of Opera Buffa in Mozart's Vienna: A Poetics of Entertainment*. Princeton, NJ: Princeton University Press, 1999.

Hutchings, Arthur. *A Companion to Mozart's Piano Concertos*. Oxford: Oxford University Press, 1948.

Immerwahr, Raymond. "Diderot, Herder and the Dichotomy of Touch and Sight." *Seminar* 14 (1978): 84–96.

Irmscher, Hans. "Die geschichtsphilosophische Kontroverse zwischen Kant und Herder." In *Hamann-Kant-Herder*. Acta des vierten Internationalen Hamann-Kolloquiums im Herder-Institut zu Marburg/Lahn 1985. Ed. Bernhard Gajek, 111–92. Frankfurt am Main: Verlag Peter Lang, 1987.

Irving, John. *Mozart's Piano Concertos*. Burlington, VT: Ashgate, 2003.

———. *Mozart's Piano Sonatas: Contexts, Sources, Style*. Cambridge: Cambridge University Press, 1997.

Jahn, Otto. *Life of Mozart*. Trans. Pauline D. Townsend. 3 vols. London: Novello, Ewer & Co., 1882.

Jakobson, Roman. *On Language*. Ed. Linda R. Waugh and Monique Monville-Burston. Cambridge, MA: Harvard University Press, 1990.

Jameson, Fredric. *The Prison-House of Language: A Critical Account of Structuralism and Russian Formalism*. Princeton, NJ: Princeton University Press, 1972.

Jesperson, Otto. *Language: Its Nature, Development, and Origin*. London: Allen & Unwin, 1922.

Johnson, Mark. *The Body in the Mind: The Bodily Basis of Meaning, Imagination, and Reason*. Chicago: University of Chicago Press, 1987.

Joly, Henry. "Condillac et la critique de l'âge de raison." In *Condillac et les problèmes du langage*, ed. Jean Sgard, 7–25. Geneva: Slatkine, 1982.

Kant, Immanuel. *Critique of Practical Reason.* Trans. Lewis White Beck. Indianapolis: Liberal Arts Press, 1956.

———. *Critique of Pure Reason.* Trans. Norman Kemp Smith. New York: St. Martin's Press, 1965.

Keefe, Simon. "'An entirely special manner': Mozart's Piano Concerto No. 144 in E flat, K. 449, and the Stylistic Implications of Confrontation." *Music and Letters* 82, no. 4 (2001): 559–81.

———. *Mozart's Piano Concertos: Dramatic Dialogue in the Age of Enlightenment.* Rochester, NY: Boydell Press, 2001.

Kerman, Joseph. "Mozart's Piano Concertos and Their Audience." In *On Mozart,* ed. James M. Morris, 151–68. New York: Woodrow Wilson Center Press, 1994.

Kim, Dae Kweon. *Sprachtheorie im 18. Jahrhundert: Herder, Condillac, Süssmilch.* St. Ingbert, Germany: Röhrig, 2002.

Kirkendale, Warren. *Fugue and Fugato in Rococco and Classical Chamber Music.* Trans. Margaret Bent and Warren Kirkendale. Durham, NC: Duke University Press, 1979.

Kline, A. David. "Berkeley's Divine Language Argument." In *Essays on the Philosophy of George Berkeley,* ed. Ernest Sosa, 129–42. Dordrecht, Netherlands: D. Reidel, 1987.

Knepler, Georg. *Wolfgang Amadé Mozart.* Trans. J. Bradford Robinson. Cambridge: Cambridge University Press, 1994.

Koch, Heinrich Christoph. "Instrumentalmusik." In *Musikalische Lexicon.* Frankfurt am Main: August Hermann, 1802.

Kristeva, Julia. *Revolution in Poetic Language.* Trans. Margaret Waller. New York: Columbia University Press, 1984.

Kuehn, Manfred. "The Early Reception of Reid, Oswald, and Beattie in Germany, 1768–1800." *Journal of the History of Philosophy* 21 (October 1983): 479–96.

———. *Scottish Common Sense in Germany, 1768–1800: A Contribution to the History of Critical Philosophy.* Kingston, Ontario: McGill-Queen's University Press, 1987.

Küster, Konrad. *Mozart: A Musical Biography.* Trans. Mary Whittal. Oxford: Clarendon Press, 1996.

Lacan, Jacques. *Écrits.* Trans. Alan Sheridan. New York: W. W. Norton, 1977.

Lakoff, George, and Mark Johnson. *Metaphors We Live By.* Chicago: University of Chicago Press, 1980.

Lamy, Bernard. *La rhétorique ou l'art de parler.* Ed. Benoît Timmermans. Paris: Presses Universitaires de France, 1998.

Landon, H. C. Robbins. *Haydn: Chronicle and Works.* 5 vols. Bloomington: University of Indiana Press, 1988.

Leeson, Daniel, and Robert Levin. "On the Authenticity of K. Anh. C 14.01 (297 b), a Symphonia Concertante for Four Winds and Orchestra." In *Mozart-Jahrbuch 1976/77*, 70–96. Kassel, Germany: Bärenreiter, 1978.

Le Guin, Elisabeth. *Boccherini's Body: An Essay in Carnal Musicology*. Berkeley and Los Angeles: University of California Press, 2006.

Leibniz, Gottfried Wilhelm. *New Essays on Human Understanding*. Trans. Peter Remnant and Jonathan Bennett. Cambridge: Cambridge University Press, 1996.

———. *Philosophical Essays*. Ed. Roger Ariew and Daniel Garber. Indianapolis: Hackett, 1989.

Lerdahl, Fred, and Ray Jackendoff. *A Generative Theory of Tonal Music*. Cambridge, MA: MIT Press, 1983.

Lessing, Gotthold Ephraim. *Werke*. 8 vols. Munich: C. Hanser, 1970–79.

Lidov, David. *Elements of Semiotics*. New York: St. Martin's Press, 1999.

———. *Is Language a Music? Writings on Musical Form and Signification*. Bloomington: Indiana University Press, 2005.

Lippmann, Friedrich. "Der italienische Vers und der musikalische Rhythmus. Zum Verhältnis von Vers und Musik in der italienischen Oper des 19. Jahrhunderts, mit einem Rückblick auf die 2. Hälfte des 18. Jahrhunderts" 2. Teil, *Analecta musicologica* 12 (1973): 253–369.

Little, Meredith, and Natalie Jenne. *Dance and the Music of J. S. Bach*. Expanded ed. Bloomington: Indiana University Press, 2001.

Locke, John. *An Essay Concerning Human Understanding*. Ed. John W. Yolton. London: David Campbell, 1961.

Lukács, György. "Zur Ästhetik Schillers." In *Beiträge zur Geschichte der Ästhetik*, 11–96. Berlin: Aufbau, 1965.

Mac Intyre, Bruce C. *The Viennese Concerted Mass of the Early Classic Period*. Ann Arbor: University of Michigan Research Press, 1984.

Man, Paul de. *Allegories of Reading: Figural Language in Rousseau, Nietzsche, Rilke, and Proust*. New Haven, CT: Yale University Press, 1979.

Maniates, Maria Rika. "*Sonate, que me veux-tu?* The Enigma of French Musical Aesthetics in the 18th Century." *Current Musicology* 9 (1969): 117–40.

Marazzini, Claudio. *Storia e coscienza della lingua in Italia dall'umanesimo al romanticismo*. Turin, Italy: Rosenberg and Sellier, 1989.

Markis, Dimitrios. "Das Problem der Sprache bei Kant." In *Dimensionen der Sprache in der Philosophie des Deutschen Idealismus*, ed. Brigitte Scheer and Günter Wohlfart, 110–54. Würzburg, Germany: Königshausen & Neumann, 1982.

Mattheson, Johann. *Der Vollkommene Capellmeister*. Trans. and ed. Ernest C. Harriss. Ann Arbor, MI: UMI Research Press, 1981.

McClary, Susan. "A Musical Dialectic from the Enlightenment: Mozart's *Piano Concerto in G Major, K. 453,* Movement 2." *Cultural Critique* 4 (Autumn 1986): 129–69.

McGowan, William. "Berkeley's Doctrine of Signs." In *Berkeley: Critical and Interpretive Essays,* ed. Colin Turbayne, 231–46. Minneapolis: University of Minnesota Press, 1982.

Mercado, Mario. *The Evolution of Mozart's Pianistic Style.* Carbondale: Southern Illinois University Press, 1992.

Miel, Jan. "Pascal, Port-Royal, and Cartesian Linguistics." *Journal of the History of Ideas* 30, no. 2 (1969): 261–71.

Miller, Jonathan, ed. *Don Giovanni: Myths of Seduction and Betrayal.* New York: Schocken Books, 1990.

Monelle, Raymond. *Linguistics and Semiotics in Music.* London: Harwood Academic Publishers, 1992.

———. *The Musical Topic: Hunt, Military, and Pastoral.* Bloomington and Indianapolis: Indiana University Press, 2006.

———. *The Sense of Music: Semiotic Essays.* Princeton, NJ: Princeton University Press, 2000.

Montfrans, Manet van. "An Orange on a Pine Tree: French Thought in Herder's Linguistic Theory." In *Yearbook of European Studies* 7 (1994): 55–76.

Mooney, Michael. *Vico in the Tradition of Rhetoric.* Princeton, NJ: Princeton University Press, 1985.

Moser, Walter. "Jean-Georges Sulzer, continuateur de la pensée sensualiste dans l'Académie de Berlin." *Modern Language Notes* 84, no. 6 (1969): 931–41.

Mozart, Leopold. *A Treatise on the Fundamental Principles of Violin Playing.* 2d ed. Trans. Editha Knocker. Oxford: Oxford University Press, 1985.

Mozart, Wolfgang Amadeus. *Briefe und Aufzeichnungen. Gesamtausgabe hrsg. von der Internationalen Stiftung Mozarteum, Salzburg.* Ed. Wilhelm A. Bauer and Otto Erich Deutsch. 8 vols. Kassel, Germany: Bärenreiter, 1975.

Mueller-Vollmer, Kurt. "From Sign to Signification: The Herder-Humboldt Controversy." In *Johann Gottfried Herder: Language, History, and the Enlightenment,* ed. Wulf Koepke, 9–24. Columbia, SC: Camden House, 1990.

Mülder-Bach, Inka. *Im Zeichen Pygmalions. Das Modell der Statue und die Entdeckung der "Darstellung" im 18. Jahrhundert.* Munich: W. Fink, 1998.

Muratori, Lodovico Antonio. *Della regolata divozione de' cristiani.* In *Dal Muratori al Cesarotti,* vol. 1, ed. Giorgo Falco and Fiorenzo Forti, 929–63. Milan: Riccardo Ricciardi Editore, 1960.

Nagel, Ivan. *Autonomy and Mercy: Reflections on Mozart's Operas.* Trans. Marion Faber and Ivan Nagel. Cambridge, MA: Harvard University Press, 1991.

Neubauer, John. *The Emancipation of Music from Language: Departure from Mimesis in Eighteenth-Century Aesthetics.* New Haven, CT: Yale University Press, 1986.

Neumann, Frederick. "A New Look at Mozart's Prosodic Appoggiatura." In *Perspectives on Mozart Performance*, ed. R. Larry Todd and Peter Williams, 92–116. Cambridge: Cambridge University Press, 1991.

Newton, Isaac. *Opticks, or A Treatise of the Reflections, Refractions, Inflections and Colours of Light.* New York: Dover, 1952.

Nicolai, Friedrich. *Beschreibung einer Reise durch Deutschland und die Schweiz.* 4 vols. Berlin: Stettin, 1784.

Norton, Robert E. *Herder's Aesthetics and the European Enlightenment.* Ithaca, NY: Cornell University Press, 1991.

Noverre, Jean-Georges. *Lettres sur la danse et sur les ballets.* 1760. Facsimile reprint, New York: Broude Brothers, 1967.

Palézieux, Nikolaus de. *Die Lehre vom Ausdruck in der englischen Musikästhetik des 18. Jahrhunderts.* Hamburg: Verlag der Musikalienhandlung Karl Dieter Wagner, 1981.

Pappas, George. *Berkeley's Thought.* Ithaca, NY: Cornell University Press, 2000.

Parini, Guiseppe. *Prose.* Ed. Egidio Bellorini. 2 vols. Bari, Italy: G. Laterza, 1913–15.

———. *Prose.* Ed. Silvia Morgana and Paolo Bartesaghi. 2 vols. Milan, Italy: Edizioni Universitarie di Lettere Economia Diritto, 2003–5.

Parker, Roger. *Leonora's Last Act: Essays in Verdian Discourse.* Princeton, NJ: Princeton University Press, 1997.

Pauly, Reinhard G. "The Reforms of Church Music under Joseph II." *Musical Quarterly* 43 (1957): 372–82.

Peirce, Charles Sanders. *The Collected Papers of Charles Sanders Peirce,* 8 volumes. Ed. Charles Hartshorne and Paul Weiss. Cambridge, MA: Harvard University Press, 1931–58.

Pompa, Leon. *Vico: A Study of the "New Science."* Cambridge: Cambridge University Press, 1990.

Potts, Alex. *The Sculptural Imagination: Figurative, Modernist, Minimalist.* New Haven, CT: Yale University Press, 2000.

Powers, Harold S. "Reading Mozart's Music: Text and Topic, Syntax and Sense." *Current Musicology* 57 (1995): 5–44.

Quintilian, Marcus Fabius. *Institutio Oratoria.* Trans. H. E. Butler. 4 vols. Cambridge, MA: Harvard University Press, 1921–22.

Raphael, D. D. *The Impartial Spectator: Adam Smith's Moral Philosophy.* Rev. ed. Oxford: Clarendon Press, 2007.

Ratner, Leonard G. "*Ars Combinatoria:* Chance and Choice in Eighteenth-Century Music." In *Studies in Eighteenth-Century Music: A Tribute to Karl Geiringer on His Seventieth Birthday.* Ed. H. C. Robbins Landon, with Roger E. Chapman, 343–63. New York: Oxford University Press, 1970.

———. *Classic Music: Expression, Form, and Style.* New York: Schirmer Books, 1980.

————. *Music: The Listener's Art.* New York: McGraw-Hill, 1957.

————. *Music: The Listener's Art.* 2d ed. New York: McGraw-Hill, 1966.

————. "Topical Content in Mozart's Keyboard Sonatas." *Early Music* 19 (November 1991): 615–19.

Redekop, Benjamin W. "Reid's Influence in Britain, Germany, France, and America." In *The Cambridge Companion to Thomas Reid*, ed. Terence Cuneo and René van Woudenberg, 313–36. Cambridge: Cambridge University Press, 2004.

Reichert, Georg. "Mozarts Credo-Messen und ihre Vorläufer." In *Mozart-Jahrbuch 1955*. Salzburg, Austria: Salzburg Drückerei, 1955.

Reid, Thomas. *Essays on the Intellectual Powers of Man.* Cambridge, MA: MIT Press, 1969.

————. *An Inquiry into the Human Mind on the Principles of Common Sense.* Ed. Derek R. Brookes. Edinburgh: Edinburgh University Press, 1997.

Richards, Annette. *The Free Fantasia and the Musical Picturesque.* Cambridge: Cambridge University Press, 2001.

Ricken, Ulrich. *Grammaire et philosophie au siècle des lumières. Controverses sur l'ordre naturel et la clarté du français.* Arras, France: Publications de l'université de Lille, 1978.

————. *Linguistics, Anthropology, and Philosophy in the French Enlightenment: Language Theory and Ideology.* Trans. Robert E. Norton. London: Routledge, 1994.

Riley, Matthew. *Musical Listening in the German Enlightenment: Attention, Wonder, and Astonishment.* Aldershot, UK, and Burlington, VT: Ashgate, 2004.

Rosand, Ellen. "The Descending Tetrachord: An Emblem of Lament." *Musical Quarterly* 65, no. 3 (1979): 346–59.

Rosen, Charles. *The Classical Style: Haydn, Mozart, and Beethoven.* New York: Viking Press, 1972.

Rosenfeld, Sophia. *A Revolution in Language: The Problem of Signs in Late Eighteenth-Century France.* Stanford, CA: Stanford University Press, 2001.

Rousseau, Jean-Jacques. *Écrits sur la musique.* Paris: Éditions Pourrat, 1833. Reprint, Paris: Stock, 1979.

————. *Émile, or On Education.* Trans. Allan Bloom. New York: Basic Books, 1979.

————. *Essay on the Origin of Languages and Writings Related to Music.* Trans. John T. Scott. Hanover, NH, and London: University Press of New England, 1998.

————. *Oeuvres complètes de Jean-Jacques Rousseau.* Ed. Henri Coulet, Bernard Gagnebin, Bernard Guyon, and Marcel Raymond. 5 vols. Paris: Gallimard, 1959.

Rousseau, Nicolas. *Connaissance et langage chéz Condillac.* Geneva: Librairie, 1986.

Rudowski, Victor Anthony. "The Theory of Signs in the Eighteenth Century." In *Language and the History of Thought*, ed. Nancy Struever, 83–90. Rochester, NY: University of Rochester Press, 1995.

Rumph, Stephen. "Beethoven and the *Ut Pictura Poësis* Tradition." *Beethoven Forum* 12, no. 2 (2005): 113–49.

———. "Unveiling Cherubino." *Eighteenth-Century Music* 4, no. 1 (2007): 129–38.

Rushton, Julian, ed. *W. A. Mozart: "Don Giovanni."* New York: Cambridge University Press, 1981.

Rushton, Julian. "Mozart's Art of Rhetoric: Understanding an Opera Seria Aria ('Deh se piacer mi vuoi' from *La clemenza di Tito*)." *Contemporary Music Review* 17, no. 3 (1998): 15–27.

Saisselin, Rémy. *The Rule of Reason and the Ruses of the Heart: A Philosophical Dictionary of Classical French Criticism, Critics, and Aesthetic Issues.* Cleveland: Press of Case Western Reserve University, 1970.

Scaglione, Aldo. *The Theory of German Word Order from the Renaissance to the Present.* Minneapolis: University of Minnesota Press, 1981.

Searle, John. *Expression and Meaning: Studies in the Theory of Speech Acts..* Cambridge: Cambridge University Press, 1973.

Seidel, Wilhelm. "Essay von Adam Smith über die Musik. Eine Einführung," *Musiktheorie* 15, no. 3 (2000): 195–204.

———. "Zählt die Musik zu den imitative Künsten? Zur Revision der Nachahmungsästhetik durch Adam Smith." In *Die Sprache der Musik. Festschrift Klaus Wolfgang Niemöller zum 60. Geburtstag am 21. Juli 1989.* Ed. Jobst Peter Fricke, with Bram Gätjen and Manuel Gervink, 495–511. Regensburg, Germany: Gustav Bosse Verlag, 1989.

Shapiro, Michael. *Asymmetry: An Inquiry into the Linguistic Structure of Poetry.* Amsterdam: North Holland Publishing, 1976.

———. *The Sense of Grammar: Language as Semeiotic.* Bloomington: Indiana University Press, 1983.

Sisman, Elaine R. "After the Heroic Style: Fantasia and the 'Characteristic' Sonatas of 1809." *Beethoven Forum* 6 (1998): 67–96.

———. "Genre, Gesture, and Meaning in Mozart's 'Prague' Symphony." In *Mozart Studies* 2, ed. Cliff Eisen, 27–84. Oxford: Clarendon Press, 1997.

———. *Haydn and the Classical Variation.* Cambridge, MA: Harvard University Press, 1993.

———. "Learned Style and the Rhetoric of the Sublime in the 'Jupiter' Symphony." In *Wolfgang Amadé Mozart: Essays on His Life and His Music,* ed. Stanley Sadie, 213–38. Oxford: Clarendon Press, 1996.

———. "Memory and Invention at the Threshold of Beethoven's Late Style." In *Beethoven and His World,* ed. Scott Burnham and Michael P. Steinberg, 51–87. Princeton, NJ: Princeton University Press, 2000.

———. *Mozart: The "Jupiter" Symphony.* Cambridge: Cambridge University Press, 1993.

Smith, Adam. *Essays on Philosophical Studies.* Ed. W. P. D. Wightman and J. C. Bryce. Oxford: Clarendon Press, 1990.

———. *An Inquiry into the Nature and Causes of the Wealth of Nations.* Ed. R. H. Campbell, A. S. Skinner, and W. B. Todd. 2 vols. Oxford: Clarendon Press, 1976.

———. *Lectures on Rhetoric and Belles Lettres.* Ed. J. C. Bryce. Oxford: Clarendon Press, 1983.

———. *The Theory of Moral Sentiments.* Ed. Knud Haakonssen. Cambridge: Cambridge University Press, 2002.

Spaethling, Robert. *Mozart's Letters, Mozart's Life: Selected Letters.* New York: W. W. Norton, 2000.

Spitzer, Michael. "Inside Beethoven's 'Magic Square': The Structural Semantics of Op. 132." In *Les Universaux en Musique,* ed. Costin Miereanu and Xavier Hascher, 87–125. Actes du 4e Congrès International sur la signification musicale. Paris: Publications de la Sorbonne, 1999.

———. *Metaphor and Musical Thought.* Chicago: University of Chicago Press, 2004.

Spongano, Raffaele. *La poetica del sensismo e la poesia del Parini.* Bologna, Italy: Patron, 1964.

Steinberg, Michael P. *Listening to Reason: Culture, Subjectivity, and Nineteenth-Century Music.* Princeton, NJ: Princeton University Press, 2004.

Stieler, Kaspar. *Teutsche Sekretariat-Kunst.* 3 vols. Nuremburg, Germany: J. Hofmann, 1673.

Strohm, Reinhold. *Dramma per musica: Italian Opera Seria of the Eighteenth Century.* New Haven, CT: Yale University Press, 1997.

Stückenrath, Jörn. "Der junge Herder als Sprach—und Literaturtheoretiker— ein Erbe des französischen Aufklärers Condillac?" In *Sturm und Drang. Ein literaturwissenschaftliches Studienbuch,* ed. Walter Hinck, 81–96. Kronberg, Germany: Athanäum, 1978.

Sulzer, Johann George. "Observations sur l'influence réciproque de la raison sur le langage et du langage sur la raison." In *Histoire de l'académie royale des sciences et des belles lettres de Berlin: avec les mémoires pour la même année, tirez des registres de cette Académie,* vol. 23 (Berlin: Ambroise Haude, 1768): 413–38.

Taruskin, Richard. *The Oxford History of Western Music.* 6 vols. New York: Oxford University Press, 2005.

Taylor, Charles. *Philosophical Arguments.* Cambridge, MA: Harvard University Press, 1995.

Terezakis, Katie. *The Immanent Word: The Turn to Language in German Philosophy, 1759–1801.* New York and London: Routledge, 2007.

Thomas, Downing. *Music and the Origins of Language: Theories from the French Enlightenment.* Cambridge: Cambridge University Press, 1995.

Till, Nicholas. *Mozart and the Enlightenment: Truth, Virtue, and Beauty in Mozart's Operas.* New York: W. W. Norton, 1993.

Tomlinson, Gary. "Music and Culture: Vico's Songs: Detours at the Origins of (Ethno) Musicology." *Musical Quarterly* 83, no. 3 (1999): 344–77.

Tovey, Donald Francis. *Essays in Musical Analysis*. 6 vols. London: Oxford University Press, 1972.

Trabant, Jürgen. "Herder's Discovery of the Ear." In *Herder Today: Contributions from the International Herder Conference, Nov. 5–8 1987, Stanford, California*, ed. Kurt Mueller-Vollmer, 345–66. Berlin: W. de Gruyter, 1990.

———. "Inner Bleating: Cognition and Communication in the Language Origin Discussion." In *Herder Jahrbuch: Herder Yearbook 2000*, 1–19. Stuttgart, Germany: Metzler, 2000.

Treitler, Leo. *Music and the Historical Imagination*. Cambridge, MA: Harvard University Press, 1990.

Trummer, Johann. "Zur Situation der Liturgie im katholischen Reichsgebiet zu Beginn der Wiener Klassik." In *Mozarts Kirchenmusik, Lieder und Chormusik*, ed. Thomas Hochradner and Günther Massenkeil, 21–40. Laaber, Germany: Laaber-Verlag, 2006.

Tull, James Robert. "B. V. Asaf'ev's 'Musical Form as a Process': Translation and Commentary, Volume III." Ph.D. diss., Ohio State University, 1976.

Turbayne, Colin Murray. *The Myth of Metaphor*. New Haven, CT: Yale University Press, 1962.

Turino, Thomas. "Signs of Imagination, Identity, and Experience: A Peircian Semiotic Theory for Music." *Ethnomusicology* 43, no. 2 (1999): 221–55.

Tyson, Alan. *Mozart: Studies of the Autograph Scores*. Cambridge, MA: Harvard University Press, 1987.

Varwig, Bettina. "One More Time: Bach and Seventeenth-Century Traditions of Rhetoric." *Eighteenth-Century Music* 5, no. 2 (2008): 179–208.

Vaugles, Claude Favre de. *La Préface des "Remarques sur la langue Françoise* [1646]." Ed. Zygmont Marzys. Geneva: Droz, 1984.

Verene, Donald Phillip. *Vico's Science of Imagination*. Ithaca, NY: Cornell University Press, 1981.

Vico, Giambattista. *The Art of Rhetoric (Institutines Oratoriae, 1711–1741)*. Trans. and ed. Giorgio A. Pinton and Arthur W. Shippee. Amsterdam and Atlanta, GA: Rodopi, 1996.

———. *The First New Science*. Ed. and trans. Leon Pompa. New York: Cambridge University Press, 2002.

———. *On Humanistic Education (Six Inaugural Orations, 1699–1707)*. Trans. Giorgio A. Pinton and Arthur W. Shippee. Ithaca, NY: Cornell University Press, 1993.

———. *On the Most Ancient Wisdom of the Italians Unearthed from the Origins of the Latin Language*. Trans. L. M. Palmer. Ithaca, NY: Cornell University Press, 1988.

———. *On the Study Methods of Our Time.* Trans. Elio Gianturco. New York: Bobbs-Merrill, 1965.

———. *New Science.* Trans. David Marsh. 3rd ed. London: Penguin Books, 1999.

Wackenroder, Wilhelm Heinrich. *Confessions and Fantasies.* Trans. Mary Hurst Schubert. University Park: Pennsylvania State University Press, 1971.

Waldoff, Jessica. *Recognition in Mozart's Operas.* New York: Oxford University Press, 2006.

Webster, James. "The Analysis of Mozart's Arias." In *Mozart Studies,* ed. Cliff Eisen, 101–99. Oxford: Clarendon Press, 1991.

———. "Between Enlightenment and Romanticism in Music History: 'First Viennese Modernism' and the Delayed Nineteenth Century." *19th-Century Music* 25, no. 2/3 (Autumn 2001–Spring 2002): 108–26.

———. *Haydn's "Farewell" Symphony and the Idea of Classical Style: Through-Composition and Cyclic Integration in His Instrumental Music.* Cambridge: Cambridge University Press, 1991.

Wellbery, David E. *Lessing's "Laocoon": Semiotics and Aesthetics in the Age of Reason.* Cambridge: Cambridge University Press, 1984.

White, Hayden. *Tropics of Discourse: Essays in Cultural Criticism.* Baltimore and London: Johns Hopkins University Press, 1978.

Williams, Peter. *The Chromatic Fourth During Four Centuries of Music.* Oxford: Oxford University Press, 1997.

Wolterstorff, Nicholas. *Thomas Reid and the Story of Epistemology.* Cambridge: Cambridge University Press, 2001.

Yolton, John W. *Locke and French Materialism.* Oxford: Clarendon Press, 1991.

Zamito, John H. *Kant, Herder, and the Birth of Anthropology.* Chicago: University of Chicago Press, 2002.

Zbikowski, Lawrence M. "Dance Topoi, Sonic Analogues and Musical Grammar: Communicating with Music in the Eighteenth Century." In *Communication in Eighteenth-Century Music.* Ed. Danuta Mirka and Kofi Agawu, 283–309. Cambridge: Cambridge University Press, 2008.

Zeuch, Ulrike. *Umkehr der Sinneshierarchie. Herder und die Aufwertung des Tastsinns seit der frühen Neuzeit.* Tübingen, Germany: Max Niemeyer Verlag, 2000.

Zinzendorf, Karl Graf von. *Aus den Jugendtagebüchern: 1747, 1752, bis 1763.* Ed. Maria Breunlich and Marieluise Mader. Based on work by Hans Wagner. Vienna: Böhlau Verlag, 1997.

Index

Text: 10/14 Palatino
Display: Univers Condensed Light 47, Bauer Bodoni
Compositor: Integrated Composition Systems
Indexer: Sharon Sweeney
Printer and binder: Maple-Vail Book Manufacturing Group

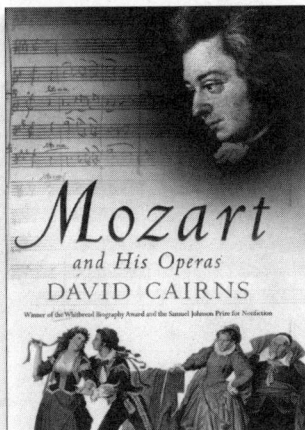